BIG DIGITAL HUMANITIES

T0329628

DIGITAL HUMANITIES

The Digital Humanities series provides a forum for ground-breaking and benchmark work in digital humanities, lying at the intersections of computers and the disciplines of arts and humanities, library and information science, media and communications studies, and cultural studies.

Series Editors:
Julie Thompson Klein, Wayne State University
Tara McPherson, University of Southern California
Paul Conway, University of Michigan

Manifesto for the Humanities: Transforming Doctoral Education in Good Enough Times
Sidonie Smith

Teaching History in the Digital Age
T. Mills Kelly

Hacking the Academy: New Approaches to Scholarship and Teaching from Digital Humanities
Daniel J. Cohen and Tom Scheinfeldt, Editors

Writing History in the Digital Age
Jack Dougherty and Kristen Nawrotzki, Editors

Pastplay: Teaching and Learning History with Technology
Kevin Kee, Editor

Interdisciplining Digital Humanities: Boundary Work in an Emerging Field
Julie Thompson Klein

Web Writing: Why and How for Liberal Arts Teaching and Learning
Jack Dougherty and Tennyson O'Donnell, Editors

Digital Rhetoric: Theory, Method, Practice
Douglas Eyman

Ethical Programs: Hospitality and the Rhetorics of Software
James J. Brown Jr.

Big Digital Humanities: Imagining a Meeting Place for the Humanities and the Digital
Patrik Svensson

DIGITALCULTUREBOOKS, an imprint of the University of Michigan Press, is dedicated to publishing work in new media studies and the emerging field of digital humanities.

Big Digital Humanities

IMAGINING A MEETING PLACE FOR THE
HUMANITIES AND THE DIGITAL

Patrik Svensson

University of Michigan Press

ANN ARBOR

Published in the United States of America by the
University of Michigan Press
Manufactured in the United States of America
⊗ Printed on acid-free paper

2019   2018   2017   2016   4   3   2   1

A CIP catalog record for this book is available from the British Library.

Library of Congress Cataloging-in-Publication data has been applied for.

ISBN 978-0-472-07306-1 (hardcover : alk. paper)
ISBN 978-0-472-05306-3 (paper : alk. paper)
ISBN 978-0-47212174-8 (e-book)

http://dx.doi.org/10.3998/dh.13607060.0001.001

Contents

Preface

This is a book about how the humanities intersects with the digital. This engagement is richly multifaceted, intersectional, technical, critical, and hopeful. The digital can be seen as a material or a property that permeates much (but not all) of contemporary culture and society as well as the humanities as an institutional and scholarly endeavor. Humanistic questions about materiality, embodiment, prosthesis, gender, identity, privacy, space, aesthetics, and ethnicity all relate to the digital in one way or another, and such questions must shape the digital humanities. Some of these questions will necessarily be discipline-specific, while others will require joint efforts across disciplines and areas. At the same time, the humanities needs to engage with technology and maintain its critical potential when creating technological infrastructure. The technology itself is intertwined with instrumentation, methodologies, expert competence, expressions, research challenges, and analytical possibilities. Examples include map-based analyses, critical readings of databases, visualization, textual analysis, and academic installations.

The status of the digital humanities as a field has been debated for decades but now seems to have reached a certain size, level of maturity and level of visibility. At the same time, the digital humanities is still being formed, negotiated, and envisioned, which makes this a particularly good time to explore the field in depth. Disciplinary and epistemic tension exists, as do multiple possible paths forward, making this book not just a discussion of an existing field but also a far-reaching engagement with the ideational and practical shaping of that field, not in a dogmatic or exclusionary way but rather in an exploratory and inclusive fashion. This is also a book about how individual students, experts, and scholars can become involved in making the digital humanities.

One of the key challenges for the digital humanities is the integration of critical and technological engagement. For example, this requires humanists to look critically at big data as a phenomenon while considering how big data methodology may or may not be useful to humanities research and education. This may prompt the humanities to redefine what big data is and even to develop new methodologies. The bigness of big data in the humanities may refer to the number of perspectives inherent in the material and the richness of critical inflection rather than the sheer quantity of data.

In addition, the digital humanities has also come to be seen as a site for challenging and renewing the humanities and academy. This is a controversial position open to attack on several fronts. Some of the digital humanities community would state that envisioning the future of the humanities is not what the field is about given its focus on building and on managing day-to-day project works. Some mainstream humanists would argue that the digital humanities is not a serious humanistic endeavor because it simply includes too little humanities. Others would point out that digital humanities is a top-down strategy implemented by administrators and other leaders to "help" the humanities even though many other investments would make much more sense.

At the same time, the digital humanities has actually become a place of hope, open debate, and progressive energy, with strong critical potential. There is value to the debate and frenzy surrounding the digital humanities. Early career scholars are coming to the field not just because there may be jobs there but also because it is seen as a place to engage with the future of the humanities. And what if we see the support for the digital humanities not as a way of controlling and "helping" the humanities but rather as a possible way to strengthen both the humanities and the digital humanities? I see embracing this aspect of the digital humanities as a responsibility, and we need to incorporate all of these facets in our vision of the digital humanities. I also believe that we will likely reach a decisive point for the field in the near future and that some of the choices we make over the next five years will not only decide the fate of the digital humanities but influence the future of the humanities and the academy.

This book suggests a model for the digital humanities ("big digital humanities") that draws on the humanities; on being placed in the space between ideas and institutions; on the traditions and emerging configurations of the digital humanities; and on the coming together of intellectual and technological curiosity. Many of the pieces are already there, and I hope that this volume will help us think about what we are, where we could be going, and how we can get there.

The State of the Field

There are many indications of the contemporary reach and energy of the digital humanities as a field. One simple example is that at the end of the first week of December 2013, at least three international workshops on the field took place simultaneously. The conference Cultural Research in the Context of "Digital Humanities" in St. Petersburg, Russia, coincided with the workshop Sorting the Digital Humanities Out in Umeå, Sweden, and the conference (Digital) Humanities Revisited—Challenges and Opportunities in Hanover, Germany. These events demonstrate that the digital humanities also lives outside the Anglo-American sphere. The titles alone also give us a sense of the ongoing reconfiguration, and the event programs point to different directions and interests. It is also telling that the key international organization for the digital humanities, the Alliance of Digital Humanities Organizations, did not support any of these events, even though the Hanover conference included many speakers from that community.

As these gatherings demonstrate, the digital humanities is not one thing, and although the field's footprint has increased over the past decade, it does not incorporate everything that could be labeled *digital humanities*. Furthermore, not everyone who might be identified as doing digital humanities may want to be labeled a *digital humanist*. In this sense, the field is not a blank slate but rather a narrative or a series of narratives. As an institutional structure, the field has a predominant (and privileged) epistemic tradition that has shaped many of the institutional parameters that now configure it. This tradition, humanities computing, has a substantial investment in engaging with information technology as a tool, in privileging textual analysis and encoding, and in promoting a particular set of technologies and methodologies. These are important competencies and areas, but they are not the only ones. The recent expansion of the field, however, has challenged this structure on a number of points, which is a healthy and necessary development. For example, the perceived lack of gender, ethnic, or environmental engagement has been noted. Ideally, in intersecting with other traditions and disciplinary backgrounds, these areas will also be challenged and negotiated. For example, we see exciting development in areas such as environmental humanities and sound studies.

Given that the range of the digital humanities extends from technological instrumentation to transforming the academy, we should not be surprised that there is no clear consensus about what it entails. When Jeffrey Schnapp announced "A Short Guide to the Digital_Humanities" in January 2013,[1] Mark Sample tweeted, "I've got 99 problems and the Short Guide to Digital_Humanities is about a dozen of them."[2] And when discussing a definition of "digital humanities" on the same day, Ted Underwood said, "Fantasizing about a lead-walled chamber deep in stable Precambrian rock, where the term 'Digital Humanities' could be sealed away forever."[3] Natalia Cecire offers a different kind of argument when she problematizes the stress on "niceness" in the digital humanities and discusses the focus on building, noting the field's "complicity with exploitative postindustrial labor practices."[4] These examples point to different positions, and one of the key arguments of this book is that we need to reconcile various traditions and positions without losing their substance and sharpness.

Big Digital Humanities

Big digital humanities describes a broadly defined, open, and challenging field that exists between humanities departments, disciplines, and epistemic traditions, between the humanities and other knowledge domains, and between the academy and the world outside. This position is driven by intellectual curiosity, technological imaginaries, historical sensibility, scholarly challenges, and a willingness to engage critically and technologically across issues, perspectives, and needs relevant to understanding and improving the human condition.

Big digital humanities facilitates multiple modes of engagement between the humanities and the digital, stretches across all of the humanities and outside, and functions as a platform for the humanities. According to this model, the digital humanities engages with the digital as a tool, as an object of inquiry, and as an expressive medium. These modes of engagement increasingly need to come together in intellectually driven and materially sensitive amalgams. In this way, the digital humanities can address some of the most important current and future challenges: achieving far-reaching scholarly advancement, creating a rich nonservile connection to the rest of the humanities and outside, furthering the humanities, pushing development of all the modes of engagement, and tackling some of the scholarly and methodological issues facing the humanities today.

Naturally, not all digital humanists or digital humanities initiatives will do all of these things at the same time, and a multitude of positions and institutional realities will necessarily exist. This model is open and moves beyond the big-tent framework of the digital humanities and some of the territorial struggles. Indeed, the notion of a big tent is problematic in a number of ways, and I believe that we need to get rid of the tent altogether. Big digital humanities is not a new label, but rather a framework for envisioning and making the digital humanities. The digital humanities is seen as a liminal[5] operation or space, placed in between, with considerable integrity. This position is easier to maintain if we do not see the digital humanities as a fully fledged discipline. At the same time, we need to be sensitive to the heterogeneity of local contexts and avoid proclaiming a one-size-fits-all model for the digital humanities.

The solution to this problem does not box us in but allows us to maintain multiple identities at the same time, respect others, be critical toward both the humanistic and the digital, and continuously renew ourselves. This solution is a broadly conceived, multifaceted, inclusive, nonterritorial, and intersectional digital humanities that can further humanities research and education, stimulate methodological and technical engagement, function as a meeting place and innovation hub, and be a place for engaging with the future of the humanities and higher education. Herein lies the bigness of big digital humanities.

The fact that the digital humanities is not very well defined can be seen as problematic in some ways, but it is also a strength. Liminal, networked operations depend on a certain degree of instability and adaptability. As outlined in this book, big digital humanities reaches across a large territory but has no precise territory of its own. The field also has a very large range, from societal challenges and the role of the humanities to the exact materiality of archival interfaces and the cultural conditions that continuously shape underlying data structures.

The Place of the Digital Humanities

The digital humanities cannot be seen in isolation from the rest of the humanities, the academy, and the planet that we inhabit. Even though the field as traditionally historicized was not institutionally stable or safe, it did have a clearer sense of institutional position and place. The increased institutional centrality of the field over the past ten years and the growing realization inside and outside the academy that the digital, broadly conceived, matters intellectually, technologically, and humanly has created pressure on the field to be more strongly and diversely connected to the outside (humanities disciplines, the rest of the academy, so-called big challenges) than in the past. This is not to say that the field has not previously been collaborative or involved in outreach; rather, we may need a different kind of collaboration in terms of scale, quality, and questions asked.

While the digital humanities seems to have been unable to respond to some of these challenges, a great deal of development and an influx of new perspectives have undoubtedly occurred over the past decade. Not only has the digital humanities adapted to its new reality, but its interlocutors and collaborators have adapted to and interrelated with the core of the digital humanities. From the perspective that the digital humanities is a liminal place, such interactions and continuous exchanges are operationally critical.

Unsurprisingly, hurdles may prevent such rich interaction. The tendency for the humanities to look at the digital humanities in instrumental terms (as a service) is one such hurdle. Another is that since the expansion of the field in the mid-2000s, the digital humanities seems somewhat stuck between top-down perspectives emanating from the supposedly agentive role of the digital in potentially reforming the humanities and bottom-up perspectives grounded in the practice of decades of humanities computing work. While this bifurcation is obviously not strict or simple, it has contributed to the partial blocking of two important pathways for the digital humanities.

First, disciplinary perspectives have been slow to emerge as a consequence of a tendency to focus on either the large picture or on a largely technological and instrumental relation to the humanities disciplines as manifested in projects. This means that certain kinds of humanities work—in particular, traditional interpretative scholarship—has not played a major role in the development of digital humanities. A more general lack of disciplinarily driven issues and questions has also existed in the digital humanities, even in the presence of disciplinary subfields such as digital history. The overall consequence has been a weak or dissonant connection with the disciplines. This is not to say that the digital humanities should have adopted a disciplinary perspective or that the traditional disciplines should necessarily serve as role models; instead, having a rich connection between the digital humanities and the humanities disciplines is critical to both parties.

Second, the weak integration between overarching humanities perspectives, disciplinary vantage points, and humanities computing practice has resulted in a lack of intellectually and materially grounded agendas for the digital humanities. Among other things, this explains the digital humanities' limited capacity to be an intellectual and technological partner in collaboration with areas such as environmental humanities and ethnic studies and with various university-wide and global initiatives. The digital humanities has started to move more in this direction, but such developments often remain in the relatively early stages. The 2013 discussion of "digital materialism" on the Humanist list is a good example of different worlds clashing within the expanding field of digital humanities, and Whitney Trettien's comment manifests a certain degree of frustration: "If digital materiality is a cute oxymoron, please tell that to the noisy CPU fan that incessantly huffs hot air from my poorly thermoregulated laptop."[6] Trettien indirectly draws our attention to another, related perspective rarely discussed in the digital humanities: the environmental impact of the technologies used. And while Bethany Nowviskie's characteristically thought-provoking "Digital Humanities in the Anthropocene" at the Digital Humanities 2014 conference provides a refreshing and rare perspective on the field's place in relation to large time spans and major challenges, she still proposes strategies and a forward path largely internal to the digital humanities rather than relating to areas such as environmental humanities.[7]

The digital humanities has become a place where the humanities are made, for better or worse, and such a place requires solid intellectual, methodological, and technological engagement and outreach across the humanities, the humanities disciplines, the academy, and the public sphere. The digital humanities is not a discipline, not a big tent, not a service function, not a methodological commons. Rather, it is an inclusive meeting place for the humanities and the digital, a contact zone for a range of epistemic traditions and expert competencies, and an infrastructure for empowering participants, creating scholarship of many types, building technological solutions and methodology, and curating meaningful intellectual exchange. In this view, scholarship, education, and technology are intrinsically intertwined, whether in performing critical analysis of online learning platforms, developing tools for exploring and deconstructing historical 3-D constructions, creating alternative metadata ontologies to allow for postcolonial readings of legal documents, exploring the use of visual frames architecturally and computationally, or challenging the traditional attribution of gender in computer game history. Such work is always both humanistic and technological.

If the digital humanities is at heart a humanistic endeavor, the field has to have a sense of what it means to be part of the humanities in our time. While this question unavoidably speaks to all of the humanities, it is particularly relevant for the digital humanities, given the place and potential of the field. David Theo Goldberg says, "I understand the power of the humanities, traditionally and today, to be an engagement in translating the human to ourselves: what it is to be, what it means and has meant to be, and what it ought to be human?"[8] The response to such questions can never be just technological, but in an increasingly digital world, the response is fairly likely to have some kind of digital inflection. The digital humanities must work with the humanities (and other) disciplines and various intersectional areas around such questions. Many intellectual and technological partnerships can be created and strengthened through placing the digital humanities between rather than at the center or the periphery.

Understanding the place of the digital humanities also means being open to the traditions, complexity, dynamism, and innovation in the humanities. The digital part of the digital humanities seems often to be assumed to be more dynamic, progressive, and agentive than the humanities part. The assumption of the unchanging nature of the humanities is not new and was questioned as early as 1967 by Walter J. Ong, and although he writes that this assumption "hardly lingers in informed circles today," it still seems prevalent.[9] While some aspects of the humanities may not change very quickly and disciplinary structures may condition scholarship to a significant degree, the humanities is not static. Important findings certainly continue to emerge in the traditional disciplines, although much of this work can seem incremental and highly specialized. And while a need certainly exists for more collaborative scholarly output in the humanities and for a larger engagement with digital modalities, among other examples, it is also important to acknowledge the value of individual scholarly production and other modalities associated with the traditional humanities. Sometimes the frustration with the humanities among digital humanists and others results in calls for a full overhaul of the humanities, but it seems more productive and realistic to work with the disciplines and include them in visions of the future humanities. This is not to say that the disciplinary landscape cannot change or that old structures must prevail; rather, there is an intellectual and strategic rationale for aligning what is already there, including the intersectional work carried out under rubrics such as queer studies, critical disability studies, software studies, and sound studies.

The humanities seems more amenable to structural shifts within and outside the academy than do other domains, perhaps as a consequence of the relatively small size of the humanities and a perception that the humanities has a marginal position, at least in relation to the way higher education has been transformed over the past two decades. In Sweden, for example, a changed allocation system since the mid-1990s has put a low value on most humanities and social science students in favor of funding to tackle certain "big challenges" (typically not at all humanities-driven), funding for "large" research environments (a few of which have been geared toward social sciences/humanities), a multiple-funding initiative to support the environmental humanities, long-term investments in gender studies, and arts-based research, and massive investments in science infrastructure (including the European Spallation Source). Overall, the size of higher education in Sweden has increased significantly over this period, but there has also been a distinct redistribution of resources and an increased focus on utilitarian, instrumental, and innovation-framed perspectives. This redistribution has clearly not benefited the humanities and the interpretative social sciences. The development of higher education has also increasingly been driven by a sense of international competition, which has made the prioritization of science, engineering, and medicine even more pronounced and has emphasized concepts such as employability and bibliometrics.[10]

Somewhat sadly, one of the constant factors since at least the 1970s seems to be the framing of the humanities as a domain in crisis. This framing has a very real and factual foundation, but it is also a matter of narrative, perspective, and outlook. Despite their discursive and conceptual expertise, the humanities clearly have not been able to articulate a convincing rationale and path forward. Multiple factors explains this inability, including the limitations of disciplinary thinking, a high degree of specialization, a reluctance to use humanities knowledge to change the academic lifeworld, and the positioning of the humanities as marginal and resistant to what is perceived as coming from the outside (including a neoliberal agenda and science-based models for knowledge production).

The digital humanities contributes to the development of the humanities and the academy through simultaneously challenging and being challenged by the humanities. The digital humanities as a liminal place is much more than a platform for digital studies and implementations; it is a means to articulate, further, and revitalize the humanities—not as digital humanities by itself but as a vision of the human sciences where the digital humanities can contribute to taking on the intellectual, social, and technological challenges of our time. Goldberg argues that given the new landscape of information, we need "revisioned modes of translating ourselves to ourselves."[11] The humanities thus need to reconfigure and rethink themselves, which will take a concerted effort, and the digital humanities has much to contribute to such an effort, as do other areas and initiatives both inside and outside the humanities. Indeed, the digital humanities needs to occupy this place to reach its scholarly, technological, and societal potential.

HUMlab as a Testing Ground

My conception of the digital humanities has been shaped through more than ten years' experience of running HUMlab at Umeå University, researching the field, visiting a large number of institutions and individuals, and taking an active part in a national and international dialogue.

This book tells the story of big digital humanities through a range of perspectives or facets that come together, many of them filtered through HUMlab as an experience and as an intersectional point for reflection, experiments, and the articulation of what digital humanities and the humanities at large can be. In this way, HUMlab has partly been a collaborative laboratory for testing ideas that led to the conception of big digital humanities as presented in this book. I have used HUMlab as a networked platform for probing, challenging, discussing, articulating, building, and making the digital humanities. This does not mean, however, that big digital humanities can only be implemented through building HUMlab-like environments at comprehensive universities; rather, experiences from building HUMlab have contributed to my understanding of big digital humanities.

Since the late 1990s, I have traveled extensively and seen many operations around the world and, more important, have had the opportunity to engage in in-depth conversations with hundreds of people interested in the humanities and information technology. Furthermore, I have carefully followed a number of international developments and have learnt from these, and I draw on a large amount empirical material. As a result, the narrative presented in this book has many kinds of contexts and elements.

Presentation of the Book

Big Digital Humanities is intended to be a central piece for establishing, discussing, and envisioning the field of digital humanities. The book proposes a comprehensive model of digital humanities that I hope will help the field move forward. This model is based on seeing the digital humanities not as an operation mostly concerned with established technology and tools but as an endeavor making strong intellectual arguments intertwined with technological engagement. This does not mean that every digital humanist needs to code or that every coder needs to write lengthy analytical articles, but the digital humanities brings together these perspectives and traditions in such a way as to further scholarship, enhance learning, and create new academic opportunities. Big digital humanities is also about renewing the humanities and the academy. Doing so requires openness, negotiation, a willingness to learn, and curiosity. Engagement is a critical component of making big digital humanities happen.

My engagement is demonstrated through eight personal interludes interspersed throughout the book. The main argument of the book, presented in five chapters, is constructed by looking at the intersection of the humanities and the digital, exploring the field of digital humanities, identifying the central premises of big digital humanities, proposing a framework for creating academic infrastructure to support these premises, and suggesting what processes and perspectives are most important for making the digital humanities.

Structure of the Book

The first chapter introduces the digital humanities, explores the intersection of the humanities and the digital, discusses digitally inflected challenges and the role of technology, analyzes some recent statements about the field, and traces possible directions of the field.

Chapter 2 looks at the history and wider context of the digital humanities to provide a basis for a deep understanding of the current landscape of the field, epistemic commitments, and tensions. The development of the landscape is explored through engaging with contemporary debates, looking at the role of major digital humanities associations and initiatives, and suggesting that we need to think beyond big-tent digital humanities.

The third chapter presents the foundation of big digital humanities through three basic premises: the field and the humanities disciplines benefit from engaging broadly with the digital, the digital humanities needs to be a meeting place with broad humanistic and deep academic investment, and the digital humanities is well placed to be a site of engagement for all of the humanities.

Chapter 4 considers how academic infrastructure can facilitate big digital humanities and support the humanities more broadly. Infrastructure plays a key role, and it is necessary to challenge the templates suggested by science and technology infrastructure and by the cultural heritage sector. The humanities need to engage not just in terms of building and using infrastructure but also, and equally important, in terms of conceptualizing and critiquing infrastructure.

The final chapter is about making the digital humanities and starts out from an interlude describing a day in HUMlab. Making the digital humanities is about building institutions, curating the digital humanities, empowering the humanities, and making spaces. Ultimately, the digital humanities offers a significant site for learning and knowledge building and for connecting the conceptual level with the material and technological level.

Acknowledgments

I feel most fortunate to have a rich collegial network of people who have contributed to this book. Many of these people have become close friends and intellectual comrades. Per-Olof Ågren, Thomas Augst, Mats Dahlström, Cathy Davidson, Johanna Drucker, Emma Ewadotter, Anna Foka, Zephyr Frank, Matt Gold, David Theo Goldberg, Katherine Hayles, Stephanie Hendrick, Lorna Hughes, Torbjörn Johansson, Kjell Jonsson, Finn Arne Jørgensen, Lauren Klein, Simon Lindgren, Cecilia Lindhé, Alan Liu, Shannon Mattern, Tara McPherson, Jenna Ng, Thomas Nygren, Andrew Prescott, Jessica Pressman, Rita Raley, Matt Ratto, Erica Robles-Anderson, Geoffrey Rockwell, Nishant Shah, Pelle Snickars, Jonathan Sterne, Lisa Swanstrom, Fred Turner, and many others have helped me shape these arguments. I have enjoyed and benefited from working with an excellent technology, methodology, and communication group in HUMlab, including Elin Andersson, Emma Ewadotter, Karin Jangert, Mattis Lindmark, Roger Mähler, Magnus Olofsson, Fredrik Palm, Jim Robertson, Jon Svensson, and Johan Von Boer. Stephanie Hendrick read, commented on and proofread most of the manuscript, and provided very useful pointers and help. Anne Drewett proofread the whole manuscript more thoroughly than I thought possible. Her linguistic and discursive sharpness has been invaluable. Pelle Snickars also read the full manuscript and helped me make this into a better publication. Matt Ratto, Anna Foka, Finn Arne Jørgensen, Cecilia Lindhé, Thomas Nygren, and Erica Robles-Anderson read and commented on parts of the manuscript. Fred Turner read one chapter and predictably gave me great advice. Many others have read sections of the manuscript and I thank them all. I also thank my academic mentors: David Theo Goldberg, Kjell Jonsson, Fred Turner, and Johanna Drucker. My friends and colleagues have provided the grounding on which I stand. I sincerely hope that this book makes some sense to all of you.

I also thank the staff and leadership at the Digital Humanities Quarterly, and Arts and Humanities in Higher Education where earlier versions of some of this material were shaped and published.

I finished the book while a Distinguished Visiting Fellow at the Advanced Research Collaboratory at the Graduate Center at City University New York, whose spirit, generosity and intellectual strength helped me greatly.

This book is a direct result of generous support from Umeå University, the Baltic Group, and the Wallenberg Foundation.

ONE

Introducing the Digital Humanities

This chapter introduces the humanities and information technology as an area and the digital humanities (DH) as an institutional endeavor. It starts out with an overview of the field, some personal key encounters, and a working definition of the digital humanities. Important questions addressed in the chapter are: Why should we care about "the digital?" What do "the digital" and "the humanities" bring to the digital humanities? What does it mean to be a digital humanist? What are the scholarly and institutional challenges? How can we think about the role of technology and infrastructure in the digital humanities? The final section of the chapter approaches the digital humanities as a field through descriptions of three books from 2012 to illustrate different perspectives associated with the establishment of the digital humanities as well as by addressing some possible future directions for the field.

Introduction

As the history of the printing press tells us, humanists are not new to engagement with information technology or "new media."[1] And there is a rich critical literature on older media and technologies within the humanities. Although humanists may not have been the foremost adopters of new layers of digital technology, this pattern also applies to other parts of the academy. In any case, we should not see the digital humanities as a way of curing technophobia in the humanities or graciously bringing technology to the humanities. This approach would only strengthen a split between the humanities and the digital humanities that does not seem overly productive. There are good reasons for a certain level of resistance, but at this point, the humanities clearly need to engage with the digital both critically and in terms of material engagement. A number of entangled forces are giving renewed currency to the meeting between the humanities and information technology.

For example, research materials in most humanities disciplines are increasingly available in digital formats. This is true not only of cultural records that have been and are being digitized but also of digitally born materials that are becoming more and more relevant for humanities research and teaching. Both types of materials typically require careful digitization processes, encoding, and systematization. Such processes are methodologically laden and come with competing worldviews and assumptions. Expertise, collaboration, and well-thought-out practices are needed to ensure the quality and rigor of the materials.[2]

With large and often heterogeneous digital materials comes the need for tools and expertise to manage, retrieve, and search these data. Such tools can be modern forms of analog tools, systems such as concordances or library catalogs,[3] or new kinds of tools that draw more distinctly on the attributes of modern digital technology. As Johanna Drucker and others have argued, tools are not neutral artifacts, and here methodological and epistemic awareness is critical.[4] This is particularly important if we see tools and their shaping as an integral part of research and learning processes rather than as something used to produce results or presentations at a specific point in such processes. Discussing visualizations in spatial history, Richard White makes the important and sometimes difficult point that visualization is not "about producing illustrations or maps to communicate things that you have discovered by other means. It is a means of doing research."[5]

Digitally born material includes relatively recent materials—such as archived e-mails, websites, online fan fiction, old games, surveillance data, online video, dance performance sensor data, and live data feeds—that can be useful for humanistic inquiry. The management and curation of such materials may call for what Matthew Kirschenbaum calls computer or digital forensics: a deep understanding of digital data both as material and as abstract, symbolic identity.[6] Some of the actual material may integrate well into existing analytical models, whereas other types of data and questions may call for new methodologies, material awareness, or critical frameworks. As Jonathan Sterne emphasizes, the humanities has a long tradition of engaging with different kinds of materials, and on one level, engaging with digital materials is a logical extension of this tradition.[7]

Looking at the level of output or production, traditional academic publishing may still have a fairly strong position in the humanities, but the system faces considerable pressure and the terrain is shifting quickly.[8] This is very clear from the ongoing debate about open access, digital distribution, the business model of academic publishing, the emergence of various online publishing platforms, and requirements from some funding agencies. Moreover, if digital tools and methods are to become a more integral and iterative part of scholarly work, traditional modalities may simply not suffice as they do not allow integrated dynamic content and access to data or media environments. This development overlaps with an increased interest in alternative types of academic production, pushed by accessibility to digital production means and interest in experimental modes of expression. There is also a potentially fruitful connection to art-based research and associated practices.[9] However, we should be careful not to overestimate the speed and impact of these changes. Modes of knowledge production are embedded in epistemic, institutional, and economic structures that will not change quickly. And the traditional monograph has value not merely because of its placement in this structure but also because of the argumentative potential and individual engagement in such artifacts (whether physical or digital).

The entanglement of the digital extends to the subject matter of humanistic inquiry. While essentially true for all humanities disciplines, this interconnection is more apparent in some disciplines or areas than others. For example, disciplines such as media studies, English, and comparative literature are directly affected by digital media, expressions, and inflections. As Fred Turner argues, media studies comes from a single-screen paradigm and needs to engage with a world where screens are pervasive.[10] Journalism studies can hardly avoid being concerned with the role of the web, pace, mobile devices, and paywalls—essentially a changed (but not new) logic for this sector—in current media production and consumption.[11] From the disciplinary perspective of English, Katherine Hayles emphasizes how the way we read is being challenged by digital media and how literature is affected by the digital in multiple ways,[12] while literature scholar Cecilia Lindhé points to how the digital can function as an interpretative-experiential perspective on the medieval church space and Virgin Mary as a role model in medieval Sweden.[13] In her project, it is difficult to draw the line between sophisticated tool and object of analysis, but the enacted church space is clearly an object of study as well as a research tool.

Thus, the humanities is affected by digital materials and tools as well as by new modes of expression and digitally inflected scholarly questions. These aspects are not distinct but rather are entangled. Different individuals, initiatives, and disciplines will be entangled in different ways, but on an institutional level, the digital humanities needs to engage with the digital on multiple levels (tool, study object, and medium). This is the promise of the inclusive variety of digital humanities advocated in this book, big digital humanities. This intellectually driven and materially sensitive enterprise is well positioned to take on major scholarly, societal, and cultural challenges inside and outside the humanities.

My background in linguistics in the department of English at Umeå University provides an example of this multiple engagement. In my studies of nominal number, I used large-scale text databases (corpora) and various tools to extract use patterns and produce visualizations. This work required a fair amount of methodological awareness and involvement with the development of tools. When studying communication patterns in digitally enabled communication situations, the digital was not only a material but also an object of study. For example, how does turn-taking work in digitally mediated communication situations? At the same time, as a teacher, I worked with colleagues on a project that encouraged English students to create a graphical virtual world installation around a rich theme instead of writing a traditional bachelor's degree paper.[14] The rationale was to bring together linguistics, literary studies, and cultural studies and to empower students to create their own academic manifestations in a shared world. Here, the technology functioned as an expressive medium and an arena. For me personally, these different engagements all fed into each other naturally; moreover, they were easily integrated and synergized in the same physical and digital spaces.

What Is the Digital Humanities?

The field of digital humanities has a reputation for being difficult to define and for being preoccupied with defining itself. The instability and impreciseness of the term *digital humanities* results not only from the field being new and growing but also from a set of uncertainties and a reliance on binary oppositions (such as individual-collaborative and methodological-critical). Some of these uncertainties and oppositional pairs must be overcome, while others may well be constructive and useful to the development of the field.

The size of the digital humanities is a significant factor. A field that was previously significantly smaller and more unnoticed has expanded, not only in terms of the number of proponents and institutions but also in scope. Scope is most critical for the current discussion of how to define the digital humanities. Big digital humanities relies on a large scope and an inclusive notion of the digital humanities. According to this definition, the field encompasses the area in between the humanities, in its full richness, and "the digital." The digital is taken to include information technologies, digital media and different types of digitally enabled modalities, tools, and expressions. Being in between (liminal) is an important quality for facilitating this kind of digital humanities. This liminal position possesses stability at the same time that its dynamism complicates any effort to predict what will emerge. Some scholarly work may not even be particularly digital but may nevertheless contribute to the field and the humanities at large. This expansive view does not suggest that everyone in the digital humanities has to do everything. Different institutions, initiatives, and people place themselves differently in relation to their self-defined space, and no one-size-fits-all model exists.

One of the advantages of seeing the digital humanities as a liminal space or contact zone is that it can accommodate many different interests and perspectives. There is no need to be aggressively territorial or to give people only one label. One can be many things at the same time, and those multiple identities are productive for the furthering of knowledge across epistemic traditions. The digital humanities is never about only one field or tradition changing or being challenged; rather, it is about allowing curiosity, exchange, and sharpness to drive intellectual and material development.

There are many ways of describing and understanding the digital humanities. I use the notion of "modes of engagement" as a means of describing the interrelation between the humanities and the digital. One important mode of engagement is technology as a tool, and much of the tradition of digital humanities has been built up around this mode: building archives, developing metadata schemes, creating and using tools of different kinds, and focusing on methodology. Other modes of engagement include technology as an object of analysis and as an expressive medium. These modes of engagement are embedded in different epistemic traditions. Big digital humanities, as developed in this book, suggests that we need to respect the integrity of these traditions at the same time as supporting the further intertwining of intellectual perspectives, disciplinary practices, and modes of engagement in a dynamic contact zone, which will itself lead to changes in the perspectives, people, and traditions it brings together.

While the label *digital humanities* is important in itself and is used consistently in this book, there is no guarantee that the label or the field will prevail indefinitely. Indeed, a previous denomination, *humanities computing*, is now used fairly rarely, and *digital humanities* does not necessarily correspond to *humanities computing*. This does not mean that *humanities computing* has disappeared or has simply changed into something different. The digital, however, has a particularly large scope and range that contributes to the plasticity of the digital humanities as well as to the usefulness of the term *digital humanities*. And once an area or label has been institutionalized, it can be pervasive even if it no longer seems fully descriptive.

The particular history of the field (as normally narrated) also conceals alternative traditions of work that may well qualify as digital humanities but have not been a significant part of the trajectory of humanities computing and what later became the digital humanities. Examples include much work on new information technologies in critical studies, media studies, gender studies, and ethnic studies and areas such as rhetoric and composition. We cannot change the historical trajectory of the past, but we can be sensitive to the multiple genealogies of the area and make every effort to be as inclusive as possible when moving the field forward. Indeed, doing so is a necessity for enabling the kind of digital humanities this book advocates, and such a trajectory is likely to result in negotiations, changes, and realignment of positions across the board.

Interlude 1: Some Personal Starting Points

Three points in time have affected my personal thinking about the digital humanities and have been formative in shaping my understanding of the field: in 1999, when we were in the process of launching HUMlab; in 2005, when we had Katherine Hayles do a talk at Umeå University and I asked myself why the *Blackwell Companion to the Digital Humanities* did not include her work; and in 2006, when I attended a cyberinfrastructure workshop in San Diego and ended up moderating a heated debate between humanists and supercomputer experts.

In the fall of 1999, I was involved in establishing HUMlab at Umeå University under Torbjörn Johansson, the founding director. Torbjörn had a very strong idea about an open meeting place for the humanities, culture and technology, and while I was very supportive, I was also more distinctly attached to the Faculty of Arts and the Department of English. At this time, I was working on a concept for a digital language laboratory outside of but potentially linked to HUMlab. This process highlighted the difference between my position and Torbjörn's. He pushed to make the new language lab a more general resource for the faculty and part of HUMlab's overall mission, while I sought to build a more closed resource for language studies. Looking back, I think there were pros and cons to both models, but this example illustrates the territoriality of institutional work. I had come from the Department of English and had a substantial investment in its perspective. It took me some time to go from "Yes, this open meeting place is a great idea" to fully embracing the basic idea. I did change my mind fairly quickly, however, and I think that this shifting of positions was educational in itself. It was also inspirational and productive to work with someone based in mathematics and university IT administration who strongly believed in the value of the humanities and culture. It did not hurt that Torbjörn's long hair and cowboy boots also made clear his belief in the importance of self-expression and in not necessarily conforming fully with all rules at all times.

September 21, 2005, was a pleasant fall day in Umeå, Sweden. Katherine Hayles was just about to start her talk, "My Mother Was a Computer: Digital Subjects and Literary Texts." Despite that title, her formal credentials as a professor of English and her demeanor before starting to talk seemed to make some of the audience (unaware of much of her research) categorize her as a fairly traditional literary scholar. She certainly surprised some of the audience when she started to talk about the machine on which the universe may be running. The first time she came to Umeå, three years earlier, Hayles had talked about "Computing the Human"; on a 2012 visit, her talk was titled "Economic Infrastructure and Artificial Intelligences: The Case of Automated Trading Programs." Hayles is clearly a foremost figure in thinking about the intersection of computation and what it entails to be human, and her work touches on many intellectual questions that are central to the humanities. She has been important to my thinking about what the digital humanities can be, and she is one of the first scholars we invited to HUMlab.

At the time of her 2005 visit, I had started to look at the discourse of the field of digital humanities (and humanities computing) more closely, and I found it surprising that Hayles did not really seem to be part of that discourse. For example, she is represented in the *Companion to the Digital Humanities* (2004) only by two bibliographic references in a section on further reading in one of the chapters, and when the field's achievements are summed up, the *Companion* says, "If one humanities computing activity is to be highlighted above all others, in my view it must be the TEI [Text Encoding Initiative]. It represents the most significant intellectual advances that have been made in our area, and has influenced the markup community as a whole."[15] The TEI is a consortium that works to develop and maintain standards for how to represent texts in digital form, and the guidelines for how to codify texts produced by this community have no doubt been important to the development of the digital humanities. But while TEI is a major achievement, one might well argue that Hayles's work was equally worth mentioning in this context.

I found, however, that her absence was not only a matter of someone having been left out of the account; rather, very different epistemic traditions were at work here. Hayles was not so much excluded as not part of the map in the first place. This did not quite make sense to me, as I thought the field needed to engage with her work as well as with the TEI, and this realization has remained central for my conception of the field.

The final discussion at the Cyberinfrastructure Summer Institute at the University of California at San Diego, was held on July 28, 2006, a hot and sunny day in Southern California. The institute had been advertised as a series of workshops to allow humanists, artists, and social scientists to engage with new digital tools and infrastructural resources. The workshops involved "demonstrations of new technological devices, and their applications as well as scholarly practices," and participants worked together in a laboratory to "engage important and creative thought and application."[16] A mix of humanities scholars, supercomputer representatives, and others interested in the intersection of the humanities and large-scale computing were present. In many ways, this was an ideal setup to explore possibilities for furthering humanities research collaboratively and making interesting use of available and emergent technologies. I had arrived late to the event and was asked to moderate the final session on short notice.

I still remember the contained energy among the participants during my introduction to the session. I quickly became aware that this was not the contained energy of wanting to continue a harmonic and constructive dialogue but rather a deep sense of lack of dialogue. Many of the humanities and social sciences scholars felt that their questions and perspectives had not been taken into account, and they were most eager to engage in a conversation about this fact. They had come to the workshop with research issues and with an interest in learning more about the possibilities of large-scale computing. However, they thought that the technological perspective had been foregrounded at the expense of their research-driven interests. Moreover, even when a sense of a common goal exists, a very substantial gap can remain between the infrastructural level (such as robust distributed access rights) and the research questions scholars may want to ask. The discussion went well after the initial surge of energy, and it became a critical component of the workshop. I was greatly helped by a young computer science major interested in classics, who helped bridge the gap between the technologists and the humanists. I still remember the negative energy of the event, however, and the sense that it could have gone very wrong. The stakes were high—probably higher than they needed to be—and the encounter further developed my curatorial interests. It would have been useful if the setup had allowed some of this energy to be channeled earlier and if some of the discussion could have been provoked at the beginning of the program. Chapter 5 discusses the role of curatorship in the digital humanities.

These three encounters taught me the value of a truly open meeting place and of retreating from a position, the importance of epistemic traditions and different worldviews in the development of a field, and how tension can both be destructive and constructive. While this book is not primarily about disciplinary tension, differences and unrest undoubtedly point to significant issues in the formation of a field and are important in forwarding the development of a field. Such tensions may well be an integral part of the future of the digital humanities.

Digital Humanities and Digital Humanists

Digital technology, or the digital, is relevant to the humanities for several reasons: it is an integral part of life in large parts of the world, an increasing amount of material is digital, and digital media offer expressive potential. The digital reaches across the humanities and beyond and thus provides useful points of connection. Since digital technology is interwoven into our daily lives, expressive modalities, corporate structures, and societal concerns, it is a powerful intersecting property and a boundary object. The usefulness of the digital can be seen in the way it can incorporate different perspectives, modes of engagement, and disciplinary connections. In this sense, the digital can be seen as a material or an inflection that is relevant to much (but not all) humanities work. This extended and plastic meaning of the digital is one of several reasons for the comparatively large leverage of the digital humanities.

A basic question is whether a field that singles out the digital can incorporate other technological layers such as nanotechnology and moveable type. The brief answer is clearly affirmative, because otherwise the digital humanities would not make sense as an enterprise. We cannot even begin to understand present-day digital technologies (and even less the digital) without relating to both the predigital and the postdigital. Chandra Mukerji, a historian of early modern technology, makes this point when she connects the logistical tradition manifested in the Garden of Versailles under Louis XIV to digital media. She argues that both the digital revolution and the logistical revolution of the early modern period have "restructured selves, social identities and global relations of power through material innovation."[17]

As for the second part of the denomination *digital humanities*, Natalia Cecire makes an important point when she observes that we "seem to have a tendency to think that the "humanities" part of DH is stable, that we sort of already have it squared away, while the tech skills are what we need to gain."[18] The humanities, with its investment in the human condition and cultural expression, is also a type of boundary object, and as Cecire emphasizes, it is not a completely stable one. Traditionally, digital humanities and humanities computing seem to have interacted to a larger extent with more stable parts of the humanities—in particular, departments and disciplines (some more than others)—rather than with other humanities-related hubs and centers (such as gender studies, ethnic studies, queer studies, medical humanities, environmental humanities, or "neurohumanities"). These areas are more likely to be dynamic and intersectional but are also typically more theory-driven and less dependent on large digitized material collections, which would help explain why the connection has traditionally been fairly weak. Digital humanities and some of these centers or departments may also have been competitors for resources. A description of a roundtable discussion at a 2011 American Studies Association conference demonstrates some of the tension:

> In an era of widespread budget cuts at universities across the United States, scholars in the digital humanities are gaining recognition in the institution through significant grants, awards, new departments and cluster hires. At the same time, ethnic studies departments are losing ground, facing deep cuts and even disbandment. Though the apparent rise of one and retrenchment of the other may be the result of anti-affirmative action, post-racial, and neoliberal rhetoric of recent decades and not related to any effect of one field on the other, digital humanities discussions do often elide the difficult and complex work of talking about racial, gendered, and economic materialities, which are at the forefront of ethnic and gender studies. Suddenly, the (raceless, sexless, genderless) technological seems the only aspect of the humanities that has a viable future.[19]

This account brings up the recurring critique that there is not enough humanities in the digital humanities.[20] It can hardly be disputed that the digital humanities has not richly and consistently incorporated gender, ethnic, queer, or environmental perspectives into its operation and agenda, and these sensibilities and scholarly areas clearly must be considered central to the field. Furthermore, these and other clearly intersectional areas of the humanities can be good partners for the digital humanities. In return, the digital humanities can contribute to the development of these areas and more generally to the development of the disciplines that make up the humanities. An excellent example of this kind of exchange can be seen in some recent work on sound studies at the interface of cultural studies of sound and the use of digitally driven methodologies. According to a panel presentation at the 2014 Digital Humanities Conference,

> A wide range of interdisciplinary scholarship on sound has sparked investigations into the cultural histories of aurality and sound reproduction, the politics of the voice and noise, urban soundscapes, ethnographic modernities, acoustemologies, and the sonic construction of gender, race, and ethnicity. . . . These important qualitative studies, moreover, have in recent years been supplemented by large-scale quantitative analyses of speech and music datasets. . . . Yet a lingering textual bias within digital humanities—largely a product of the field's emergence from textual and literary studies—has obscured the significance of this work for the field, often preventing meaningful overlap. . . . It is against this backdrop that leading sound theorist Jonathan Sterne has argued that "existing digital humanities work has largely reproduced visualist biases in the humanities." . . .
>
> By identifying and highlighting four research initiatives clustered around audio artifacts, this panel aims to bring sound scholarship and digital humanities into a more meaningful conversation with each other.[21]

While Sterne is right about the visual basis in the humanities being perpetuated in the digital humanities,[22] the digital humanities has not had a predominant visual studies interest (for some of the same reasons that sound studies has not had a strong place in digital humanities). In some cases, visual elements have come into the digital humanities through the textual (for example, through images of textual elements), through information attached to artifacts in archives and libraries, and increasingly through a growing interest in visualization and spatial humanities. There is much potential in developing the intersections between digital humanities and areas such as sound studies and new forms of visual studies. Such work must be based on the further development of both the digital humanities and the other areas.

There is also a sense that the landscape has shifted and is continuing to shift. Ethnic studies departments are not necessarily seen as having as promising a future as the digital humanities, and some fields and centers that used to occupy the privileged position of the digital humanities may no longer do so. A tension naturally exists between operations that are prioritized and others that are not. At the 2011 UCLA Queer Studies Conference, Micha Cárdenas reflected on a comment from Karen Tongson:

> Tongson was discussing how Queer Theory used to be seen as a "hip, trendy" field to be in, when people still thought it was ripe with possibility for disruption and that now it seemed more institutionally tamed. (It's hard to convey here the combination of sarcasm and actual sense of dissolusionment [sic]) Similarly, she said, with a bit of irony perhaps, that the Digital Humanities is the new hot, sellable commodity. (If so, then perhaps our panel was the most hipster thing around, Ha!)[23]

The digital humanities can learn from this story in terms of thinking about its longevity and institutional position. What happens if (when?) the digital humanities loses its current privileged status? Does becoming more institutionalized also mean that there is a risk of becoming too tame? And while the field needs to incorporate gender, ethnic, queer, and environmental perspectives much more strongly into its operation and agenda,[24] the digital humanities also needs to have a long-term coevolutionary relationship with fields for which such engagement is the core. The discussion of the digital humanities as a field has a great deal to do with what is seen as the core of the field in relation to other fields and disciplines. Is the field focused on developing methodologies for analyzing humanities materials, producing media artworks, critiquing the gendered and political inflection of digital knowledge structures, or redefining the humanities? Or all of the above? From the point of view of big digital humanities, the answer to the last question would be, "Yes, all of these aspects can and probably should be part of the field." It is not surprising, however, that uncertainty exists and debate is ongoing concerning the subject matter of the digital humanities given the multiple epistemic traditions of the field and the size of the territory indicated by these questions.

This debate also necessarily relates to the question of identity. The fact that the number of people identifying with the field has increased significantly is one reason why instability exists. The community is more heterogeneous, and more work is taking place at the boundaries of the field. Ted Underwood has argued that digital humanities is not an identity category and that graduate students should not have to declare themselves digital or analog humanists,[25] and while this may be a worthwhile sentiment, the digital humanities clearly is an identity category. The fierceness and extension of the debates surrounding the digital humanities can partly be linked to the making and negotiation of identities. Some people will place themselves within the identity category of digital humanities, others will not, and many (if not most) will simultaneously subscribe to several professional identity categories. Even negative or open definitions, such as Jesse Stommel's "For me, what counts as digital humanities, ultimately, is work that doesn't try to police the boundaries of what counts as digital humanities,"[26] build on identity formation. As chapter 2 discusses, there is added complexity here because the name *digital humanities* is also relatively new to those who structurally were (and still are) the core of the institutional buildup of the digital humanities.

So who are the digital humanists? Is this question at all relevant? Yes, it probably is, although not primarily to work out how many digital humanists there are but to discuss the dynamics of an expanding field that is closely interrelated to a range of disciplines and platforms. A simple answer to this question would be, anyone who answers yes when asked, "Are you a digital humanist?" This issue is more complex, however; for one thing, many respondents would probably say, "Yes, but I am also a . . ." Or "Not really, but some of my work is aligned with the digital humanities." The people most likely to answer affirmatively without much reservation are individuals involved in a digital humanities center or organization or invested in potential careers in the field of digital humanities. The denomination seems to be sharply increasing even in a negative sense—that is, when individuals are explaining why they are not or are not becoming digital humanists.[27]

While we should not use the label *digital humanist* for people not interested in identifying as belonging to the field, we need to make sure to accept new people interested in the field, even if they may not initially identify as digital humanists. This is particularly important if the field is seen as a meeting place across disciplines and different modes of engagement. Indeed, under such a model, the question of exactly who is a digital humanist becomes less of an issue. What is important is that scholars and experts across a range of disciplines and specialties come together and contribute to humanities-driven exploration of digitally inflected research and education.

This is partly a discussion of time-sensitive labels and labeling. But while on one level it does not extend beyond packaging and intuitional framing, it is also about issues that are very central to the formation of the field, scholarly identity, and conceptual framing. We rarely are only one thing at one time. If we see the digital humanities as an intersectional meeting place, allowing for multiple affiliations and identities is the best way forward.

Interlude 2: Do I Have to Be a Digital Humanist?

I sometimes have mixed feelings about being identified as a digital humanist or representing the digital humanities. In a Swedish context, the term for the field (*digital humaniora*) is still not used frequently, and it tends to be mostly associated with the packaging of what we do and where we want to go for funding agencies, policy making, deans, and others. This can be a very useful strategic move. For example, it permits one to make a case for national doctoral program in digital humanities or a chair in digital humanities in a way that is difficult if there is no sense of a discipline or established area. Having a platform provides leverage.

But we also need to be skeptical about platforms and platforming. David Goldberg points out that platform thinking tends to flatten complex interrelations, and Shannon Mattern critiques the entrepreneurial epistemology of the platform metaphor.[28] In addition, the more one packages oneself as something, the more one becomes associated with that packaging or operation. I have hesitated to become too heavily involved with specific scholarly associations within the digital humanities—with varying degrees of success—because I relish an outside position. At the same time, the formation of a field is a process that necessarily implies pinning down, establishing territories, and often losing some of the flexibility and openness associated with a more undefined enterprise. Is it possible to have both a strong institutional platform and a relatively free role?

Being seen as a representative for the digital humanities sometimes comes with certain expectations, particularly from the rest of the humanities. One common expectation is that one will fight to defend the field in its entirety. Another expectation is that representatives of the digital humanities should be able to articulate the value and impact of the field in a way that is rarely expected of representatives of established disciplines and fields. A third expectation is that the digital humanities is mostly about tools and databases. These expectations may not be surprising given the relative newness of digital humanities as an institutional player and the field's history, but they also demonstrate the tendency to see digital humanities as separate from the disciplines and as an outlier fairly insignificant to the furthering of the humanities as a project.

I once attended a lunch with the director of a major humanities and social sciences institution, and I found myself not only pressured to defend the whole of the digital humanities but also to give a rationale for the field in a way that would probably never have happened if I had represented another area. While this fierce discursive approach did not surprise me, it felt peculiar in several ways, not least because my work is partly a critique of the field and because the assumptions presented about the digital humanities were both uninformed and tendentious. In such discussions, established disciplines are normally not questioned. I found myself defending something that I do not really represent, though I am of course largely sympathetic to the digital humanities as a project. In hindsight, the situation reminded me of Anne Balsamo's description of representing a traditional notion of the humanities at a school of technology, although she was not quite comfortable doing so from her position of "progressive humanities."[29]

This outside pressure to motivate and rationalize a field is natural, since curiosity and territorial tensions are not only inevitable but warranted since resources are being invested in the field. However, when such humanities representatives ask the digital humanities to present their "killer application" or explain why they are relevant, these questioners use a discursive frame that they often strongly resist when it comes from outside the humanities.

We want discussions of the field to be respectful and sharp and to be based on interest and curiosity. It is an advantage that the digital humanities seems more talked about, discussed and questioned than many other fields. This means that people in the field need to be capable of talking about their work, the field and its interrelation to other knowledge areas. It is useful to have a good sense of the digital humanities as a whole, including both scholarly and technological layers, an awareness of the intersectional quality of the field, and a familiarity with a couple of key projects and results.

Digitally Inflected Challenges

Part of the critique of the digital humanities draws on a perceived lack of connection to research questions that are meaningful to the humanities. Alan Liu writes that the digital humanities rarely extends its "critique to the full register of society, economics, politics, or culture."[30] This critique comes not only from within the field[31] but also from outside. In a controversial *New Republic* article, Adam Kirsch categorizes the digital humanities as being understood in two different ways: the application of computer technology to traditional scholarly work (a minimalist reading) and changing the substance of humanistic matter (a maximalist reading). He argues that the (extreme) maximalist version of digital humanities has "less to do with ways of thinking than with problems of university administration" and suggests (through a rhetorical question) that the minimalist version helps us illustrate what we already know rather than gives us new ways to think.[32] While Kirsch's critique is sweeping and dogmatic, it addresses some important questions. The questions are more relevant than the conclusions, and the digital humanities would do well not to just simply refute such critiques.[33] Kirsch raises two broad key questions: What is the grounding of the visionary type of digital humanities? What is the intellectual gist of the methodological type of digital humanities?

Much discussion in the digital humanities tends to focus either on general and overarching perspectives or on very specific and often technical or methodological issues. Though important, these perspectives are not necessarily what is paramount to scholars or anyone interested in the richness of the subject matter beyond the structural level or individual projects.

As a scholarly field, the digital humanities will have to better articulate what it is, where it comes from, and how its work contributes to our collective knowledge. What makes good work is not simply what it is about but how it is done, the questions asked, the insights, the quality of the arguments made, the novelty of the ideas uncovered, and the arguments that sustain them. One never conjures a field out of thin air; rather, one extends what has gone before, what has worked, even as one breaks with it.[34] A major challenge for the digital humanities as a field is to demonstrate the depth, innovativeness, and quality of the work.

The digital humanities, however, is not just about grand challenges and disciplinary insights. We also need to acknowledge that an important part of the fabric of the field is the infrastructural work, the methodological competence, and the building of tools that contribute to understanding our past, shaping arguments, and formulating questions. This type of work can sometimes be mostly instrumental through supporting other types of work but is often an integral part of a discovery process. To some extent, tools and infrastructure shape the questions we can ask, and just like with other work, the quality of such work will vary. And while it may be tempting to separate the infrastructural level from other levels, in most cases doing so is neither possible nor desirable.

This argument goes both ways. Scholarly focused work needs to be aware of the important and integral role of infrastructure and methodological competence, and infrastructural work by itself is not enough without anchorage in the context of exciting scholarly and archival challenges. The story and the project of digital humanities need to incorporate both these perspectives.

The digital humanities is about work that has some digital inflection, whether through the use of technology as a tool or research challenges that somehow significantly incorporate both a digital or technological dimension and a human and cultural one. The digital humanities seemingly will be hard-pressed to accomplish this task without engaging with media studies, cultural studies, environmental humanities, and other parts of the institutionalized humanistic endeavor. And, of course, digital humanities also needs to engage with computer science, engineering, design, and other disciplines outside the humanities.

What research challenges may emerge at the intersection of disciplines and the digital humanities? There is no simple answer to this question, but some challenges from a few different disciplines exemplify perspectives relevant to the digital humanities. Lisa Gitelman at New York University is interested in the cultural work performed by or with the technology of paper.[35] While the digital inflection here is not predominant, it is certainly relevant to the digital humanities. Jennie Olofsson of Umeå University investigates the life of screens from component to postrecycling.[36] She is also interested in the meaning invested in screens when they are used. Her work aligns with media theory and environmental humanities. Richard White and his colleagues at Stanford University explore how historic perceptions of space in the newly settled West were not just a question of Cartesian geography but were decided by patterns of landholding, commerce, and communication.[37] Digital mapping can be quite useful here, and according to the group, leads to new questions being asked. Media scholar Jonathan Sterne at McGill University offers a history of the MP3 format in relation to a more general history of compression.[38] He questions how our ideas about what it means to hear and listen are tied to the development of twentieth-century media. Philosopher Peter Asaro at the New School researches questions of identity, social practice, and responsibility in relation to teleoperated and autonomous war systems.[39] He also made a film about robot love, thereby demonstrating the "making" part of digitally enabled work.[40] Archaeologist Thomas Larsson at Umeå University explores the social and environmental context of rock carving sites based on a research tool that layers maps, carefully vectorized rock carvings, and other data.[41] Individual rock carving characteristics can be combined to visually show configuration and distribution over expansive sites. Such examples can help the digital humanities describe what is at stake intellectually.

As these examples indicate, different disciplines and scholarly traditions engage with the digital in different ways. These patterns are complex, and a detailed look at the discipline of history (itself a large and diversified construct) may be instructive. We would expect history to have a more infrastructural and instrumental relation to the digital than a discipline such as media studies since history lacks a strong focus on digitally inflected study objects and since it increasingly needs tools to manage and mine large quantities of digitized materials. According to the website for the Roy Rosenzweig Center for History and New Media, digital history constitutes

> an approach to examining and representing the past that takes advantage of new communication technologies such as computers and the Web. It draws on essential features of the digital realm, such as databases, hypertextualization, and networks, to create and share historical knowledge.[42]

Technology clearly serves as a tool in this description. It is not surprising that history does not engage extensively with the digital as an object of analysis since most relevant material was not digitally born and research questions are typically less digitally inflected as they are in some other disciplines. History of technology is an exception, although this area tends not to engage primarily with digital technologies. Nevertheless, the history (and philosophy) of technology has much to contribute to the digital humanities. Other examples of when the focus of the work is not limited to the instrumental use of technology include some science and technology studies work, some environmental humanities work, and recent research on digital culture and history didactics.

The relation between the technological layer and disciplinary questions can be seen, for example, in Kaci Nash's report from the panel "Hardtack and Software: Digital Approaches to the American Civil War" at the 2012 American Historical Association conference:

> During the comments section of the panel, Robert Nelson asserted that the challenge is to produce scholarship that is going to be of interest to

scholars of the subject not the technology. We must focus on historical questions and historical moments, not on techniques.

This thought was one that stayed with me more than any other aspect of the session. If we want the discipline of history to be receptive of works created through and with the digital medium, it is essential that we emphasize the scholarship that is being produced, not the way in which it is being produced.[43]

It seems likely that the digital humanities will always be placed between the technological-methodological and the disciplinary, and while Nash's point is valid, we also need to be concerned with the *how*. We must to be careful not to lean over too much one way or the other. The way in which scholarship is carried out is also important, but without historical questions and historical research, we run the risk of failing to go beyond infrastructure and demonstration projects.

Cameron Blevins claims that digital history has "over-promised and under-delivered" as a result of being too preoccupied with methodology.[44] He demonstrates this point by looking at two examples of his own previous work in a rare and illuminating self-critical analysis. The first study (published as a blog entry) used topic modeling to analyze a large number of diary entries by a Maine midwife. This is the most widely read piece of historical writing Blevins has ever produced: it has reportedly been viewed more than ten thousand times and been included in the syllabi of at least twenty different courses. But the interest raised by the blog entry was mainly methodological, and he claims that the piece did not really add any disciplinary knowledge. The other study was a more traditional scholarly article on an imagined geography of the nation based on data from one newspaper. Here there was a clear historical argument, but in trying to address the fact that computational methods helped produce these results (presented in a separate online piece), he found himself framing the issue in terms of methodology, thus again getting caught in a methodological nexus where most of the outside comments related to the methodology rather than the content. Blevins usefully illustrates the tensions among disciplinary perspectives, methodological perspectives, and epistemic traditions. The chosen modes of publication, associated conventions, and intended audiences both shaped his own articulation of the subject matter and filtered the reading of the pieces. We need scholarly processes where the intellectual questions and the methodology are not separated in this way and instead are combined to create a stronger, entangled space somewhere in between.

Mainstream history includes a whole range of work that does not focus on the digital but draws on digital sources, digital tools, and accessible infrastructure. The likelihood of a digital denomination is much stronger if the output also has a digital component. For example, use of a digital archive or tool to address a research challenge may not be apparent in a resultant journal article unless the use is heavy enough to warrant a discussion of the methodology and tools used. Brian Donahue's The Great Meadow: Farmers and the Land in Colonial Concord is an example of important mainstream history work featuring an argument that is partly based on digital mapping but that would probably not readily be classified as digital humanities.[45] The tool is not in the foreground, though it is clearly acknowledged, yet there is no question that the research question and the main argument (challenging the idea that farmers of colonial New England degraded the land) are the driving factor. Digital modes of expression are becoming increasingly common and will undoubtedly change the future repertoire of scholarship. This is particularly relevant for history given the accumulation of digital archives, materials, and representations. The gap between such content and traditional publication formats is quite distinct, and we should not expect things to change quickly.

The entrenchment of digital databases and archival resources in in studies of history is an important part of the infrastructure of the discipline. This is not surprising given that historians examine historical materials (seen as fragments of the past) critically, pay attention to what is not there as well as to what is there, and base interpretation on the fact that history is manifested in complex contexts that we cannot fully understand. Hence, one challenge is to create digital platforms that can handle uncertainty and materials that are not fully described or easily encoded.

We also see an increase in research using large demographic databases, even if there is still skepticism in the history community regarding the perceived quantitative focus of such work.[46] As Hayles observes, tension exists between the narrative quality of history and the database as genre.[47] In a subfield such as ancient history or classics, however, the use of digital materials and tools seems to be much more accepted.[48] This can partly be ascribed to a long history of using such resources in a way that has been close to the development of the discipline, the establishment of authoritative digital resources such as the Thesaurus Linguae Graecae and the Perseus Digital Library, and a strong dependency on a comparatively small and limited array of material.

Whether we look at ancient history or history more generally, digitally enabled spatial representations are becoming increasingly accessible and important. Maps and spatial representation have been important in the past, but there is considerable power to the combination of historical materials, use of spatial modalities, and digital mapping systems. Also, the methodology behind geographical information systems (GIS) offers some powerful tools for navigating rich data sources.

As Hayles observes, most geographical information software is built on a Cartesian grid, and she points to the tension between this underlying conception of space and the view of space as a social construction or a set of dynamic interrelations as articulated by Henri Lefebvre and Doreen Massey, among others.[49] Hayles looks at spatial history in this context and points to uses of geographical software that may not conform to a non-Cartesian conception of space but that still adds layers and networks to the representation, distorts the Cartesian model in different ways, and adds time as a significant variable. The material qualities of specific computational structures to some extent determine what conceptions of space can be instantiated. Zephyr Frank discusses this "sweet spot" between historical GIS and space as a historical and social construct, writing that the "shared commitment to interpreting the past with reference to space and spatial meanings is what draws the two approaches together and, perhaps in the right hands, makes them compatible."[50]

Digitization of map resources can also lead to the questioning of printed map practices. As historian Patricia Seed shows, well-established cultural heritage institutions may not control the process leading up to a printed map.[51] For example, maps may be professionally adjusted as if they were images, or digitization services may put together map parts without clear acknowledgement.

Ancient history can offer examples of some other types of visualization used in the field. The Rome Reborn project seeks to digitally reconstruct the entire city of ancient Rome.[52] The intention is to study urban development, but the project started in 1997 at 320 AD and has not yet moved beyond this date. It is an example of an initiative embedded in a realist framework, where the detail of the visual representation can at times seem more important than raising research questions. It is telling that the polygon count is given as an important indicator of progress.[53] This may not be surprising given the character of the project, and high-quality reconstructions of course can have a distinct value, but many assumptions seem not only to be built into the model but also not to be much problematized. It might, for example, have been useful to include other kinds of visual layers that could bring in other datasets or social dynamics or that could make us step out of the frame of the visualization. Johanna Drucker discusses "a rhetoric taken wholesale from the techniques of the empirical sciences that conceals their epistemological biases under a guise of familiarity."[54] With many of these reconstructions, the familiarity lies in the use of platforms such as Google Maps, game-style 3-D modeling, and GPS technology.

This realist frame also seems at times to hold when historians move to a more multisensory approach. Eleanor Betts rightly points to the visual bias in representations such as Rome Reborn, presenting a highly useful and knowledgeable narrative about how Rome might have smelled, tasted, and sounded.[55] However, there is also a tendency to move to a reconstructive sensibility here that seems fairly positivistic when the digital project is described. Examples include trying to simulate noise levels in decibels, using GPS surveys to model data, and simulating sound, smell, and colors:

> By recreating and measuring the combination of sounds, smells, tastes and sensations described by the sources and mapped onto specific areas of Rome, a more accurate and representational understanding of the everyday experience of the city can be established.[56]

Even though this approach supposedly adds an experiential layer to existing visual models, the underlying positivistic push seems to be the same: reconstruct as much as possible in as detailed, scientific, and objectivistic a way as possible. The difference is that Betts's work contains real narrative and historical questions that probably are considerably more useful and richer than any realist model. While such a technical project could probably be fruitful if done well, many problems would have to be overcome. One example is that the intention is to build this sensory model on top of established visual representations, which are already laden reconstructions. Another question is the feasibility of getting the work done given the kind of chronological trajectory of large-scale projects such as Rome Reborn.

Even if these types of tools and perspectives can be useful, other models may be more effective if they are less invested in realist reconstruction and instead are built on a conceptually strong basis with a level of detail, layering of data, and experimentation appropriate for this foundation and for real research questions. For instance, rapid prototyping can provide a quicker and more conceptual approach to reconstruction work.[57] While there is no one process or blueprint for carrying out intellectual-material work, putting effort into conceptual and exploratory work is often time well-spent, which increases the chance of the intellectual questions not being locked down at an early stage or disregarded. There needs to be a continuous interplay between scholarly questions, materials and data structures, and aesthetic-material manifestations. Such work is hard and often requires us to challenge epistemic traditions and assumptions about technology and computational systems.

Innovation in such processes works on multiple levels, as demonstrated in the discussion of geographical information systems. Research questions and argument paths can be innovative, but so can methodological perspectives and infrastructural implementations. A useful example concerns the importance of a longue durée perspective in digitally supported historical work. Jo Guldi argues that digital technologies enable the combination of scale and scrutiny over large extents of time and space.[58] David Armitage develops a similar position:

> Even to more traditional analogue humanists, the promise of the digital humanities for transforming the work of intellectual historians is immense. The increasing availability of vastly larger corpora of texts and the tools to analyse them allows historians to establish the conventions that framed intellectual innovation, and hence to show where individual agency took place within collective structures. And with ever greater flexibility for searching and recovering contextual information, we can discover more precisely and persuasively moments of rupture as well as stretches of continuity. In short, we now have both the methodological tools and the technological means to overcome most, if not all, of the traditional objections to the marriage of intellectual history with the *longue durée*. We can at last get back to studying big ideas in a big way.[59]

This combined methodological and intellectual claim goes far beyond digitizing already existing processes or materials. Indeed, it uses some of the visionary terminology sometimes associated with the digital humanities to make this point, but there is a real conceptual foundation here, expressed as "discover[ing] more precisely and persuasively moments of rupture as well as stretches of continuity."[60] This is partly a matter of scale and change of scale (or zooming), and Hayles argues that this is one of the most important aspects of the transformation associated with the digital humanities.[61] Her discussion of reading also relates to scale when she refers to the sheer number of books available, the limitations on a person's lifelong reading and algorithmic processing of literary material. Even the term *reading*, she argues, is being challenged by distant reading as conceptualized by Franco Moretti and others. In arguing that the tension between close reading and algorithmic analysis should not be overemphasized, Hayles thus seems to align with Armitage's position as well as Frank's point about combining different mapping traditions. Approaching this tension is a key challenge not only for these disciplines but also for the humanities more generally and for the interpretative social sciences.[62]

The Role of Technology

Armitage puts considerable emphasis on the technological layer (tools, search capabilities, methodology, and so forth) when discussing the potential impact of digital humanities on the discipline of history. This line of argumentation has a factual foundation, as we are seeing the emergence of very large databases and powerful tools, but technology also serves as an enabler and a means of discussing the far-reaching development of a discipline beyond the impact of specific technologies. In this sense, technology can have imaginary power, which sometimes leads to an overly technoromantic discourse but which can also be useful in thinking about and designing possible futures.

On a material level, different types of digital humanities engage quite differently with technology as a consequence of different modes of engagement and epistemic traditions. Much of the work of humanities computing has focused on tools and standards and has been manifested, for example, as stand-alone software, web applications, and text encoding schemes. Such production requires access to technology but not necessarily large-scale laboratory installations.

The digital humanities generally has engaged in relatively little experimentation with computation outside the computer. Most digital humanists do not engage with physical computing such as sensor technology, 3-D printing, or the so-called Internet of Things (multitudes of connected entities). The rich infrastructure associated with areas such as media arts or scientific visualization is rarely seen in the digital humanities. While this is changing, many digital humanities centers still do not seem very technologically advanced or experimental, at least on the surface. One primary reason for this is that the experimentation often takes place inside the computer (typically on the web and in terms of back-end systems and data structures) and intellectually and that there is often not a large investment in the physical materiality of computing. One exception is the growing interest in maker labs and similar enterprises in the digital humanities and in libraries. One example (among several) is the Maker Lab in the Humanities at the University of Victoria, Canada.[63] Again, the digital humanities consistently needs to bring a critical perspective to its practices, not least when they buy into established frameworks. Hackathons, THATcamps, and maker labs are not neutral enterprises, and the recurring descriptions of them as devoid of hierarchies seem problematic. Combining an explorative, playful relation to technology with a critical dimension can be challenging but is necessary.

The service function of some traditional digital humanities operations may have discouraged play as a justified and projectable part of the operation. Most central computing service departments or similar functions at universities are quite functional and take care to avoid engaging too much in seemingly playful experimentation and activities that may not seem like well-spent money. Indeed, as Willard McCarty points out, academic legitimacy historically often came from the service function, making it important within the field.[64]

Digital humanists coming from a critical tradition are less likely to use considerable technological infrastructure. Again, this territory is changing, but mainstream humanists who study the digital often maintain a certain distance from what they study, and strong technological engagement is not very common. An exception is the area of scholarly production, where we see examples such as Scalar, a system for multimodal scholarship, developed by Alliance for Networking Visual Culture.[65] Media production can also be part of educational programs. The use of digital tools beyond personal and organizational use would seem to be fairly uncommon, even if specialized software packages exist for methods and practices such as qualitative analysis, topic modeling, and network analysis. This area would seem to offer substantial potential gain from seeing the digital humanities as an intellectual and technological meeting place operating across different modes of engagement and most of the humanities disciplines.

Whatever technology is used and whether or not it is inside the computer, real technological engagement is vital to the digital humanities. As Matt Ratto explains, his idea of "critical making," highlights the reconnection of two modes of engagement with the world that are typically held separate: critical thinking, traditionally understood as conceptually and linguistically based, and physical "making," goal-based material work.[66]

Technological engagement and critical work need to be brought together, and doing so requires allowing digitally inflected exploration and experimentation. We also need a conceptual foundation for humanities infrastructure that is not just built on science and engineering models but makes deep sense from the point of view of humanities-based questions and activities.[67] Such infrastructure may include web platforms used to present and question multiple perspectives on a research issue, performance spaces that enable academic installations and artistic projects, floor screens that challenge traditional screen thinking and facilitate vertical engagement with materials, systems for critically analyzing database structures and testing alternative ontologies, and maker spaces that question the idea and history of making. Moreover, technology can also serve as a boundary object and enabler of imaginary discourse for a broadly conceived digital humanities that functions as an intersectional meeting place.

Writing the Digital Humanities

One output for imaginary discourse is descriptions of the digital humanities, and with a steady stream of books and articles on the digital humanities since 2010, there is plenty of material. Looking at specific texts about the digital humanities is one way of getting a better sense of what the digital humanities is and how the field is being framed and formed.

Texts of this kind can help us understand a developing field as well as how institutional questions are linked to other concerns and factors. However, we need to exercise analytical caution and see these texts in their context. They are commercially driven descriptions rather than scholarly texts, and their relative brevity puts pressure on what can be included. In addition, the authors may not be fully in control of the texts, which are likely seen as the press's responsibility. At the same time, these texts grapple with relating to a "new" field and attracting a reasonably large audience. Here I examine three books published in 2012: *Debates in the Digital Humanities* (University of Minnesota Press), *Understanding Digital Humanities* (Palgrave Macmillan) and *How We Think: Digital Media and Contemporary Technogenesis* (University of Chicago Press).

The existence of *Debates in the Digital Humanities*, edited by Matthew Gold, demonstrates a certain level of institutional maturity. The press's promotional material for the book presents it as reflexively discussing the digital humanities in terms of promise, tension, critique, and grounding:

> Encompassing new technologies, research methods, and opportunities for collaborative scholarship and open-source peer review, as well as innovative ways of sharing knowledge and teaching, the digital humanities promises to transform the liberal arts—and perhaps the university itself. Indeed, at a time when many academic institutions are facing austerity budgets, digital humanities programs have been able to hire new faculty, establish new centers and initiatives, and attract multimillion-dollar grants.
>
> Clearly the digital humanities has reached a significant moment in its brief history. But what sort of moment is it? *Debates in the Digital Humanities* brings together leading figures in the field to explore its theories, methods, and practices and to clarify its multiple possibilities and tensions. From defining what a digital humanist is and determining whether the field has (or needs) theoretical grounding, to discussions of coding as scholarship and trends in data-driven research, this cutting-edge volume delineates the current state of the digital humanities and envisions potential futures and challenges. At the same time, several essays aim pointed critiques at the field for its lack of attention to race, gender, class, and sexuality; the inadequate level of diversity among its practitioners; its absence of political commitment; and its preference for research over teaching.[68]

This text does not question the existence of digital humanities as a field and signals the maturity of the field by bringing in established figures and declaring that it has reached a "significant moment." However, that moment is situated against a "brief history," which could be taken to indicate a possible lack of historical perspective. The foundational narrative of digital humanities (as the tradition of humanities computing) usually goes back to the late 1940s, whereas most media studies programs, in comparison, were started in the 1960s and 1970s. Some of this history is indeed covered in Matthew Kirschenbaum's chapter in the volume.[69]

This text emphasizes the comparative strength of the field by talking about large grants and major expansion at a time when many institutions of higher education are facing significant cuts. Such discourse is common for new or developing fields, of course, offering a way of asserting the institutional power of an enterprise that does not necessarily have full acceptance or support from the broader community. The book clearly is about the formation of a new field rather than engaging with what goes on outside the field or trying to contribute to mutual development of the digital humanities and other disciplines. In addition, the text gives a sense of the field's major potential, declaring that the digital humanities has the capacity to transform the liberal arts as well as possibly the university itself. The digital humanities is the main agent in this process. This is a strong visionary statement, and such statements are common in contemporary digital humanities.

This description presents *Debates in the Digital Humanities* as representing a fairly inclusive notion of the digital humanities. However, the text also has only a limited focus on the digital as an object of inquiry and devotes fairly little attention to the technological layer (apart from invoking new technology)—perhaps understandable given the focus on the field's development.

Understanding Digital Humanities, edited by David M. Berry, seems more grounded in a technological tradition:

> The application of new computational techniques and visualisation technologies in the Arts and Humanities are resulting in fresh approaches and methodologies for the study of new and traditional corpora. This "computational turn" takes the methods and techniques from computer science to create innovative means of close and distant reading. This book discusses the implications and applications of "Digital Humanities" and the questions raised when using algorithmic techniques. Key researchers in the field provide a comprehensive introduction to important debates surrounding issues such as the contrast between narrative versus database, pattern-matching versus hermeneutics, and the statistical paradigm versus the data mining paradigm. Also discussed are the new forms of collaboration within the Arts and Humanities that are raised through modular research teams and new organisational structures, as well as techniques for collaborating in an interdisciplinary way.[70]

While the existence of some overlap with the previous description is not surprising, a fairly different concept of the digital humanities is clearly presented here. In this text, *Digital Humanities* is capitalized and accompanied by quotation marks, a treatment that could be taken to indicate a certain level of newness and unfamiliarity.

However, this description is much shorter, more specific, and more methodological than the description of *Debates in the Digital Humanities*, reflecting the different foci of the two books. This is a much more instrumental, computationally oriented, and data-driven approach to the digital humanities that has roots in the tradition of humanities computing as well as in computational theory, media archaeology, and philosophy. A central concept in the description of *Understanding Digital Humanities* is "algorithmic techniques," which are portrayed as providing the basis for a discussion that not only is restricted to the immediate application of these techniques but also encompasses various penetrating issues such as the contrast between databases and narratives. This algorithmic approach would seem to lend more focus to this book than to the first example. There is also a more distinct disciplinary emphasis on literary studies and neighboring fields and implicitly on areas such as software studies and platform studies. This text also argues that new work practices and organizational models generate new types of collaboration in the humanities and arts. This relates to the discussion in the description of *Debates in the Digital Humanities* about the impact on the humanities at large as well as the academy but is less focused on far-reaching transformation.

The third book does not include *digital humanities* in the title, although it is clearly signposted as a book that relates to the field. *How We Think: Digital Media and Contemporary Technogenesis*, by Katherine Hayles, is also the only monograph among the three books. Hayles is a well-known thinker on the intersection between literature, the humanities, and the digital, but with this work, she chooses to indicate a closer affinity to digital humanities as a project. According the publisher's book description,

"How do we think?" N. Katherine Hayles poses this question at the beginning of this bracing exploration of the idea that we think through, with, and alongside media. As the age of print passes and new technologies appear every day, this proposition has become far more complicated, particularly for the traditionally print-based disciplines in the humanities and qualitative social sciences. With a rift growing between digital scholarship and its print-based counterpart, Hayles argues for contemporary technogenesis—the belief that humans and technics are coevolving—and advocates for what she calls comparative media studies, a new approach to locating digital work within print traditions and vice versa.

Hayles examines the evolution of the field from the traditional humanities and how the digital humanities are changing academic scholarship, research, teaching, and publication. She goes on to depict the neurological consequences of working in digital media, where skimming and scanning, or "hyper reading," and analysis through machine algorithms are forms of reading as valid as close reading once was. Hayles contends that we must recognize all three types of reading and understand the limitations and possibilities of each. In addition to illustrating what a comparative media perspective entails, Hayles explores the technogenesis spiral in its full complexity. She considers the effects of early databases such as telegraph code books and confronts our changing perceptions of time and space in the digital age, illustrating this through three innovative digital productions—Steve Tomasula's electronic novel, TOC; Steven Hall's The Raw Shark Texts; and Mark Z. Danielewski's Only Revolutions.

Deepening our understanding of the extraordinary transformative powers digital technologies have placed in the hands of humanists, How We Think presents a cogent rationale for tackling the challenges facing the humanities today.[71]

This text presents a scholarly challenge. How do we think in relation to media, and how do humans coevolve with technology? According to this description, Hayles believes that the answers involve a comparative media perspective, looking at "changing perceptions of time and space in the digital age" as well as discussing the neurological implications of engaging with digital media when doing hyperreading or using machine algorithms to do analysis. This approach is focused in that it incorporates distinct if large research questions and expansive in that it encompasses not only large humanities-based issues but also neural research and media history. The description has a revolutionary sensibility when it discusses the end of the age of print, the challenges facing the humanities, the rift between print and digital scholarship, the new technologies appearing every day, and the changing perceptions of time and space.

This description presents a clear institutional perspective relating to the challenges facing "traditional print-based disciplines" and the humanities. Hence, Hayles's book engages clearly with the future of the humanities as a whole, not merely the digital humanities or specific issues. Digital technology receives considerable agency—or, rather, the technology is said to give humanists "extraordinary transformative powers." The book thus very clearly sets out to engage with the future of the humanities, and technology is a critical ingredient of that engagement rather than simply the institutional frame of the digital humanities.

While Hayles's interest in the digital humanities is much deeper than simple alignment (which is very clear in the book itself), she nevertheless might not readily call herself a digital humanist. And it is not likely that comparative media studies, advocated by Hayles as an important part of the "solution," would be easily incorporated into the digital humanities, even if such integration could have clear potential. Indeed, digital humanities and media studies are often described as separate projects.

However, invoking *digital humanities* eases connections between transformative sentiment and the current state and future of the humanities writ large. If so, *digital humanities* may have more leverage at this time than *comparative media studies* does in relation to discussing and rethinking the humanities. In this sense, the *humanities* part of *digital humanities* is quite significant.

These three books all point to the transformative potential of the digital humanities in relation to the development of the humanities and the liberal arts. *Debates in the Digital Humanities* does so through a largely institutional perspective, *Understanding Digital Humanities* describes an algorithmic turn, and *How We Think* looks at the close interrelation of thinking and technology from the point of view of a print-based discipline. This sample shows the breadth of the field and the directions it follows as it is emerging as well as to some extent its lack of consolidation. The two edited volumes have very little overlap in terms of authors—of the sixty-four contributors to the books, only one, Lev Manovich, is included in both volumes.

Three Possible Directions for the Digital Humanities

The analysis of the three book descriptions demonstrates the distinct differences and commonalities in how the field of digital humanities is approached and conceptualized. The institutional position and trajectory of the digital humanities is clearly a pivotal issue.

One possible trajectory is a relatively self-sufficient discipline of digital humanities with its own agenda, faculty, conferences, educational programs, and status. From such a position, being a "digital humanist" may seem quite natural. Many of the necessary characteristics are already in place. However, the digital humanities has normally depended on working with other actors within and outside the humanities to an extent that is not present in most other disciplines. It is also not clear what would make up the core of digital humanities as a discipline.

What would a discipline based mainly on tools and methodology look like? It would clearly depend on working with others but would have more integrity and status and would probably also be accountable in a different way than a humanities computing or digital humanities center would be. Accountability would likely be more closely linked to measurements and standards applied to traditional departments and disciplines.

A second disciplinary model could center on studies of digital culture, artifacts, and processes. This position is less likely given the history of digital humanities, and it would require a fairly major reorientation. The question is also whether it is the most productive way forward. Such a strategy would challenge existing disciplines and formations much more clearly. Even though the current disciplinary structure is partly a historical artifact, there is always contemporary alignment and concern about turfs and jurisdiction. And although traditional disciplines may not yet have engaged fully with digitally inflected materials and issues, they are likely to protest if a new discipline were to challenge their core domain, especially if they are already reconfiguring themselves in a more digital direction. This scenario has already played out with game studies, and we would be hard-pressed to say that a richly implemented discipline of game studies currently exists.

Another possibility within a disciplinary model would be to imagine the discipline of digital humanities as starting anew, without buying into the genealogy of the present field, thus opening up the field in a way that would otherwise be impossible. But who would get to define and shape the new discipline, since there is no such thing as a neutral institutional construct? And in practice it seems quite difficult (or even impossible) to start from scratch in this way, even though such a solution would have clear benefits.

While a change from "field" to "discipline" or "center" to "department" may seem on one level a matter of linguistics or labeling, the long-term consequences can be far-reaching. A "center" may certainly seem to be competing with "departments" and "disciplines" but is usually recognized as a different type of entity. If the digital humanities more generally were to become a discipline, it would likely be competing alongside other disciplines and eventually become structurally integrated in a way that most centers or labs are not. The result may be more stability and integration as well as a higher degree of conformity and less maneuverability.

A second trajectory and institutional direction is for the digital humanities to occupy an in-between position rather than moving toward a more distinct disciplinary position. This position is by no means new, but it could be institutionalized more strongly than before, given the current leverage and interest in the digital humanities. Such a model draws on collaboration with existing disciplines and centers and is not based on fulfilling a service function.

The focus of such a model could be methodology and tools, disciplinary and interdisciplinary challenges with a digital inflection, or both. Researchers, teachers, and practitioners placed at the core of such institutions might call themselves "digital humanists," but most people involved in the digital humanities would probably see themselves not solely as digital humanists but rather as disciplinary scholars with a strong engagement in the humanities and the digital. Double or triple affiliation would be a useful organizational model. If flexible, such institutions could accommodate some of the work and perspectives that would not align with traditional disciplines. While starting such centers or initiatives may not be easy, they would likely be perceived differently than a newly created discipline. Such institutions ideally should foreground much of the work taking place in the traditional disciplines as well as provide a place for discussing and promoting the humanities writ large.

This book places big digital humanities in such a liminal position based on the notion that this position has clear advantages, as does the incorporation of multiple modes of engagement between the humanities and the digital, ranging from big data tools to experimental expressions. In this way, the digital humanities offers an infrastructural and intellectual platform for carrying out work placed between the humanities and the digital. This platform seeks deep connections with humanities disciplines and areas as well as with other fields and initiatives. These multiple epistemic traditions and perspectives contribute to making the digital humanities a dynamic and diverse field. Such curiosity-driven work must be based on respect, intellectual sharpness, and technological innovation. Big digital humanities gets leverage from a combined intellectual, material, and political engagement and can serve as an experimental contact zone for the humanities.

However, such a broad and inclusive model offers challenges. For example, the absence of the clear institutional position that a disciplinary or departmental status would give can create difficulties and uncertainty. Another challenge is to accommodate a range of epistemic traditions and to balance long-term thematic or methodological directions with the shifting dynamics of a meeting place.

A third institutional direction predicts that the digital humanities will get absorbed by the humanities. According to this trajectory—often offered from outside the digital humanities—there is simply no need for a separate "digital humanities" project since the traditional humanities disciplines will incorporate digital elements into their practice and agenda. A different and in some ways more sophisticated argument holds that the digital humanities focuses too much on the digital at the expense of a richer cultural, technological, societal, and historical context and that the disciplines should take on this rich context in a way that is digitally aware.

This projection is not unwarranted, but it also depends on what kinds of digital humanities are being discussed. A type of digital humanities focused on the study of the digital would probably be more at risk (as a consequence of the considerable overlap with existing disciplines) than a methodology-focused endeavor. Conversely, a digital humanities that emphasized methodology would be at risk if the methodologies and technological competence became naturalized by traditional departments or central information technology functions, but this scenario is probably not very likely given that technology-methodology is a moving target and that the issues of encoding, managing, and interpreting large (and small) collections of digital materials are complex and fall outside the scope of most disciplines and information technology centers. These issues also extend across disciplines, so it would seem to make sense to focus efforts across departments or schools, although institutional reality is not particularly predictable. Digital humanities, implemented as a meeting place and in-between player, will likely not be absorbed by any department or discipline. This version of digital humanities would be somewhat more likely to be subsumed by humanities centers and advanced institutes.

Regardless of the institutional makeup of the field, absorption and integration seem unlikely to occur anytime soon, as Matthew Kirschenbaum tweeted in response to the question, "When we can we start calling the digital humanities just 'the humanities?'":

Not for a long, long time.[72]

The complexity of the full interrelation of the digital and the humanities as well as the particularities of institutional landscape may call for an institutional arrangement outside of the traditional disciplinary structures.

The future path of the digital humanities will probably not be decided at some specific point. Instead, a great many decisions, institutional alignments, and individual choices will shape the future of the field. Regardless of the model chosen, the humanities could no doubt survive without the digital humanities, but it would be a different humanities.

Conclusion

A rich intersectional space exists between the humanities and the digital. It is filled with scholarly challenges, infrastructural concerns, institutional uncertainty, and intersectional work. We need to develop and extend this space to meet the intellectual, material, and institutional challenges and opportunities facing the digital humanities.

There is value in allowing the digital humanities to remain a relatively imprecise notion for a variety of reasons: the humanities and the digital entangle in different ways, there are useful points of interaction between the digital and most of the humanities, scholarly work needs to be aware of infrastructure and vice versa, approaches such as critical making presuppose simultaneous intellectual and technological engagement, and there might be an institutional advantage to having the maneuverability and flexibility associated with not being a traditional institution. This does not mean that the intersectional position is unproblematic or is the only possible model. However, this conceptual and institutional blurriness can be an asset. The next chapter turns to the historical and epistemic reasons for this blurriness and the current state of the field.

TWO

Digital Humanities as a Field

No field exists without its history, and no field is merely a reflection of its history. Academic fields are historical, contextual, and dynamic. They are also consistently shaped by institutional, societal, and cultural logics. This chapter looks more closely at the digital humanities as a field, an institutional endeavor, and a historical trajectory, arguing that the field cannot move forward productively without historical sensibility, self-awareness, and genuine openness.

A major reconfiguration of the field has occurred over the past ten years, and this chapter investigates this reconfiguration. It tells the story of a dominant player, humanities computing, that reinvented itself through a series of moves. One critical move was the renaming of the field from *humanities computing* to *digital humanities*. For some members of the humanities computing community, this reconfiguration was not much more than a change of names, and in actuality, the epistemic tradition of humanities computing has remained strong in the digital humanities. This has partly been made possible through the major role played by the scholarly associations connected with humanities computing in terms of doing institutional work, hosting conferences, supporting journals, and providing a platform. Indeed, if anything, the associations have increased their footprint through new constituent organizations and a fairly elaborate territorial strategy.

At the same time, the reinvented field and the new name came with certain expectations and responsibilities, which the digital humanities has not necessarily been able to meet. Over the years, the associations in the Alliance of Digital Humanities Organizations have faced increased pressure to be more inclusive, and one resultant rhetoric has been that of "big-tent digital humanities," which supposedly would help to open up the field to newcomers. However, the big tent never was truly big, and we need to look at other models.

The chapter begins with an extended discussion of the institutional status of the digital humanities. Is it a field or a discipline? These two main institutional forms offer different possibilities for the development of the digital humanities, and other possible institutional pathways also exist. One way of getting a sense of the variation and development of the field is to look at typologies that have been suggested for the digital humanities. The trajectories of such typologies are often situated in the disciplinary standpoint of the writer and defined by and against such frames of reference.

The chapter explores the role of scholarly associations as a lead-in to an examination of the history of the field and particularly the shift from humanities computing to digital humanities. Furthermore, it traces the epistemic tradition of humanities computing at some length, and contrasts that tradition with the vision presented in this book (big digital humanities). Returning to the current situation, I look at how the territorial ambitions of the digital humanities organizations and of more recent movements such as #transformDH play out.

Even a big-tent notion of digital humanities is restricted and epistemically structured, so it would be wise to eliminate the tent altogether and position digital humanities as an intersectional and liminal field with multiple genealogies.

Changing Circumstances

The field of digital humanities has been emerging for a long time. If we include humanities computing as part of the history of digital humanities, the field was certainly described as emerging as early as in the 1980s. In the initial 1987 welcome message for the *Humanist* e-mail list, Willard McCarty wrote that "computing in the humanities is an emerging and highly cross-disciplinary field."[1] The quality of being emergent is often associated with the uncertain institutional and disciplinary status of the field as well as with much discussion about what it is and what it can be. It is not surprising, perhaps, that we can detect a certain amount of weariness among old-timers who have been debating these issues for a long time, especially now when there is a sense of a stronger institutional position and the possibility of leaving behind some of the uncertainty and hardships.

The weariness and wanting to move forward are understandable and a worthwhile sentiment, but the tension and associated discussions about the field will not go away anytime soon, if ever. For one thing, the influx of new people to the field is likely to create instability and negotiation as these newcomers will not necessarily subscribe to the same set of core values as people with a long history in the field. If we are going to argue for digital humanities as an inclusive and intersectional project, we need to accommodate newcomers and open up the field not only to a larger constituency but also to new ideas and epistemic traditions. This responsibility accompanies the new, larger territory and substantial investments in the field and applies on one level to anyone involved in the digital humanities. At the same time, we need to acknowledge that some people do not share this vision.

Rafael Alvarado describes the situation aptly as a small town that has recently "been rated as a great place to raise a family."[2] Such a situation is bound to feature tension and negotiation. The original community must be accommodating, while newcomers must be interested enough to acquire a sense of the history of the town and its community. Not every newcomer will function well in the new community, and not every original resident will be willing to adapt to the new situation. On another level, basic structures and rules may be challenged, and in the long run, there may be a need to work toward a new charter or common platform that speaks both to original residents and to newcomers.

We should not take this metaphor too far, but it is true that any inclusive notion of digital humanities is not likely to succeed without a sense of the history of the field and without accommodating a range of different traditions. A unified vision may not be possible, but there should at least be a sense of direction, grounding, and differences. This sense cannot be achieved without a continued discussion of the field both inside and outside the institutions that are most integral to the long tradition of digital humanities and humanities computing. We also need to acknowledge that some traditions close to the digital humanities, such as rhetoric and composition, have not necessarily become part of the genealogy of the field and that other neighboring and overlapping areas exist.

Another way of approaching this issue is to argue that the digital humanities currently gives us a window of opportunity for influencing and shaping our own academic and personal futures. For various reasons, the digital humanities has become a reasonably powerful platform, and it is our responsibility to make the most of it. The 4Humanities Initiative, a website and platform devoted to the advocacy of the humanities drawing on digital technologies, is one example of this kind of thinking.[3] We need to look ahead and think ahead, and we need to be aware of different traditions, positions, and trajectories. This chapter provides some of the necessary context and tools for this work.

Unrest and disciplinary debate may not be the best long-term instruments for creating and sustaining a field, but the dynamic character of the digital humanities makes it an exciting and hopeful place for many people. I refer not to polarized debates and harsh exchanges but to the relative openness and exploration that come with something that has not been fully defined and negotiated and that offers a range of positions and possibilities.

Field or Discipline?

Before going into more detail concerning the landscape of the digital humanities, it will be useful to establish some basic concepts. One important question concerns the institutional label of digital humanities. A number of different terms are used, including *discipline, field,* and *area.* A simple Google Search on September 3, 2014, gave the following frequencies for the frame "X of /the/ digital humanities": "discipline" (about 77,700 instances), "field" (216,900), and "area" (142,500). This is not a surprising distribution given that *area* is the most generic, noninstitutional term and that *field* has a generic quality while pointing to a stronger institutional structure. According to Julie Thompson Klein, a field is a "descriptor of shared interests across a wider sphere than specialized domains and full-fledged disciplines."[4] *Discipline* is by far the least frequent term, and it indicates the most institutionalized trajectory.

Again, this is a matter of words and institutional tactics, but it is very relevant to how we think of the digital humanities and future trajectories. The history of digital humanities has been characterized by a certain degree of institutional instability, and there is understandably an accumulated need for a more secure and independent position. We face a major challenge in balancing this legitimate need with the advantages of maintaining an intersectional position, at least if the goal is a broadly conceived and open digital humanities—big digital humanities, in between the humanities and the digital, between disciplines, between the university and outside interests, and between different modes of engagement. But even such a model of the digital humanities obviously also requires a core operation and some of the powers that come with the status of discipline.

Disciplinary formation in the modern sense is a relatively new phenomenon going back to the 1800s, and as Peter Weingart emphasizes, disciplines are social communities as well as historical constructs.[5] There is no blueprint as to what actually makes an academic discipline, but the digital humanities fulfills some of the criteria sometimes used to identify disciplines. For example, the digital humanities has scholarly associations, departments at universities, conference and book series, and dedicated funding streams as well as a unified visibility and a sense of a community. We would be hard-pressed, however, to argue that the digital humanities as a whole is characterized by shared methods and theories, a preferred institutional model, or the ability to reproduce itself with the help of educational programs from undergraduate to graduate education.

The lack of a shared conception of the digital humanities is the cause of fervent discussions about the field, frequent territorial negotiations, and reactions from established disciplines and fields. No matter which institutional model is advocated, there is a real need for some kind of demarcation (the digital humanities cannot be everything) and for introducing institutional elements normally associated with academic disciplines. It makes sense that digital humanities institutions can employ and tenure faculty, given that local and national regulations make doing so possible. This does not mean that all digital humanities faculty must be employed by digital humanities institutions. It is quite possible to imagine a dual-affiliation model in which many faculty are based in other institutions and departments.

In fact, the current discussion of the scope and direction of the digital humanities is intimately linked to questions of institutionalization. In other words, our ideas about what the digital humanities should be are likely to align with some but not all institutional models. On one level, this is about what the digital humanities community (or communities) wants, and no broad consensus currently exists, which is one reason why the digital humanities cannot be a discipline, although some observers call for that status:

> DH is a discipline now—with universities granting degrees in it, and federal organizations dedicated to funding it—and that brings boundaries, and how the boundaries get drawn sparks turf wars. It's a boring narrative, really, and I don't have much stake in any of it; but if we're going to agree DH is a discipline, we should start having conversations about its disciplinarity at appropriately disciplinary venues. [The Modern Language Association] is not that.[6]

In this blog entry, written a couple of weeks after the 2013 Conference of the Modern Language Association (MLA), Whitney Trettien argues that this venue is not the best place to discuss the future of the digital humanities. This sentiment is sound in some ways, but the question of whether the digital humanities really is and should be a discipline is not so easy to resolve.

Institutions are complex formations, and there is no clear line between field and discipline. There is no simple checklist of features for disciplinarity because we are concerned with a social-institutional phenomenon. It is fairly easy to recognize a fully developed discipline, however, and the digital humanities simply does not qualify, at least not across the board. There is too much heterogeneity, lack of institutional stability, and at least partial resistance to being a discipline. This is not to say that the digital humanities cannot become a discipline. But is that what we want?

Also, within the digital humanities are various subfields or groups with their own identities, including the text encoding community, library-associated communities, and digital history. These may never become disciplines in their own right, but they have or will acquire certain disciplinary qualities. A less territorial meeting-place model of the digital humanities may well be better placed to align productively with such subfields than a more disciplinary development of the field.

In this book, the term *field* is used consistently for the digital humanities to indicate a position that is not fully disciplinary. Such a position is compatible with the intersectional and inclusive notion of the digital humanities suggested by big digital humanities, and it would arguably be a mistake to move toward a model where the digital humanities is a discipline on par with other disciplines. This does not mean that the digital humanities should not have disciplinary qualities or that some subfields will not have such qualities, but there is a definite advantage to the field having and maintaining an in-between institutional position.

A Dynamic Landscape Exemplified

The digital humanities as a field has a dynamic and exciting quality that comes from the fact that it is not determined or fully institutionalized and that the communities engage in intense discussion. Some of this discussion may seem like dramatic play and self-promotion, but there is also much well-developed thinking about the state and the future of the field.

Two examples from approximately the same point in time demonstrate some of the dynamic and unsettled status of the field and highlight what is at stake here.

Example 1:

Andrew Prescott, newly appointed director of the Department of Digital Humanities at King's College London, offered a surprising description of his department in the summer of 2012:

> The type of humanities represented by the directory of projects undertaken by the Department of Digital Humanities at King's College is one which would have gladdened the heart of Ronald Crane. Of the 88 content creation projects listed, only 8 are concerned in any way with anything that happened after 1850. The overwhelming majority—some 57 projects—deal with subjects from before 1600, and indeed most of them are concerned with the earliest periods, before 1100. The geographical focus of most of the projects are on the classical world and western Europe. The figures that loom largest are standard cultural icons: Ovid, Shakespeare, Ben Jonson, Jane Austen, Chopin. This is an old-style humanities, dressed out in bright new clothes for the digital age.
>
> For all the rhetoric about digital technologies changing the humanities, the overwhelming picture presented by the activities of digital humanities centres in Great Britain is that they are busily engaged in turning back the intellectual clock and reinstating a view of the humanities appropriate to the 1950s which would have gladdened the heart of Ronald Crane. One of the great achievements of humanities scholarship in the past fifty years is to have widened our view of culture and to have expanded the subject matter of scholarship beyond conventional cultural icons. There is virtually no sense of this in digital humanities as it is practiced in Britain.[7]

This is both a far-reaching critique of the current state of the digital humanities as well as a vision for the field and the department. Focusing on Great Britain, Prescott questions many of the cornerstones of digital humanities operations (including his own): the centrality of projects, the importance of collaboration as a distinctive feature of the field, the predominant focus on "core" cultural heritage, and the focus on method. This is an example of a lively discussion of what the field can be, which institutional models may work, and what it means to do humanities work. Prescott's proposed solution is to develop an intellectual agenda for the digital humanities, to move away from having an auxiliary or service function, to engage more with digitally created material, and to deemphasize the focus on collaboration and interdisciplinarity.

While Prescott's analysis of the current status is largely convincing if somewhat dogmatic, not all archival work is traditional, not all "new" work is good, and traditional digital humanities has never just been a service function. Despite some hedging, his is still a very sharply articulated position. And the solution Prescott advocates, a stronger intellectual agenda, would indeed seem beneficial.

Example 2:

In a much-discussed column in the *Chronicle of Higher Education,* "No DH, No Interview," William Pannapacker reflects on the digital humanities after having participated in the 2012 Digital Humanities Summer Institute at the University of Victoria. The Summer Institute is a largely practice-focused activity with a long tradition in the field. The column's title refers to Pannapacker's tweet on considering digital humanities competence as a requirement for any humanities job. He juxtaposes digital humanities and critical theory and refers to the keynote speech at the Institute, which was delivered by Laura Mandell, director of the Initiative for Digital Humanities, Media, and Culture at Texas A&M University:

> Mandell said DH is partly a turn against the dominance of critical theory, which she called "a PR failure and an intellectual failure: an excessive and unexamined lock-step discipline." DH provides a rigorous alternative to the seemingly exhausted scholarly approaches of the previous generation. Moreover, DH is a culture of building projects that serve a wide audience rather than—to paraphrase Mandell—engage in knee-jerk denunciations of capitalism while depending on its dwindling largess for our employment.[8]

Like Prescott, Mandell had recently been appointed, and she, too, was speaking in the summer of 2012. However, their positions differ markedly. While Mandell describes digital humanities as a reaction to critical theory, Prescott suggests that the digital humanities can learn from established disciplines such as media studies. According to Pannapacker, Mandell points to the importance of building and creating accessible projects, while Prescott problematizes a project-based tradition and suggests that the field needs to become more experimental. Although their statements and this comparison may make the differences seem larger than they actually are, they are still two very different visions of the future of the field and specific institutions.

Pannapacker notes the discouraging comments from digital humanists in relation to his tweet about a digital humanities requirement outside of digital humanities programs proper. And he agrees that a core digital humanities requirement may be problematic. This is essentially a question of inclusion and exclusion. What are the boundaries of the field? This question is also evident in Pannapacker's discussion of young scholars coming to the digital humanities because there may be a better job market here than in other parts of the humanities:

> So even though I've been excited about the digital humanities since my first visit to the summer institute, I want to urge job candidates: Don't become a DH'er out of fear that you won't get a position if you don't. You may not get a job if you do. There are already many outstanding people in the field, with publications and good postdocs, who are not permanently employed, and the rapidly growing number of DH'ers seems likely to exceed the number of available positions in the foreseeable future.[9]

On one level, this might seem like sensible advice: do not get into the digital humanities without a keen interest in the field. However, this piece of advice has an unfortunate exclusionary and gatekeeping sentiment. Pannapacker presents both the humanities and the digital humanities as uniform entities, but there is no single type of digital humanist, and not everyone will be equally attractive on the job market. Hence, it is impossible to know whether a junior or incoming scholar with a specific set of qualifications and skills will be competitive. Prescott and his department, for example, might be interested in recruiting outside the traditional field to move in the direction he suggests. It also seems somewhat simplistic to assume that people would change fields or choose a field only based on a projected job market. And if they do, we should probably not be moralistic about it. Whether they come for job opportunities or for other reasons, the result is an influx of potentially interesting scholars.

Most problematic, however, is the protective and conservative stance implied in statements of this kind. Pannapacker is essentially saying that there are already many good ("outstanding") and deserving people in the digital humanities, and until they have permanent employment, newcomers are not welcome. Pannapacker also indirectly advocates for a closed-off type of digital humanities, since newcomers are likely to come from outside the established community. This type of gatekeeping would seem incompatible with the vision of digital humanities as an inclusive field under competitive pressure.

The Back Story: Humanities Computing

Gatekeeping is related to the history of the field and multiple traditions at play. In particular, the tradition of humanities computing has been quite influential in shaping and influencing contemporary digital humanities. This is a question not just of historical traces but also of the texture and genealogy of contemporary digital humanities. Big digital humanities depends on incorporating many different epistemic traditions and positions, a process that requires discussing the particulars of such traditions.

Moreover, history repeats itself: the current discussion of digital humanities as a field is not at all new. Under the name *humanities computing*, the field was negotiated and partly institutionalized, as is evidenced by the description of a 1999 panel organized by the Association for Computers and the Humanities (ACH):

> Empirically, humanities computing is easily recognized as a particular academic domain and community. We have our professional organizations, regular conferences, journals, and a number of centers, departments, and other organizational units. A sense for the substance of the field is also fairly easy to come by: one can examine the proceedings of ACH/ALLC conferences, issues of CHum and JALLC, the discussions on HUMANIST, the contents of many books and anthologies which represent themselves as presenting work in humanities computing, and the academic curricula and research programs at humanities computing centers and departments. From such an exercise one easily gets a rough and ready sense of what we are about, and considerable reassurance, if any is needed, that indeed, there is something which we are about.[10]

The listed achievements are those typically associated with the establishment of a new discipline.[11] The final sentence could be read as both asserting communal identity and indicating that an undisputed sense of the practice of humanities computing did not necessarily exist. In other words, humanities computing was never a fully homogenous enterprise, although the discourse surrounding the field may give such an impression. Communal identity is an important factor and is built over time. The foundational narrative of humanities computing is based largely on Father Roberto Busa and work going back to the 1940s:

> During World War II, between 1941 and 1946, I began to look for machines for the automation of the linguistic analysis of written texts. I found them, in 1949, at IBM in New York City.[12]

In her classic study of the printing press, Elizabeth Eisenstein demonstrates that a major change that is often perceived as a technological shift depends on a set of complex circumstances.[13] Similarly, much is left out of the standard narrative of the emergence of the digital humanities, although a growing scholarship exists on this matter. Julianne Nyhan points to the role of the operation associated with Busa's collaboration with IBM, including the punch card operators, most of whom were female.[14] Steven Jones addresses the complexities of Busa's project (and the digital humanities) evident in the coming together of academic and corporate cultures and in the change of technological conditions and platforms over the span of the project.[15]

This foundational story establishes two important epistemic commitments of humanities computing: the role of information technology as a tool, and written texts as the primary dataset within the framework of linguistic analysis. The automation also required systematic management of materials, pointing to the long-standing interest in the marking-up of materials and methodology as an organizing principle. Such commitments contribute to framing what are legitimate types of questions and study objects for the field and how work and relevant institutions are organized.

This heritage is evident in the programs of the annual Digital Humanities Conferences. An earlier study shows that the conferences were dominated by workshops and papers on textual analysis, methodology, tagging, and tools.[16] A simple frequency analysis of conferences based on titles of papers and sessions from 1996 to 2004 showed that frequent content words included *text* (56, total number 1996–2004), *electronic* (53), *language* (30), *markup* (28), *encoding* (27), *TEI* (23), *corpus* (22), *authorship* (18), *XML* (18), *database* (13), and *multimedia* (11). A follow-up investigation of the programs of the 2011–12 conferences largely confirmed this pattern, although only a fairly small amount of material is analyzed. The most common content words are *text* (23), *tool* (17), *project* (15), *language* (14), and *edition* (12).[17] A decrease in references to tagging and markup may be occurring, however, since the 2011–12 material contains only a few uses of *markup* (5), TEI (4), *encoding* (3), and XML (1). It may be that this activity has partly moved to more specialized contexts and venues.

Scholarly journals play an important role in establishing a field or discipline, and the journal *Computers and the Humanities* was started in 1966. Early issues were not as textually oriented as might have been assumed, featuring articles such as, "PL/I: A Programming Language for Humanities Research," "Art, Art History, and the Computer," and "Musicology and the Computer in New Orleans" (all from 1966–67). The journal seems to have become more textual over time, but the sample from 1966–77 certainly invokes a big-tent notion of the field.[18]

Another significant journal, *Literary and Linguistic Computing* (LLC), has from its inception focused on textual and text-based literary analysis, as would be expected from its title. It was established in 1986 by the Association for Literary and Linguistic Computing (ALLC). In 2008, the publication's name was changed to *LLC: The Journal of Digital Scholarship in the Humanities*; since the beginning of 2015, the journal has been known as *Digital Scholarship in the Humanities* (DSH).

This journal has clearly played an important role in establishing the field of humanities computing, not only by offering a publication venue, institutional structure, and academic exchange but also by publishing reflective articles on the role, organization, and future of humanities computing. The journal has been used to define the digital humanities in calls for the Digital Humanities Conference, thus in a sense transferring the epistemic culture of the journal and associated field to the "new" field. LLC/DSH has a partnership with the Alliance of Digital Humanities Organizations (ADHO), meaning that subscribers to the journal are ADHO members. So there is a strong economic-administrative rationale for the institutional place for this journal.

LLC remained very text-oriented, and the editors were impressively resilient. In a 2008 report to the ADHO, ALLC, and ACH, editor Marilyn Deegan wrote, "We do tend to focus on text primarily, we don't publish too much on music, art, archaeology, or even history."[19] However, the equivalent document from 2012 suggests a more open focus, with a stronger commitment to the total field of digital humanities and interdisciplinary work across the humanities as well as a note that the main focus will "reside with the textual, visual, artefactual, and performative disciplines."[20] The initial position of *text* is not surprising, and this focus can be exemplified by four articles listed on the journal's website on September 8, 2013. They deal with log-normal distributions of shot lengths in films, language and gender in congressional speech, a word sense disambiguation system, and a review of a book that makes use of word frequency and distribution data for work in social psychology.[21] The article on filmshot length is the only one that does not focus on textual analysis, but it uses some of the methods and discourse of such articles.

While DSH, with its central role for ADHO, remains fairly traditional and text-centered, the development of *Digital Humanities Quarterly* (DHQ) is one of the best examples of institutional digital humanities successfully adapting to an expanding and different digital humanities. DHQ is an open-access journal also supported by ADHO, but with a freer role and not as institutionally laden. It started out with a strong engagement with the tradition of humanities computing,[22] and has retained that focus while expanding the territory of the journal significantly. This has partly been done through special issues curated by scholars in the field. Examples include "The Literary" (2013), Feminisms in Digital Humanities (2015), and "Comics as Scholarship" (2015). Early ambitions included becoming an experimental publishing platform, but it seems that the journal has found a place through maintaining a relatively traditional online journal format and building strong academic credentials while also slowly and naturally engaging with new perspectives in the field.

While journals, conferences, and academic associations play an important role in creating and maintaining an academic field and community, another important factor is the ways in which a field has been organized and institutionalized in academe. In the case of humanities computing, this long and partly uncertain process has clearly shaped the field. The most common institutional configuration has been different kinds of centers, which are often institutionally different and in some cases unstable, leading to recurring challenges regarding questions of tenure, career pathways for experts, and evaluation of alternative types of scholarship. Stephen Ramsay usefully illustrates the issues when he says that for most of the history of humanities computing and digital humanities, there has been "an incredible amount of anxiety over whether our activities would be accepted in academia."[23] And in terms of institutional anxiety and institutional pressures, many centers have struggled to survive.

Some of these centers, however, have existed for a comparatively long time. They tend to have an acronym, physical premises, a fairly inclusive mission (not just one specialty area), an infrastructural function, resource personnel, and a range of programming activities. The activities vary but often include seminars, fellowship programs, and ways of initiating new projects and external applications. Examples include the Center for Computing in the Humanities at the University of Toronto (started in 1986), the Department of Digital Humanities at King's College (1991), the Institute for Advanced Technology in the Humanities at the University of Virginia (1992), and the Maryland Institute for Technology in the Humanities at the University of Maryland (1999). An earlier and more computationally focused institution is the Centre for Literary and Linguistic Computing at the University of Cambridge (1963).

Several of the principal institutions for contemporary digital humanities thus come from a humanities computing tradition. They are not the same, of course, but the historical trajectory is highly relevant, not least because many key people in digital humanities come from this tradition.

Interlude 3: Academic Road Trips and Textured Visitors

There are many ways of finding out about the emergence of a field and how work can be done in between the humanities and the digital. This chapter employs several strategies, including tracing historical materials, looking at ways of categorizing the field, and analyzing epistemic commitments. Another, more personal approach that I have developed over the past fifteen years has been to connect with people by visiting different types of digital humanities institutions and having visitors to HUMlab.

While road trips and visits can be seen as a personal approach, they have also represented in part an institutional engagement. When HUMlab was started, connections with milieus such as the Santa Fe Institute and ACTlab at the University of Texas were important. Sensibilities from these and other environments became part of our operation, and people from these and other institutes came to visit us in Umeå. This exchange is neither surprising nor unique—it is how these things often work when institutions have the resources to pay for travel and invite guests (a privileged position). For an intersectional field, the number of possible visitors and places to visit is larger than for a discipline, and territorial demarcation somehow becomes more difficult to uphold at the level of individuals and specific initiatives.

In October 2012, HUMlab's visitors included Molly Wright Steenson, an architecture historian and IT entrepreneur; Fred Turner, a communication studies scholar; Jake Coolidge and Ryan Heuser from the Center for Spatial and Literary Analysis at Stanford University; Anita Sarkeesian, a feminist media critic; Jennifer Brook, the experience designer responsible for the *New York Times* iPad app; and Gethin Rees from the Centre for Advanced Religious and Theological Studies at the University of Cambridge.

This may seem like a rather esoteric collection of people, but they can also be seen as part of the digital humanities. Turner's work on the history of American multimedia is highly relevant to the field, and he did a multiple-screen installation in the lab during his visit. Sarkeesian's online videos on popular culture and gender can certainly inform all of us about digital media, gender, and how academia can use digital media to reach beyond the university. Her talk was attended by 140 people, and while Coolidge and Heuser's workshops on spatial history and network analysis attracted smaller crowds, they were productive and exciting events. The tweets during Brook's workshop on prototyping for touch demonstrated how humanistic researchers, design students, and people from industry all found the exchange productive. If we see the digital humanities as a meeting place, such perspectives are part and parcel of the development of the field, even though the individuals themselves may not necessarily be seen as digital humanists.

In any case, they will certainly be involved in shaping and developing HUMlab, and I hope that they, too, have benefited from the exchange. We increasingly bring them back into the physical space through distributed means, such as Skype in full-screen mode. I like to think of guests leaving imprints in the lab and becoming part of the texture of the lab. The process works differently with different people, of course, but there really is something to the strong connection that even short-term visits build. I have also learned that showing interest in people and their work makes them likely to want to meet me, and by visiting them, I also get to see specific milieus and the modes of interaction supported by these environments. One way of building the digital humanities is to meet interesting people, see how different institutions work, and learn from others. Genuine interest in people, ideas, and meetings manifested over time is not only a good strategy but more importantly a sensible idea.

Learning how to cast a wide net takes time and openness. For example, it is often safer to go for established scholars and experts than junior people. Giving opportunities to upcoming talents is critical and good both for the individuals and the inviting institution. HUMlab has been good at supporting junior-level contributors over the years. The opening keynote speaker for one of our first large events in HUMlab (in 2005) was an MIT MA student, Ravi

Purushotma. HUMlab has also always had a fairly even distribution between male and female invitees (looking at major events organized 2010–2015, the distribution is even). Beyond metrics, one learning experience for me was to negotiate single-sex events, which to me did not easily fit with the basic idea of the lab as an open meeting place. I remember how a discussion with the organizers of the Eclectic Tech Carnival (2009) made it clear why single-sex events can make sense. The organizers explained their experience of gendered roles in participating in technology-rich learning situations, which made me see the event in a different way. The event was successfully carried out the way it has been planned by the organizers, although the lab was not closed to male (nonparticipating) users during the event. This experience made me better understand how the idea of openness can sometimes conceal layered power structures and also made me appreciate the value of running an institution where rules can be bent.

HUMlab has favored Anglo-American and, to some degree, European participation in terms of geographical distribution. HUMlab is not an exception in this respect, but there is room for development and I am glad to see a clear change toward more diversity over the last couple of years. For me personally it continues to be a learning experience to understand what deep inclusivity and diversity can be in the context of digital humanities.

Scholarly Associations and the Digital Humanities

While academic road trips may be useful, we could not do without more formal networking possibilities offered by conferences and organized networks. Here academic associations often play an important role, for the digital humanities as well as for other disciplines. Discussing some of the field's major associations helps explain the development of the field as well as some of the tensions and possible directions associated with the digital humanities.

The primary scholarly association for the digital humanities is the Alliance of Digital Humanities Organizations (ADHO), an international umbrella organization founded in 2005. The ADHO and its constituent organizations control the annual Digital Humanities Conferences as well as journals such as *Digital Humanities Quarterly*. The organization also represents the digital humanities in different contexts. In other words, ADHO is a very powerful player in the institutional life of the digital humanities.

According to the ADHO's website,

Members in ADHO societies are those at the forefront of areas such as textual analysis, electronic publication, document encoding, textual studies and theory, new media studies and multimedia, digital libraries, applied augmented reality, interactive gaming, and beyond. We are researchers and lecturers in humanities computing and in academic departments such as English, History, French, Modern Languages, Philosophy, Theatre, Music, Computer Science, and Visual Arts. We are resource specialists working in libraries, archival centres, and with humanities computing groups. We are academic administrators, and members of the private and public sectors. We are independent scholars, students, graduate students, and research assistants. We are from countries in every hemisphere.[24]

The ADHO is describing the members of their societies and their work rather than the digital humanities. The distinction may seem slight, since the ADHO is so significant in the digital humanities, but is nevertheless quite significant. The ADHO organizes three societies that form a very important part of the tradition of humanities computing and consequently present-day digital humanities: the European Association for Digital Humanities (EADH), the ACH, and the Canadian Society for Digital Humanities. It also organizes three newer organizations: centerNet, the Australasian Association for Digital Humanities, and the Japanese Association for Digital Humanities. This does not mean, however, that the ADHO represents the digital humanities in its entirety.

The ADHO sees itself as having a constituency with considerable range and breadth and offers worthwhile inclusive rhetoric. If the ordering of items in such lists carries significance, which seems likely, text analytical work (textual analysis, electronic publishing, and document encoding) seems most prominent. The same is true of the disciplines listed first, including English, history, and modern languages. This pattern partly reflects a historical development—these areas and disciplines have been important in building the field of humanities computing and digital humanities—but it also reflects the type of digital humanities represented by the ADHO. However, the ADHO must work with its constituent organizations, and multiple positions exist within the community, including that of a more traditional flavor of humanities computing. The ADHO uses the term *humanities computing*, which is largely an older moniker replaced by *digital humanities*, in the phrase *humanities computing groups*. It is very unlikely that newcomers to the digital humanities would use this term; indeed, many may not even know it.

Of course, the ADHO is not the only scholarly association relevant to the digital humanities. Disciplinary organizations such as the American Historical Association and the MLA also have a considerable digital engagement. This engagement, however, is typically not their core mission. Other organizations, such as the Humanities Arts Science and Technology Advanced Collaboratory (HASTAC), sit closer to the intersection of technology and the humanities. HASTAC's website asks,

> What would our research, technology design, and thinking look like if we took seriously the momentous opportunities and challenges for learning posed by our digital era? What happens when we stop privileging traditional ways of organizing knowledge (by fields, disciplines, and majors or minors) and turn attention instead to alternative modes of creating, innovating, and critiquing that better address the interconnected, interactive global nature of knowledge today, both in the classroom and beyond?[25]

The ADHO and HASTAC text excerpts are not quite comparable, and they clearly reflect rather different starting points. The HASTAC description largely operates on a strategic level, and it features a transformative sentiment that is not very prevalent in most descriptions associated with the ADHO. In some ways, HASTAC represents big-tent digital humanities without the sharpness of trying to define a field or a territory. Technology receives considerable agency, and to some degree, HASTAC sets out to reform the academy using the digital as a lever. The ADHO also operates on a strategic level but resists the large-scale revolutionary sentiment often present in texts about HASTAC.[26]

Despite attempts to become more international, both the ADHO and HASTAC are fairly restricted in this sense. HASTAC is predominantly an American organization, and ADHO has historically been primarily based in the United States and Europe, although it has international ambitions. Both organizations have become more active globally over the last couple of years. More generally, the digital humanities is an Anglo-American endeavor, not only in terms of current discourse on the field but also in terms of Anglo-American models serving as a template for international ambitions and initiatives.[27] Here, I focus to a large extent on developments in America and Europe, partly as a result of the field's history and contemporary configuration. In addition, we need to be aware that humanities computing is not the only tradition or genealogy relevant to the digital humanities.

Connecting Past and Present

Two comments from a 2013 online discussion illustrate how the past and present of the digital humanities connect. David Golumbia published a blog entry on defining the digital humanities.[28] The associated discussion related to the term *digital humanities* and the development of the field. Ramsay claimed that the term came about as a way of trying to distinguish digital humanities from other fields such as game studies, media studies, and hypertext theory but became more attractive than the names of those fields.[29] Ramsay's statements essentially resist a broadly conceived digital humanities:

> So, yes: we're all stuck with it now. it would be nice, though, to go back to a term that actually makes a useful distinction between, say, media studies and the-activity-formally-known-as-humanities-computing. because there *is* a distinction there, and in my opinion, it's a very useful one.[30]

Whether he also favors recalibrating the digital humanities as humanities computing is not clear from this comment, but it is certainly a possibility. Another commentator, Alex Reid, points out that other traditions go back in time:

> The association of "big tent" dh with "newcomers" is one of these points of contention for me. as a digital rhetorician coming out of a field of computers and writing that is several decades old (and having been in the field for nearly two decades myself), i don't view myself as a newcomer to doing digital work in the humanities. at the same time, i'm not doing the same kind of work as the once-and-future humanities computing folks. i don't know that we need to be grouped under a single tent. my only complaint is that when humanities computing adopted the digital humanities name, they implied, intentionally or not, that their work encompassed the entirety of digital work being done in the humanities. now we are all stuck with the term. i don't think of myself as a digital humanist, but when others outside of humanities computing hear what i do they identify me as a digital humanist. when i want to convince my dean and provost to support the kind of work i do, they will be viewing me as a digital humanist.[31]

Reid presumably does not share most of the epistemic commitments of humanities computing. Since humanities computing can be seen as making up the principal epistemic tradition of digital humanities, Reid is thus an out-sider because he does not identify with this tradition, although he does not consider himself a newcomer because he has done this kind of work for a long time. He is also an outsider because he does not want to be grouped with the newcomers. And despite his discomfort with being identified as a digital humanist, outsiders—and his dean and provost—will identify him as such. It seems likely that Reid would capitulate and use the term about his work to align with the leadership of his school or with funding agencies. Reid's and Ramsay's comments distinguish between identity and practice, a point that Reid specifically makes. His practice places him within the digital humanities, but he does not identify with the field. Ramsay clearly identifies with the field but not necessarily with its current practice and direction.

Typologies of the Digital Humanities

One way of closing in on some of these tensions and on the digital humanities as a field is to describe it in terms of its history and evolution. A number of attempts—many of them fairly cursory—have been made to identify evolutionary stages, waves, or types of the digital humanities. Kirsch's distinction between maximalist and minimalist versions of the digital humanities (chapter 1) exemplifies a simple typology. It is useful in that it points to the difference between a strong investment in technology used for traditional scholarly work and a wish to change the humanities at its core. Nevertheless, it lacks nuance in tracing these traditions and overlapping layers, and the dogmatic nature of the typology lessens its usefulness. However, if successful, typologies add a systemic and historical sensibility to the analysis, help us understand why we are where we are, and can support us in thinking about the future of the field. Different typologies can also be contrasted, discussed, and critiqued in relation to each other. They manifest different disciplinary positions and can hence be used as a lens on the landscape of digital humanities.

Such models typically presuppose a direction of change and a moving from one stage to another, often toward something stronger and more evolved. This trajectory will differ depending on where one originates and one's basic perspective. It is part of the epistemic texture of specific positions and can sometimes be fairly subtle. For example, in a general discussion of the digital humanities, Katherine Hayles writes, "I posit the Digital Humanities as a diverse field of practices associated with computational techniques and reaching beyond print in its modes of inquiry, research, publication, and dissemination."[32] Hayles essentially advocates an inclusive notion of the field, but the trajectory she posits foregrounds "print-based" disciplines. The enterprise of moving beyond print is relevant to all of the humanities but is by far most relevant and far-reaching in relation to disciplines such as comparative literature and English. Here, print is clearly integral to what is being studied. Hayles may privilege these disciplines in the sense that she believes they have a fuller engagement with the digital framed in relation to a print tradition. The computational techniques to which she refers are presumably more general, but they arguably are less deep and diverse.

Hayles suggests a model of the digital humanities according to which some of the humanities engage on the level of text encoding, digital editions, 3-D models, archives, and spatial representations but where other parts of the humanities have a more extensive engagement. She singles out electronic literature and digital art in this respect because they have a "vibrant conversation between scholarly and creative work . . . that draws on or remediates humanities traditions."[33] This example shows some of the complexity at play here. From the point of view of another epistemic position, disciplines such as linguistics, architecture, and archeology have or could have a similarly rich engagement with the digital and could certainly host vibrant conversations. This engagement, however, might not be as fundamentally based on the notion of moving beyond print.

A somewhat similar trajectory can be found in Burdick et al.'s *Digital_Humanities* (2012). The book sketches computational developments beginning with World War II, and the narrative uses the past to emphasize how "the digital revolution entered a new phase" and how there are now "transformed possibilities."[34] At the same time, contingency across traditions is acknowledged:

> Building on the first generation of computational humanities work, more recent Digital Humanities activity seeks to revitalize liberal arts traditions in the electronically inflected language of the 21st century: a language in which, uprooted from its longstanding paper support, text is increasingly wedded to still and moving images as well as to sound, and supports have become increasingly mobile, open, and extensible.[35]

Just like Hayles, the authors refer to print culture, although they have a stronger focus on text rather than on print. This difference is significant: Hayles maintains a stronger link to print culture through using it as a distinct frame of reference. The authors of Digital_Humanities argue in favor of a less text-centered trajectory:

> And the notion of the primacy of text itself is being challenged. Whereas the initial waves of computational humanities concentrated on everything from word frequency studies and textual analysis (classification systems, mark-up, encoding) to hypertext editing and textual database construction, contemporary Digital Humanities marks a move beyond a privileging of the textual, emphasizing graphical methods of knowledge production and organization, design as an integral component of research, transmedia crisscrossings, and an expanded concept of the sensorium of humanistic knowledge.[36]

The difference in these perspectives partly comes from the different disciplinary contexts of the writers. Hayles comes from English as a discipline, whereas the authors of Digital_Humanities are more strongly situated in design, aesthetics, curatorial work, and information studies. This orientation helps to explain Digital_Humanities's considerably stronger emphasis on design and the visual, not only as a part of the text but as a distinct category different from text.

In 2009, Tara McPherson suggested a typology that also emphasizes production and design. She distinguishes among the computing humanities, blogging humanities, and multimodal humanities.[37] According to McPherson, the computing humanities focuses on building tools, infrastructure, standards, and collections, whereas the blogging humanities is concerned with the production of networked media and peer-to-peer writing. The multimodal humanities brings together scholarly tools, databases, networked writing, and peer-to-peer commentary while leveraging the potential of the visual and aural media that are part of contemporary life. McPherson's base in media and cinema studies provides a frame for this typology: media studies has not traditionally engaged with the production of multimodal expressions.

When Cathy Davidson identifies two phases of digital humanities as Humanities 1.0 and Humanities 2.0, her reference point is not so much her own discipline, English, but rather the humanities at large and higher education policy. More specifically, she is concerned that the humanities has lost its intellectual centrality at a time when it is dearly needed. This is reflected in her description of the development of Humanities 2.0 (or digital humanities): "Humanities 2.0 is distinguished from monumental, first-generation, data-based projects not just by its interactivity but also by openness about participation grounded in a different set of theoretical premises, which decenter knowledge and authority."[38] Davidson presents a well-articulated vision for the humanities where technology is a key participant in the decentering of authorship, credentialing practices, reward systems, interdisciplinarity, and collaboration. The argument extends far beyond technology and basically concerns the situation and future for the humanities more generally:

> In a time of paradigm shifts, moral and political treachery, historical amnesia, and psychic and spiritual turmoil, humanistic issues are central—if only funding agencies, media interests, and we humanists ourselves will recognize the momentousness of this era for our discipline and take seriously the need for our intellectual centrality.[39]

All of these typologies feature a general sense of the necessity of change, not just about a forward-looking variety of the digital humanities but also about the future of the humanities and the academy. At the same time, the typologies reflect particular disciplinary or academic positions. There is a sense of clear forward trajectory, and there is a risk that this trajectory conflates different epistemic traditions and goals. One particular risk is that the value of the work and epistemic tradition associated with humanities computing is downplayed because it represents an earlier iteration of the field. For example, Davidson implicitly seems to assume that Humanities 1.0 did not decenter knowledge and authority. Some of these descriptions also seem to imply that humanities computing was absorbed by newer varieties of digital humanities, which is simply not the case. For example, the tools used by the computing humanists described by McPherson are likely to different substantially from most of the tools used by multimodal humanists. And the description of Humanities 2.0 may not converge with how most members in the digital humanities community think of the future of the field.

Yet another typology more clearly addresses this issue from the point of view of the tradition of humanities computing. Ramsay proposes a division between Type I and Type II digital humanities (DH). The first category largely refers to what used to be called "humanities computing" and has been quite important in shaping present-day digital humanities. The ALLC and other organizations have played a significant role in the development of this community, and as Ramsay points out, a set of practices, including text encoding and historical GIS, is associated with humanities computing. Type II digital humanities emerged sometime after 2000 not as a community label but as a signifier both for "a very broad constellation of scholarly endeavors, and for a certain revolutionary disposition that had overtaken the academy." Ramsay argues that since this split, an ideological war has taken place between the two types.[40]

Ramsay's stance is problematic in several ways (although also usefully provocative). It seems like an attempt at turning back the clock to a time when humanities computing was digital humanities and claiming that everything outside of the communal effort of humanities computing can be separated into a type of its own. It also overlooks the fact that digital humanities as we see it today is largely a product of the humanities computing community and that the recent discussion of gender and ethnicity in relation to the field is relevant (because it is mainly driven by people outside Type I DH). Furthermore, digital humanities' current traction partly comes from a broader and more inclusive notion of the field as well as a revolutionary sentiment. Nevertheless, Ramsay's typology is helpful because it describes a very real set of tensions in the field and takes seriously the humanities computing community. It also usefully problematizes the evolutionary trajectory suggested by the other typologies presented in this section.

These typologies demonstrate the existence of a complex landscape with several concurrent epistemic traditions, associated visions, and possible trajectories. This is exactly the type of complexity that could feed fruitfully into the digital humanities as a meeting place. The challenge for big digital humanities lies not in negotiating the range of traditions or perspectives or replacing one tradition with another but rather in creating conditions for dialogue and change across traditions and perspectives that will enable rich and engaging work. This, in turn, requires a good sense of the history and development of the field.

Appropriating the Digital Humanities

The term *humanities computing* has been a strong common denominator for much of the work and community described here. In *Humanities Computing*, Willard McCarty describes the development of the field in relation to key mileposts: from "when the relationship was desired but largely unrealized" (computers and the humanities) via "once entry has been gained" (computing in the humanities) to "confident but enigmatic" (humanities computing).[41] In this 2005 book, the term *digital humanities* is not used once. According to Edward Vanhoutte, one of the first mentions of *humanities computing* in this sense was in 1966.[42] Since the publication of McCarty's book in 2005, however, *humanities computing* has gradually disappeared as an institutional label and been replaced by *digital humanities*.

Ten years after the publication of *Humanities Computing*, McCarty uses his own book and the *Blackwell Companion to the Digital Humanities* (2004) to describe the point at which the discipline of digital humanities (using that term) became self-aware.[43] While these works are important, they are still very much set in the tradition of humanities computing, and I argue that the most important factor here is how the adaption of the term *digital humanities* (in its social and institutional context) eventually opened up a new, epistemically more diverse space for renegotiating the field. This negotiation, which is still going on, has been characterized by significant external and internal pressure, and also by resistance to change. Leadership-level strategic work in the humanities computing community led to the introduction of the new name (and implicitly, new territory) in the mid-2000s, but the thinking was still strongly embedded in the epistemic tradition of humanities computing.

This change can thus be read as humanities computing strategically and rhetorically shifting to the term *digital humanities*. Matthew Kirschenbaum explains the backstory via conversations with a few key people. For example, according to John Unsworth, the term came from 2001 discussions about what to title the book that eventually became *A Companion to Digital Humanities*. The publisher, Blackwell, pressured the authors not to use *humanities computing*. Similarly, the National Endowment for the Humanities (NEH) opted for *digital humanities* when starting a new initiative in 2006. According to the agency's Brett Bobley, digital humanities was chosen partly because it "cast a wider net than 'humanities computing'" and because it came with "a form of humanism" that would make it easier to sell to the humanities community.[44] This means that it is simply wrong to claim, as Ramsay does, that the change in scope was "completely unintentional" and that "they were trying to come up with a name to describe a particular community of practitioners of the sort exemplified in the first Blackwell companion."[45]

Much of the current tension in the digital humanities comes from precisely this development. Some members of the community may have seen the shift in terminology as merely a change in name, but others certainly offered resistance since a great deal of identity had come to be associated with the term *humanities computing*. As Ramsay wrote, humanities computing is "the community that I've identified with throughout my entire career."[46] Community members had worked hard to develop their practice, identity, and position, and many saw increased leverage as a continuation of and reward for that work. Bobley's rationale, however, has a very different flavor, and the change came not solely from the NEH or Blackwell but from part of the humanities computing leadership. A small group of people from the humanities computing organizations were intimately involved in these processes. In this context, then, the change in name is not just about names but about indicating a larger scope for the field. Such change clearly comes with additional responsibilities. Indeed, the NEH could probably not have created an office for something framed as humanities computing was regardless of the name used. The name change signaled a major development in the field's direction; it was much more than a matter of cosmetics.

Kirschenbaum also retells an earlier part of the backstory involving the creation of the ADHO. John Unsworth and Harold Short came up with the idea in the summer of 2002, although the organization was not created until 2005. On August 16, 2002, John Unsworth got the ball rolling when he sent a message to an e-mail list for the Allied Digital Humanities Organizations Committee. The process was not entirely smooth, although most of the participants were key members in existing associations and presumably agreed with the basic idea of a creating a consortium. Issues raised at the time included governance, the naming of the organization, the naming of the conference, a time frame, and voting arrangements. And despite a discussion of a number of different monikers for the organization, the name selected, the Alliance of Digital Humanities Organizations, was very close to the committee's original name, the Allied Digital Humanities Organizations Committee.[47]

Renaming Work

An example of the spread of the new term *digital humanities* is the change in name of the annual conference, which beginning in 1989 was run by the ALLC and the ACH. Previously known as the joint International Conference of the Association for Literary and Linguistic Computing and the Association for Computers and the Humanities, the gathering was renamed the Digital Humanities Conference in 2006. We also started to see new book series such as Topics in Digital Humanities (University of Illinois Press), websites such as www.digitalhumanities.org, and a range of other digital-humanities-labeled initiatives. The Canadian-based Consortium for Computers in the Humanities was renamed to the Society for Digital Humanities. The name *digital humanities* had certainly been used before—at the University of Virginia, among other places—but it came to be employed more broadly and in more official and premeditated contexts. The launch of the NEH's Initiative for Digital Humanities provided a very significant indicator of the spread of the term, and this significance was reinforced when the NEH established the Office of Digital Humanities in 2008.

The relative slowness of the process is also supported through data from the long-standing e-mail list Humanist. Here *humanities computing* remained more common than *digital humanities* as late as 2006–7.[48] The retained and frequent use of the older term points to a discrepancy between the across-the-board institutional renaming of the field and the community's use of the term. One of the members of the Allied Digital Humanities Organizations Committee was outspoken about her concerns about *digital humanities* as late as in April 2005:

> First of all, what does "digital humanities" mean? Does it mean that we are only concerned with those aspects of humanities that already are digital? whatever they are. Or isn't it the case that we are interested in any humanities and how computing can enhance the understanding of humanities?[49]

This phenomenon clearly represents something more than just a name change or a simple repackaging of the field. As Kirschenbaum commented in 2011, the idea that digital humanities includes all people in the humanities doing digital work is true semantically and tautologically but not socially, materially, historically, or institutionally.[50] Kirschenbaum's response may be understood in relation to the nominal and conceptual move from *humanities computing* to *digital humanities*.

The renaming work continues: in 2012, the Association for Literary and Linguistic Computing became ALLC: The European Association for Digital Humanities.[51] As with the journal's name, *LLC*, the acronym initially was kept as a connection to the organization's past,[52] although it now seems largely to have been dropped. According to the EADH website,

> As the range of available and relevant computing techniques in the humanities increased, the interests of the association's members have broadened substantially and encompass not only text analysis and language corpora, but also history, art history, music, manuscript studies, image processing

and electronic editions. The association's new name, which was adopted in 2012, reflects this significant widening of scope. Today the EADH's mission is to represent European Digital Humanities across all disciplines.[53]

The name change is linked to a change of scope, although the list of new areas (such as manuscript studies) does not seem inclusive in any new or radical way. The reference to European digital humanities emphasizes the regional aspect of EADH and is part of the far-reaching regionalization of the ADHO associations. This development could be read as dividing up the world between different digital humanities organizations under the ADHO umbrella. The ALLC came into existence after two conferences in the United Kingdom in the early 1970s, and the organization definitely possesses European core,[54] but participants also came from other parts of the world, and the subsequent conference series alternated between Europe and the United States. In fact, in 2014, a significant number of the EADH members came from the United States,[55] which means that the link to Europe is not quite as strong as the group's name may indicate. However, a regionalized logic makes it easier to include national charters. At a 2011 ALLC meeting, Vanhoutte said that "if people want to make their own organizations, let them do so. And if they succeed, the ALLC has failed."[56] This is undoubtedly a territorial stance.

Creating the Digital Humanities

A number of strategic choices played a role in creating digital humanities as an institutional construct. The use of *digital humanities* is thus not just a question of marketing and renaming the field but also a conscious institutional move and a kind of flocking behavior as the field has gained momentum. The editors of the Blackwell volume were not just any digital humanists: they have held a number of key positions in different humanities computing and digital humanities organizations and thus wield considerable strategic power and leverage. For example, two of the editors have chaired the ADHO Steering Committee.

Domenico Fiormonte has researched the overlapping involvement of certain people in the organizational construct of digital humanities.[57] Some key scholars hold as many as five committee and board appointments. Melissa Terras, for example, has appointments in the mother organization, the ADHO, as well as in two member organizations and the two main journals supported by the ADHO. Fiormonte's data are current, but it would be quite interesting to also look at appointment patterns over time, as many of the people he lists have served on these boards and committees for a very long time. Fiormonte does not, however, clearly acknowledge that this overlapping occurs partly because the ADHO is made up of the constituent organizations, which have seats on the ADHO board and committees. Nevertheless, the distribution of power is important regardless of the exact organizational structure or history.

The clubby nature of the ADHO could be seen as an obstacle to organizational power for newcomers to the digital humanities. The only way to get on the ADHO board is through one of the constituent organizations, and the executive committees (or their equivalents) of those organizations proposes board members.[58] In other words, it is an indirect procedure. One cannot get elected to the ADHO board.

So while the field has seen considerable expansion both inside and outside the institutional umbrella of traditional digital humanities, much of the organizational anchorage is still provided by the ADHO and its member organizations. A considerable part of the digital humanities is not organized by the ADHO, however, creating tensions between the organization's main epistemic tradition and the epistemic traditions and expectations that have entered the field since the mid-2000s. The ADHO has the opportunity to admit new blood, but doing so will require more far-reaching measures than creating a big tent through fairly small actions. For example, the board structure could be changed to provide representation for other communities.

Evidence indicates that the name change from *humanities computing* to *digital humanities* occurred from the top down and that acceptance of the new moniker did not occur quite as quickly as the organizational renamings might indicate. The community held on to *humanities computing* for some time. The landmark *Companion to Digital Humanities* contains about twice as many instances of *humanities computing* as *digital humanities*. The name that appears on the cover page does not reflect the dominant usage in the book itself. In addition, the distribution of these two terms in the volume supports the view that the old term remained more important at this time. *Humanities computing* predominates in the section describing the contributors, whereas *digital humanities* primarily appears in the introduction. The former section is a place for self-representation more likely to be controlled by the individual authors, whereas the introduction is controlled by the editors. Both sections are concerned with identity and its creation, but in different ways.

A number of processes and choices, some of them strongly driven by humanities computing leaders, led to a markedly changed situation just a few years later. Each of these steps alone may not seem dramatic, but together they contributed to a new landscape. The fact that observers believed that a title without *humanities computing* for the Blackwell volume might increase readership is significant. Similarly, while the NEH's decision to start a new initiative for the digital humanities constituted a great step forward for the humanities computing community, the case that had to be made within the agency was one for the humanities rather than for a particular community. The resultant office predictably did not fully map the interests of the humanities computing community. The establishment of funding agency structures helped increase interest among university leaders, which strengthened the field in some ways but also meant that the digital humanities was being negotiated and renegotiated. An influx of new community members occurred, some from traditions and disciplines other than those traditionally associated with humanities computing. These and other factors put pressure on digital humanities as humanities computing.

So while humanities computing leaders strategically appropriated *digital humanities*, their actions have increased the difficulty of maintaining the epistemic tradition of humanities computing in light of external pressure and the field's much more heterogeneous configuration.

Humanities Computing as Digital Humanities

The heritage of humanities computing is quite visible throughout the organizational nomenclature of the digital humanities. For example, the EADH website states that the association seeks "to represent and bring together the Digital Humanities in Europe across the entire spectrum of disciplines that apply, develop and research digital humanities methods and technology."[59] Wikipedia states that "digital humanities embrace a variety of topics, from curating online collections to data mining large cultural data sets."[60]

There is a basic assumption here that the heart of digital humanities is humanities methods and technologies rather than humanistic research challenges. This position can be traced back to the tradition of humanities computing but may not harmonize with other conceptions of the field. Although interest in these challenges may exist, they are not the entry point or what is foregrounded discursively. This section examines four primary epistemic commitments of humanities computing: the instrumental focus of the tradition, a methodological orientation, the privileging of text, and the tradition's engagement with digitized cultural heritage as opposed to other study objects and materials. While this is partly a historical exercise, it is relevant to the future shaping of the field.

First, humanities computing as a whole maintained a very instrumental approach to technology in the humanities. In her introductory chapter to *A Companion to Digital Humanities*, Susan Hockey argues that this is not the place to define humanities computing: "Suffice it to say, that we are concerned with the applications of computing to research and teaching within the subjects that are loosely defined as 'the humanities,' or in British English, 'the arts.'"[61] Hockey's description indicates a paradigm in which information technology is typically not seen as an object of study, or an expressive medium. Rather, technology has this basic and epistemically grounded role as a tool, and much of humanities computing involves using these tools, helping others to use them, and to some extent developing new tools and methodologies.

Many of these tools, such as concordance programs, have a rather long and distinguished history have not necessarily changed radically over time. Traditional humanities computing focused not on innovating new tools but rather on using and developing existing ones (some of them based on analog systems). In addition, a fair proportion of the development occurred on a structural or metadata level, such as text encoding and markup systems. Of course, work on this level has fundamental implications for the development and use of tools.

Text encoding is typically seen as a core element of the tradition of humanities computing. According to Koenraad de Smedt, "Text encoding seems to create the foundation for almost any use of computers in the humanities."[62] Despite the major role that text encoding and markup have played in humanities computing, limited interest seems to have existed in critical work on encoding in the sense of reflecting on the worldviews built into such classifications (relating to factors such as gender, race, power, and epistemic traditions). Martha Nell Smith makes the important point that humanities computing "seemed to offer a space free from all this messiness and a return to objective questions of representations."[63] And even with digital humanities projects that would seem to have a clear critical potential in this regard, such as the Victorian Women Writers Project, there is a tendency not to see the encoding as an interpretative or even an "inflected" mechanism.[64] The goal becomes more a question of making accessible and building on the structure provided by the text encoding initiative than seeing the technological systems as critical devices. There are online "exhibitions" connected to the project that do important critical work,[65] but these still mostly read as critical texts at some distance from the actual encoding and data structures.

A second epistemic commitment comes from the interest in technology and methodology in humanities computing. Observers have often pointed out that what brought together humanities computing is largely a common interest in methods, methodology, tools, and technology.[66] Vanhoutte writes, "Methodology is at the basis of any transfer of knowledge about computing in the humanities, which is where Terras and McCarty locate the problem for a fruitful debate about the interdisciplinarity of the field."[67] This partly follows from the field's instrumental orientation, and there is no reason to question the methodological commons as a valuable interdisciplinary focus and productive collaborative sentiment. However, this strong methodological focus fundamentally affected the way humanities computing operated and related to other disciplines. The most serious implication was that a predominantly methodological link to other disciplines might not integrate many of the specific issues that lie at the core of these disciplines, making it more difficult for humanities computing to reach out more broadly and intellectually to traditional humanities departments and scholars. While interest will always exist in methods and technology, the actual target group—humanities scholars with an active interest in humanities computing tools and perspectives—is relatively limited. Many scholars would like to have experts help develop databases and web interfaces, but there is a risk that such engagement will involve service and technological solutions rather than a strong intellectual-material engagement. Patrick Juola argues that digital humanities has been emerging as a discipline for decades and that there is a perceived neglect on the part of the broader humanities community. While he appreciates the work done in humanities computing, he also finds that

> for the past forty years, humanities computing have more or less languished in the background of traditional scholarship. Scholars lack incentive to participate (or even to learn about) the results of humanities computing.[68]

Juola shows that citation scores for humanities computing journals are very low and points out that the American Ivy League universities are sparsely represented in humanities computing publications and at humanities computing conferences. The lack of citations can, however, result partly from the fact that humanities scholars who use humanities computing tools might not be inclined to cite the creators of these tools, especially if no written work on associated methodology or theories has been employed in the research. Also, the fact that Ivy League universities have generally been slow to engage with humanities computing and the digital humanities could reflect a certain level of traditionalism.

And although the methodological connection between the digital humanities and the humanities is important to the vision of the field advocated in this book, it is not as central as in humanities computing and many contemporary descriptions of the field. Big digital humanities sees methodology as an important boundary object and competence area but also emphasizes the research questions and intellectual challenges, whether or not they are strongly anchored in methodology, as a key connective core of the field.

The third epistemic commitment is the pronounced textual focus of humanities computing. Traditional text is clearly a privileged level of description and analysis. In her partly corpus-based study of humanities computing from 2006, Terras states, "Humanities Computing research is predominantly about text."[69] While this is true, interest in multimedia and nontextual material has certainly increased over the years. In addition to the textual focus, a tendency existed to handle other media in the same way as text (that is, to view them as different object types to encode) or to see them as merely subservient to text. Blackwell's *A Companion to Digital Humanities* offers a rather text-focused discussion of images in relation to the history (and future) of humanities computing:

> There are of course many advantages in having access to images of source material over the Web, but humanities computing practitioners, having grown used to the flexibility offered by searchable text, again tended to regard imaging projects as not really their thing, unless, like the Beowulf Project . . . , the images could be manipulated and enhanced in some way. Interesting research has been carried out on linking images to text, down to the level of the word . . . . When most of this can be done automatically we will be in a position to reconceptualize some aspects of manuscript studies.[70]

There is nothing wrong with a textual focus, but it affected the scope and penetration of humanities computing. Neither the visual turn nor the postvisual turn seemed to have a major impact on humanities computing, probably because little interaction occurred between these communities because of the difficulty of conceptualizing and developing tools for these kinds of frameworks. This does not mean that the visual has not been relevant to humanities computing (and the digital humanities), but the field has often had a text-centered and archival engagement with the visual rather than a theoretical and expressive engagement. A similar pattern exists with aural materials and perspectives. As we have seen, Jonathan Sterne notes the digital humanities' limited engagement with sound and sound studies.[71] In a promising development, however, the 2014 Digital Humanities Conference featured two panels on sound studies, and these connections should be thoroughly explored. Such exploration and negotiation across modalities and knowledge communities are essential to big digital humanities.

The final point relates to data and material used in humanities computing: the objects of study of humanities computing and associated disciplines. In his discussion of a methodological commons, McCarty distinguishes among four data types: text, image, number, and sound. He reduces the source materials and approaches of the disciplines to these four data types and a "finite (but not fixed) set of tools for manipulating them." It is essentially a formal system, and McCarty adds that these tools are derived from formal methods and that their applications are governed by such methods.[72] This viewpoint touches on the tendency to subscribe to formal and science-driven models of knowledge production in humanities computing (where text is the principal object of study):

> Applications involving textual sources have taken center stage within the development of humanities computing as defined by its major publications and thus it is inevitable that this essay concentrates on this area. Nor is it the place here to attempt to define "interdisciplinarity," but by its very nature, humanities computing has had to embrace "the two cultures," to bring the rigor and systematic unambiguous procedural methodologies characteristic of the sciences to address problems within the humanities that had hitherto been most often treated in a serendipitous fashion.[73]

Furthermore, humanities computing was interested primarily in digitized texts (or in some cases, digitized historical sites, and so forth) and not in digitally created material such as computer games, blogs, Twitter feeds, Facebook data, e-mail collections, websites, surveillance footage, YouTube films, and digital art. Most of these "objects" are studied and analyzed in different kinds of new media settings and increasingly in the digital humanities, and this is another productive intersection between the digital humanities and other fields that warrants continued exploration. However, such work—important to big digital humanities—needs to question the assumption of "systematic unambiguous procedural methodologies" as put forward by McCarty as well as the tendency of media studies to avoid deep engagements with data structures.

Territorial Ambitions

The organizations associated with humanities computing and these epistemic commitments play an important role in relation to an expansive notion of the digital humanities. Scholarly organizations are part of the fabric of academic life and institutional ecology, and building such organizations is part of establishing a field or discipline. Disciplines can be established without such organizations, but they tend to be an important tool for doing this type of work. They are useful because they operate on a strategic level and can represent their constituent members as well as help organize and create an identity for communities. Their role can be more administrative and organizational or more directly linked to scholarship and content. Digital humanities has co-evolved with a set of scholarly organizations that have played a significant part in building the field since the early 1970s.

Members of such organizations often accept even parts of the organizational agenda that may not fully conform to their own views. For example, many ADHO members likely do not care much for the idea of digital humanities as presented through the journal *Digital Scholarship in the Humanities* (formerly *Linguistic and Literary Computing*), but they nevertheless understand that the journal is both a historical artifact and a practical mechanism for securing and managing membership fees. Conflicts may arise between organizational-level strategies and the sentiment and views of scholars and constituent institutions. For people who want to take on a leadership role and work strategically, scholarly organizations can function as a platform. And for the discipline or area in question, that platform can be used to create legitimacy and leverage for further development and possibly expansion.

The three principal humanities computing organizations and later the ADHO have played an important role in shaping the field of digital humanities. On many levels, the ADHO has succeeded, and it reflects a fairly clear ambition to expand territorially. This is a worthwhile ambition for a scholarly society, but it makes the question of what type of digital humanities the

ADHO represents even more important. If the ADHO is essentially an extension of humanities computing, the territorial ambitions would equate with spreading an updated version of humanities computing under the name *digital humanities*.

The ADHO originally had two member associations, the ALLC and the ACH, with what is now the Canadian Society for Digital Humanities joining in 2007. Two other, partly overlapping initiatives were involved in the early discussions: the National Initiative for Networked Cultural Heritage and the Text Encoding Initiative Consortium.[74] In 2012, centerNet and the Australasian Association for Digital Humanities joined the ADHO as full constituent organizations, followed by the Japanese Association for Digital Humanities in January 2013. The change in name from the Association of Literary and Linguistic Computing to the European Association for Digital Humanities in 2012 represented another strategic move.[75] Two of the three original member associations have regionalized their names, and apart from centerNet and the ACH, all organizations now have regional names. Indeed, the ADHO Admissions Protocol from 2008 requires that new constituent organizations represent "a digital humanities community that has a definable geographical scope at country level or larger."[76] The ACH's name was discussed at the association's June 2011 general meeting, when the executive council had recognized that the current name "may not be as expressive of contemporary digital humanities scholarship and teaching as it might be."[77] Some discussants noted the risk that the current name might keep new people away, however, meeting participants decided to retain the old name despite its anachronistic sentiment. ACH leaders, much like those of most of the other organizations, likely wanted to adapt to the new digital humanities landscape. It is noteworthy that the only ADHO organization without a regionalized "digital humanities" name has come to include more newcomers in its leadership structure. In any case, the overall regionalization of the names of the digital humanities organizations is evidence of international growth and territorial ambitions as well as of productive and legitimate efforts to strengthen the digital humanities.

One of the recently added constituent organizations, centerNet, was affiliated with the ADHO before becoming a member. CenterNet is an "international network of digital humanities centers," leaving "the definition of 'digital humanities' up to you."[78] However, centerNet's organization around the idea of centers may impose a bias. Centers have been important in the history of digital humanities and are a common structure in some parts of the world (notably North America and the United Kingdom), but they are certainly not the only possible way of implementing the digital humanities. The centerNet website mentions labs and projects, but the main rhetoric takes centers as an institutional model.[79] This orientation is also clear in descriptions offered by Neil Freistat, a key person in the centerNet's establishment, of the digital humanities, centers and centerNet. According to Freistat, centerNet's initiatives are grounded in a "strategic vision of the place of the digital humanities center in the institutional history of the academy," and such centers can be "invaluable community resources."[80]

However, as Mark Sample pointed out in 2010, many people doing digital humanities will not have access to a center:

> And fortunately too, a digital humanities center is not the digital humanities. The digital humanities—or I should say, digital humanists—are much more diverse, much more dispersed, and stunningly resourceful to boot.[81]

Digital humanities work can be organized in many ways, including different types of network models and collaborations. And it is not clear that digital humanities centers are optimal platforms in every way. As Diane Zorich points out the many advantages of digital humanities centers as well as potential problems, such as the risks that centers will become silos, have too many resources, become unconnected to community resources, and not be ready for resource integration across geographical, disciplinary, and departmental lines.[82] A critical discussion of the built-in biases of a center model would seem to be important for an initiative such as centerNet.

Furthermore, centerNet's placement within the ADHO carries significance. What does it mean that an international network of digital humanities centers has such a strong link to the ADHO? It is a matter of epistemic alignment, as it is probably difficult to be a constituent organization without subscribing to the umbrella group's basic values. For example, the subscription model also applies to centerNet:

> In order to preserve the "subscription" principle, centerNet has agreed that from 1 January 2012 centres wishing to join centerNet will do so on the basis of an institutional subscription to LLC [now DSH].[83]

It is possible to become a member without subscribing to DSH, but this membership type is also administered through Oxford University Press. The webpage that lists the benefits of centerNet membership demonstrates that the organization has a long heritage. Among the benefits listed are eligibility for participation in the Digital Humanities Conference at a discounted rate and access to the centerNet Listserv and website, and ADHO benefits include DSH; the "seminal edited collections" *A Companion to Digital Humanities* and *A Companion to Digital Literary Studies*; and "prestigious digital humanities awards."[84] These benefits possess a substantial humanities computing flavor.

Another important part of the centerNet website is a list of roughly 200 centers (as of March 2015).[85] The criteria for inclusion on the list are somewhat unclear—my institution, HUMlab, appears even though it is not formally a centerNet member (to my knowledge). The list included 183 centers with geographical information, plus a few others (most of them organizations such as the ADHO based in the United States or Europe). Of those centers, 163 were located in the United States and Europe, with 10 in Australia and New Zealand. CenterNet's model thus comes from an Anglo-American context. More generally, it seems that much of the discussion about the field starts out from a U.S. context. Andrew Prescott points to the preoccupation with tenure and securing digital outputs in discussions of the digital humanities and sees this bias as a major problem for the field:

> I think this is possibly the true dark side of the Digital Humanities—that there is a risk that DH becomes one of the means by which an Anglophone globalization of world culture is implemented.[86]

In addition, as Domenico Fiormonte's work details, a number of problems are associated with this kind of centrism, among them the lack of multilingualism and the built-in biases of platforms such as the Text Encoding Initiative.[87] These very real concerns need to influence our thinking about the field and its future.

CenterNet is also a platform for authenticating the digital humanities and for strategically aligning with other organizations. In this way, centerNet promotes the digital humanities in different contexts. It is affiliated with the Consortium of Humanities Centers and Institutes (CHCI), which organizes humanities centers. According to the CHCI website,

> The rubric "Digital Humanities" has broadened and grown substantially in recent years to encompass an ever-widening range of practices including software for textual analysis, visualization, analysis of new media,

multimedia publications, and collaborative research conducted via the internet. This CHCI affinity group is intended for member organizations that are either engaged with digital humanities or interested in developing an approach to the area. Among other projects, CHCI is developing a program-focused relationship with our affiliate consortium, centerNet.[88]

CenterNet thus represents the digital humanities in the context of the CHCI. The CHCI seems to focus primarily on software and infrastructure, adopting a view of the digital humanities that is fairly compatible with that of the ADHO and centerNet, but this is not the only conception of the field. There is much potential in digital humanities and humanities centers working more closely together, and instead of using infrastructure as the primary link, I suggest that establishing a common intellectual and material agenda around scholarly themes with some kind of digital inflection would be a richer strategy.

Organizational structures can help to shape a field and an agenda, sometimes is fairly subtle ways. Tensions may arise if such organizations advocate directions that are not compatible with other conceptions of the field or if those organizations represent the field in various contexts.

The question of the international footprint of the digital humanities is naturally a concern beyond centerNet. In 2013, the ADHO formed a special interest group. Global Outlook::Digital Humanities (GO::DH) was formed to serve as

> the successor to various "outreach" and "North-South" initiatives proposed by ADHO members and Constituent Organisations, including SDH-SEMI (as it then was), ACH, and the ALLC (while this is its heritage, it is important to note that the initiative does not share all of the assumptions and goals of these previous initiatives: in particular, experience has shown how important it is that an initiative of this type be a peer-to-peer community rather than an "outreach" or "aid" programme).[89]

Though this description calls on and critically discusses the heritage, it offers less discussion of what kinds of digital humanities are included. Ben Brumfield addressed this question in a tweet about a GO::DH initiative, Around DH in 80 Days, that documented centers and projects worldwide: "Is #aroundDH featuring small-tent #digitalhumanities from a geographically diverse background? Which periphery is the dance around?"[90] This question also applies to centerNet. What type of digital humanities is advocated and possibly exported? These organizations tend to use a more restricted, small-tent digital humanities as a model. GO::DH is a very worthwhile initiative, and neither it nor centerNet should become a way of simply projecting a very specific model of the digital humanities to the rest of the world. The risk would seem much smaller with GO::DH than with centerNet, and engaging in dialogue with other parts of the world and other types of digital humanities clearly has enormous benefits. Furthermore, GO::DH has gradually developed into a strong platform as a Special Interest Group within ADHO with a considerable buy-in both within and outside traditional digital humanities. The position statement articulated by Élika Ortega in a 2016 paper describes an ideationally grounded, mature and self-reflective organization that struggles productively with questions of Western-ness, institutional position, and making actual change possible.[91] CenterNet has experienced a diversification and renewal that will almost certainly move the organization in a more open direction.

The #transformDH Movement as Territory

The #transformDH movement is also intended to influence and shape the digital humanities. Although #transformDH is very different, it shares some similarities in terms of territorial ambitions with the organizations discussed previously. Movements such as #transformDH are likely to be less persistent over time, although they also change to some extent. Related movements with considerable overlap in terms of people and grounding include Postcolonial Digital Humanities and Disrupting the Digital Humanities. I use *movement* to describe these initiatives to distinguish them from traditional scholarly organizations.

The #transformDH movement arose from a series of discussions but seems to have started at a roundtable session at the American Studies Association 2011 Conference, Transformative Mediations? Queer and Ethnic Studies and the Politics of the Digital. Participants perceived a lack of critical engagement in the digital humanities in relation to race/ethnic studies and gender/sexuality studies.[92] The call for the panel was framed against these areas or disciplines (studies) rather than merely issues of gender, race, and so forth, and the panel organizers unsurprisingly had backgrounds in ethnic studies and queer studies. The push, therefore, came partly from another organizational complex and of course from individuals active in both worlds.

As with older digital humanities organizations, the naming of the movement was of some concern. According to Alexis Lothian, one of six panel organizers, various hashtags were considered, but #queerDH was rejected because it took away race, while #criticalDH was deemed inappropriate because it implied that most DH was not critical. #transformDH was selected because "it seemed memorable and provocative, and because it linked to the title of our panel."[93] According to the original Tumblr description,

> #transformDH is an academic guerrilla movement seeking to (re)define capital-letter Digital Humanities as a force for transformative scholarship by collecting, sharing, and highlighting projects that push at its boundaries and work for social justice, accessibility, and inclusion.[94]

As Google confirms, the descriptor *movement* is very rarely used about the ADHO, whereas it seems appropriate with #transformDH.[95] The term implies a desire for change, and #transformDH has a clear connection to THATcamp meetings (where humanists and technologists build together in sessions that are proposed on the spot), which are also often described as a movement.[96] #transformDH challenges digital humanities as manifested by the ADHO in a way that few other voices and initiatives have managed. Junior scholars are launching fairly strong attacks, not completely buying either the big-tent implementation or the idea that the digital humanities is nice. This kind of push benefits the digital humanities, which sometimes seems to hide under a "niceness" cover. Some reactions have been negative. Roger Whitson, for one, has stated that movements such as #transformDH "baffle him":

> Do we really need guerrilla movements? Are war metaphors, or concepts of overturning and redefining, truly the right kind of metaphors to use when talking about change in the digital humanities?[97]

In Whitson's view, the collaborative and social nature of digital humanities contributed to changing the atmosphere of the Modern Language Association conference. In this light, the talk about warfare seems unnecessary. Collaboration and "niceness" are important, of course, but surely the digital humanities offers much more than just this sentiment. And while there is much discussion in the digital humanities about how to evaluate digital scholarship, practitioners remain reluctant to profoundly criticize work produced within the field and consequently hesitate to single out people, groups, or projects. This tendency could be ascribed to the collaborative and collective ethos that is part of the tradition of the digital humanities. Another factor is probably the field's historical sense of being an outsider, as it has had to construct and defend its production institutionally for a long time.

So who is conducting this war, and what does the #transformDH idea of digital humanities actually look like? And is #transformDH a strategic move from fields such as queer studies that have found themselves in more dire straits to insert themselves into the digital humanities? Or can #transformDH be seen as a more general attempt to rebrand digital cultural studies as digital humanities? As Prescott says,

> #transformDH perhaps looks too much like an attempt to turn digital hu-
> manities into another form of cultural or media studies.[98]

Despite such tendencies, it seems unlikely that #transformDH actually seeks to take over the digital humanities. Rather, the movement appears to seek to make the digital humanities more critical and to insert specific perspectives and disciplinary traditions into the field. This process should also work both ways, so that change occurs in ethnic, gender and queer studies—for example, by emphasizing the importance of digital making—as well as an honest interest in relating to and learning from digital humanities as a tradition and epistemic framework. This two-way (or multiple-way) exchange is an important prerequisite of big digital humanities.

While digital humanities has a long history and a sometimes seemingly reluctant engagement with digital media, the #transformDH community was in a sense born into the digital expressions and channels that come with the territory of digital humanities. In contrast, the ADHO's first organizational tweet did not occur until February 12, 2013.[99]

As a movement, #transformDH is not only significant but also part of a much-needed activist critique of the digital humanities as an organized effort and project. As Prescott points out, #transformDH is "fundamentally about reconnecting digital humanities with fundamental themes of current scholarship in the humanities."[100] This does not mean that #transform DH is not a territorial effort or that it covers a full range of critical perspectives. It does not appear to be explicitly exclusionary, but the subtitle of the #transformDH Tumblr site carries a clear message: "This is the Digital Humanities."[101]

Getting Rid of the Big Tent

One way the digital humanities community has tried to come to grips with the expansion of the field has been to use the metaphor of "big tent" digital humanities. This was the theme of the 2011 Digital Humanities Conference at Stanford University. While a March 2011 Google search for "small tent digital humanities" yielded no results, it seems clear that the alternative to the big-tent model is a smaller-tent model, as evidenced in Brumfield's tweet referenced earlier. Big-tent digital humanities is sometimes invoked as describing a problematic and overly large expansion of humanities computing. Vanhoutte, for example, suggests that "Digital Humanities as a term does not refer to such a specialized activity, but provides a big tent for all digital scholarship in the humanities."[102] This statement, however, does not acknowledge that the big tent is not all-inclusive and definitely does not encompass all the digitally inclined scholarship in the humanities.

The size of the big tent relates both to the disciplines or areas involved and the geographical dispersion of the field, as is evident in the call for proposals for the Stanford conference: "With the Big Tent theme in mind, we especially invite submissions from Latin American scholars, scholars in the digital arts and music, in spatial history, and in the public humanities."[103] The connection between the public humanities and the digital humanities appears to be growing, but this linkage is not normally emphasized in the tradition of the digital humanities that the annual conference represents. The examples mentioned in the call might be related to ongoing work at Stanford University, but other perspectives and questions also would have invoked big-tent digital humanities, including gender research, rhetoric, and the interface between critical studies and digital humanities.

And despite the inclusive theme of the Stanford conference and the fact that this call was more open than its predecessors, it continues to exclude.[104] According to Alex Reid, who comes from a rhetorician's perspective, the call contains "no mention of the significant digital technologies and practices that are transforming human experience on a global scale." He continues, "No, instead, we're going to talk about writing software to analyze hundreds of out of print literary texts that no one can even name."[105] Similarly, Hugh Cayless notes, "From reading my (possibly) representative sample of DH proposals, I'd say the main theme of the conference will not be 'Big Tent Digital Humanities' but 'data integration.'"[106] These comments illustrate some of the tension and range involved.

No matter how big the tent becomes, it cannot be infinite, and the border between inside the tent and outside it is fairly distinct. *Tent* comes from the Latin *tentus*, meaning "stretched." Whitney Trettien asks how much the big digital humanities tent can be stretched: "I'm not sure Digital Humanities, even a big-tent Digital Humanities, has room for all these digital humanists."[107] The discussion of the digital humanities tent focuses mainly on the size of the tent, but a more inclusive tent does not necessarily translate into more far-reaching structural change. The bringing together of different epistemic traditions will lead to change, but the metaphor and the associated discussion may not highlight these more radical aspects or, for that matter, a different basic stance. As articulated by this conference call, big-tent digital humanities remains grounded in a particular epistemic tradition.

The pressure on ADHO and institutional digital humanities has increased since the 2011 conference. The weakness of the big tent model can be traced in the minutes from the 2015 ADHO Steering Committee meeting.[108] Such documents naturally do not give the full story, in particular with regards to conflicts and institutional problematics, but can provide a useful impression of the state of health of an institution. The chair of the steering committee references fatigue in the committee and one of the committee members states that "if we don't change something, we're headed for a train wreck."

One key challenge is the growth of membership and the stress put on the organization by the overall institutional success in terms of handling increasingly large annual conferences ("Do we want to let the conference become arbitrarily large?"), journal backlogs ("excessively long turnaround time"), and new aspiring member associations ("Asks what a DH organization must do, what must its mission be, to see it as part of ADHO"). This situation cannot just be attributed to increased workload because of the larger organization; it is also about deep-going structural factors and multiple major challenges. For example, the issue of governance reform and other reform efforts runs through most of the minutes and a recurring view is that the reform process is too slow. How is representation handled? What mission should ADHO constituent organizations have? What beliefs about the digital humanities underlie ADHO decisions?

There is acknowledgment that the steering committee is seen as an insider forum and ADHO as a black box, and there is a consequent emphasis on the need for transparency, structural change, and the necessity to bring in new people. All in all, the minutes give the impression of an organization under duress whose template and model are being challenged substantially. It is clear that the big tent has not succeeded as a means of managing a larger footprint and support for more inclusivity. There are calls for more far-reaching and structural change in the document, and to some degree there seems to be a real realization of this need. Importantly, there is humility and critical reflection reflected in the minutes, which will hopefully help the organization to adapt and be more inclusive in terms of epistemic traditions and perspectives.

Their task is by no means an easy one. There is no form of digital humanities free of epistemic tradition, and we do not necessarily need to find a model that includes everyone and everything. However, the big tent is not an appropriate metaphor in arguing for an intersectional role for the digital humanities and an inclusive notion of the field—big digital humanities. I use *intersectional* in a broad sense, denoting the intellectual-material coming together of multiple epistemic traditions and perspectives around issues and challenges with some kind of digital or technological inflection. Drawing on intersectionality in the more specific sense often used in critical theory—to describe how oppression manifests through multiple categories at the same time (e.g., gender, race, and class)—Roopika Risam argues that such work must also be painful:

> This includes looking more closely at digital humanities projects, opening the black boxes to examine the imprints of intersectionality on archive, code, metadata, database, and more. In the writing and rewriting of these histories, digital humanities practitioners must situate them in the histories of Afrofuturism, digital textual recovery, new media studies, and science and technology studies, being careful not to erase or write over the contributions that scholars of race, class, gender, sexuality, disability, or other forms of difference are making to the digital humanities – or risk reaffirming the power of Western academic hegemony.[109]

Such intersectionality goes beyond the big tent and begs more far-reaching interventions. The digital humanities cannot be everything, but it can be a meeting place and contact zone centered on the digital that incorporates a broad intersectional capacity and engagement with the perspectives that Risam and others list (including those from environmental humanities and animal studies). Liminal work of this kind is both challenging and exciting. And while the emphasis is often on the digital humanities changing as a result of such work—which it will and should—the power of contact zones lies in change across epistemic traditions and perspectives including gender studies and environmental humanities.

We must respect and build on tradition, but stretching an existing tradition may not be enough to create the kind of digital humanities that engages broadly across the humanities, has integrity, is involved in reconfiguring the humanities, and allows for maximum connectivity and multiple modes of engagement with the digital.

Conclusion

Digital humanities draws on the tradition and organizational structure of humanities computing, meaning that the epistemic tradition of humanities computing has served to some extent and continues to serve as a blueprint for digital humanities. With increased interest in the field and more resources, this blueprint has faced pressure at the same time that it has been promoted through organizational structures such as the ADHO and centerNet. The dominant paradigm for digital humanities comes with a number of epistemic commitments. Over time, the digital humanities as an operation has adapted, but the question is whether a bigger tent is sufficient or whether a more major reorientation is required to help the field reach its full potential and range.

Three Premises of Big Digital Humanities

Whether or not we believe in a big-tent or stretched-tent notion of the digital humanities, an essential question concerns the size and scope of the field. This chapter further substantiates the conception of big digital humanities. This inclusive, intersectional, and infrastructural notion of the field is based on ideas that connect to the history of digital humanities, its current challenges, and its institutional trajectories. Considerable value can be gained from seeing the digital humanities as a meeting place or contact zone supporting multiple modes of engagement between the humanities and the digital. Moreover, the digital humanities needs to be a site of engagement for the humanities writ large.

Indeed, to whatever degree it is possible to find a productive institutional, scholarly, and practical "solution" for the digital humanities, big digital humanities makes a good candidate. It is based on a large and inclusive notion of the field and builds on multiple traditions and modes of engagement. Such a model must be sensitive to local conditions and cannot draw on a single institutional model, although suggestions can be made.

The big digital humanities project has considerable potential and range. It engages deeply with the humanities disciplines, has a multifaceted intellectual engagement with the digital, contributes to high-quality scholarship and methodological innovation, and provides humanistic infrastructure. Moreover, big digital humanities reaches out to the rest of the university and the world, serves as a model for a proactive humanities, and functions as a meeting place and contact zone.

It is also a day-to-day business characterized less by big words than by a combination of individual work and collaboration, coding, technical development, long-term research processes, institutional politics, and administration. The driving force is intellectual and technological curiosity, and the vision is not that everyone should be doing everything but rather that there is much power in bringing together competencies, infrastructures, and ideas. A key driving force is participants who are passionate about very different things in this large enterprise.

This chapter details three basic premises of big digital humanities:

- The field and the humanities disciplines benefit from engaging broadly with the digital.
- The digital humanities needs to be a meeting place with broad humanistic and deep academic investment.
- The digital humanities is well placed to be a site of engagement for all of the humanities.

The notion of intellectual middleware exemplifies how these perspectives can be brought together.

Why Big Digital Humanities?

Can the digital humanities ever be sorted out in terms of its institutional buildup, identity, and trajectory? The picture presented in chapters 1 and 2 might suggest that too many epistemic traditions, historical hang-ups, organizational interests, specialist communities, and intentions are at play for the field to ever come to any kind of common direction. Indeed, the scope of what is labeled *digital humanities* is quite large, ranging from the particulars of encoding schemas to the future of the humanities. The field can also at times seem almost frantically obsessed with metalevel reflections, self-referentiality, and staking out different positions in a never-ending online debate. In September 2013, Alan Liu published a three-thousand-word blog entry reiterating a two-and-a-half-year debate with Steven Ramsay.[1] Liu's well-written and forward-looking account displayed a field involved in a long-term struggle with itself, almost always manifested online. The ongoing debate, which can be traced back at least twenty-five years, demonstrates that the field is not static and stale but also shows that dialogue can become repetitive and not necessarily productive.

There is no contradiction, however, in maintaining some of this energy and intermediacy while creating more stability and better channeling the field's potential. We need to take into account the fact that the humanities and the digital are entangled in different ways and that a simultaneous intellectual and technological engagement is required to push some of the most interesting research questions and infrastructural challenges. Furthermore, whether or not we like it, the digital humanities has become a place for thinking about the humanities and a number of issues closely related to the development of the academy. This comes naturally if the digital humanities is seen as a meeting place and a place for empowerment and innovation. It would be a mistake not to embrace this possibility.

The solution is to be intellectually and materially driven, allow for multiple modes of engagement between the humanities and the digital, and make the digital humanities into an inclusive meeting place and contact zone. Epistemic inclusiveness is not just a way of getting almost everyone together; it may also actually be the only way for the humanities to engage long term with the digital in a comprehensive and meaningful way. This is not about being nice in the manner of digital humanities discourse (even if niceness is important) but rather about incorporating the different perspectives, tensions, and competences necessary to build knowledge at the intersection of the humanities and the digital. Sharpness is critical. Through being placed in between, the digital humanities can avoid becoming a new institutionalized discipline yet secure a mandate to be discipline-like, network-like, and center-like at the same time. The field needs an infrastructural and intellectual core with integrity and stability as well as a way of drawing on the collective richness of the humanities and other knowledge domains to support intellectually and materially strong and daring work.

Three Basic Premises of Big Digital Humanities

First, it is not only important but essential that the digital humanities and the humanities disciplines connect with the digital across several modes of engagement. We need to look at information technology as an object of analysis, an expressive medium, and a tool, and these modes are becoming increasingly blurred. Where they come together, we will likely find some of the most interesting future work. Separating critical studies of the digital from the building and development of technological structures is particularly unfortunate. The digital humanities has the potential to bring together data, tools, expressions, and research questions, in the process making significant contributions.

Second, the digital humanities needs to function as a meeting place and a contact zone to enable simultaneous engagement with these different modes of engagement and infrastructures as part of a broad humanistic and deep academic investment. This is particularly relevant in the context of a considerably larger field than has existed in the past. Further, we need to take seriously the responsibilities and expectations that come with this enlarged territory. The field has historically existed in part institutionally and operationally between, and the choice between building on and expanding this model and becoming more like a discipline would seem to be a decisive question for the digital humanities. There will not be only one decision or model, and all institutional contexts are not the same, but the concept of the field as a nonterritorial meeting place is arguably the most productive way of meeting many of the challenges that lie ahead: managing the enlarged community, making the most of the richness of perspectives, taking on complex scholarly and technological challenges across disciplines and epistemic traditions, and making a strong case for infrastructures for the humanities. In some ways, parallels exist between this function and that of a humanities center or advanced institute.

Third, the digital humanities is uniquely placed to become a site of engagement where all the humanities can think about and manifest their future role—a kind of laboratory and platform for the humanities. This is part of the potential of the digital humanities, and many newcomers to the field seem to be attracted by this opportunity. This is, however, a contested function of the field in several ways. Not all digital humanists look at the field in this way, and from the outside—in particular, from other humanities institutions—giving the digital humanities this privileged role might not seem to make sense. While the digital humanities is not the only platform for developing the humanities, it can certainly be an important player, and taking on this role is a responsibility.

Interlude 4: Virtual Weddings

My interest in humanities and the digital partly comes from a range of pedagogical projects in which I was involved in the late 1990s and early 2000s as faculty at the Department of English at Umeå University, during the beginnings of HUMlab. We explored how technology could help us tackle challenges, inspire students, and challenge traditions. My thinking was particularly influenced by the Virtual Wedding project, which arose out an interest in developing the equivalent of a bachelor's degree in English at Umeå University. We especially sought to break down the barriers between linguistics, literary studies, and cultural studies. Students normally had to choose just one of the three, but we wanted to work with the many rich themes that reached across these boundaries. "Weddings" was one such culturally, linguistically, and literarily embedded theme. Some of our earlier work on web-based papers for teacher trainees had shown us that collaborative online publishing was motivational. In addition, we were aware that digital media and formats could help the students and us to do things differently. Much academic convention is locked into specific formats.

After some deliberation, we chose to use virtual worlds as an arena for the project. We created a world in ActiveWorlds, a platform whose interface combined a game-like graphical world, a browser window, and a chat window. It also featured in-world building, meaning that students could fairly easily create content. Each semester we chose a different theme: in addition to weddings, themes included the city and re-creating realities. Students formed small groups, approached the theme in different ways, wrote hypertext papers, and created manifestations of their work in the world. The world started out empty except for a tower built by the teachers: the students built everything else. At the end of the semester, they presented their work simultaneously at an event in the lab and in the virtual world. For the first student presentation, about thirty people were present in the virtual world and twenty in the physical lab. The world was accumulative, which meant that new students could see what earlier students had created.

The Virtual Wedding project taught us many things. We realized how much is built into the academic paper format in terms of how one expresses oneself, what kind of media are included, how one thinks about one's own work, and how colleagues look at it. By moving the work into a virtual environment, we created a space for experimentation and empowered students to find their own expressive means and expressions. In some cases, the expressiveness of the work took too much time, while in other cases, students were unwilling to experiment, but overall we found the project quite successful.[2] ActiveWorlds provided a level of visual detail that was not photo-realistic—it looked fairly good, but the content was cartoonish enough to allow for interpretation and required less effort than would have been necessary for more realistic material. The web browser functionality allowed students to connect and integrate hypertext papers with their world. Qualities such as the level of graphical detail and the integrated web browser demonstrate the importance of material qualities for digital humanities projects.

We also learned that distinct advantages accrue from working collectively in a lab environment. Students helped each other, and the community created included not only them but also local and international participants from different fields, adding significantly to the intellectual discussions. Some students participated mostly in a distributed manner (through the virtual world), but the fact that much of the work was physically situated made the process easier. Also, from a teacher's point of view, it was useful to go to the lab and have access to most of the students at the same time. The project also overlapped with other ongoing activities.

This experience informed future projects and our thinking about HUMlab as a space and operation. HUMlab was literally being built and tested out at the time. Even so, the time factor was a challenge, and we were sometimes concerned that the project would detract from other parts of the students' educational program, but it mostly worked out well. Placing this alternative modality within the academic system also posed a challenge. We succeeded partly as a result of the validation that came with a large external grant and partly because one of the participants was a senior director of studies. With the current system for national evaluation of degree work in Sweden (where accreditation comes from an assessment of a sample of degree-related work), implementing alternative modes of knowledge production would seem much more difficult than it was at that point in time.

We also soon realized that at least some of the themes and individual student paper topics possessed a digital inflection. Students had to use a range of tools to create multimodal content for the world, and they engaged with the medium on an almost daily basis. These perspectives and practices merged fairly seamlessly and had a distinct connection to the core of the discipline. In a way, some of these basic sentiments and ideas provided an important foundation for the continued operation of HUMlab and for our thinking of the digital humanities. In addition, the project fostered a number of excellent students who embarked on doctoral projects with a digital inflection.

In some ways, although I never at the time thought of the Virtual Wedding project as digital humanities or humanities computing, this early work on educational technology shaped much of my vision for the digital humanities. As teachers, we were empowered by using technologies to approach the challenge we had identified, and we were enthused to see students doing unexpected things with this opportunity. The technologies were both enabling and constraining, and our practice was simultaneously practical, experimental, and critical. We also found that the project required simultaneous engagement with the digital as a study object, a tool, and a medium. The project was intersectional from the beginning, and interest from local and remote participants from different fields helped the students and us to see important thematic and theoretical connections. We had many interested visitors, and we became used to being involved in discussions about the humanities, knowledge production, and the intersection of the humanities and the digital.

I learned that it was important not to be (and come across) as technoromantic and revolutionary when talking to people about the project. My collaboration with Pat Shrimpton, the longtime director of studies who had taught generations of teacher trainees and built up much trust in a range of communities, was rewarding on multiple levels, and she and I complemented each other well. Her technological skepticism (or maybe more correctly, her ready expression of such skepticism) helped me gradually learn to tone down some of the revolutionary speak, which had turned out to be fairly unproductive and would often lead to comments such as "This is not really new. We heard this when they introduced the overhead projectors."

Premise: Modes of Engagement

The digital humanities benefits from engaging with the digital across many modes of engagement. Specifically, this means that the field engages with information technology and the digital as a tool, an object of study, and an expressive medium. The term *mode of engagement*[3] is used to suggest primary and paradigmatic ways in which the humanities and the digital interrelate: study object, tool, and expressive medium.

Digital technology as a tool and methodology has been a primary organizing principle for humanities computing. Although some argue that modeling rather than tools lies at the center of humanities computing,[4] it does not really change the notion that traditional humanities computing is focused on text, encoding, tool making, and methodology. Modeling is undoubtedly an important part of digital humanities work, but set in an instrumentalist framing it can appear data centric, decontextualized, and focused on perfecting the model in algorithmic and rationalistic terms, rather than stepping outside the model or allowing critical inquiry, research questions, and aesthetic interventions shape or upend the model. With its increased focus on categories such as gender, race, ability, the anthropocene, and the aesthetic, contemporary digital humanities would seem to resist seeing such rationalistic modeling as a central activity for the field. Practice-oriented work in data modeling, however, can be very rich, reflective and useful, and here modeling often assumes an assistive (rather than assertive) role. Because of the strong investment in tool making and data structures, such work may also be a good space for considering tool making and data design in terms of questioning and drawing on the divisions of model and "real world," representation and "real world," and semiotic and material.

The modes of engagement are linked to the epistemic traditions of the humanities disciplines and of the digital humanities itself. Each mode has internal complexity, and the digital as an expressive medium, for example, accentuates a variety of expressive modalities in different disciplines and fields. These are not a simple matter of tradition and choice but are to some extent "hard-wired" into the discipline or field. The digital puts pressure on these assumptions, and there are other good reasons for reevaluating traditional forms of knowledge representation. Big digital humanities can help here. Imagine a lab space where a spatial historian is interacting with a map-based visualization, an architect is building a sonic simulator, an artist is completing a sonic intervention, a textual scholar is displaying textual material on a large display wall, a media scholar is writing a book on media infrastructure, and an interpretative tool for network visualization is being tested. And what if the history department would happen to have a research meeting in the space at the same time? Even if the historians were not primarily invested in these expressive (and interpretative) modalities, they would have difficulty avoiding engagement with them on some level. Furthermore, if the space were friendly and well curated, there would be fruitful opportunities for interaction between groups and traditions.

Given that most research and educational challenges relate to several of these modes of engagement, digital humanities clearly needs to work across all the modes. Indeed, big digital humanities is built on the idea that these modes are intimately and iteratively connected. Furthermore, as different disciplines have different primary modes of engagement, such a model makes it easier to work across all of the humanities. Moreover, a far-reaching multiple-mode engagement is instrumental for enabling the combination of traditionally critical and traditionally technological perspectives. The humanities cannot afford to ignore their critical tradition in relating to digital environments, and these critical perspectives need to be grounded materially and infrastructurally. Infrastructure plays a critical role here, and incorporating multiple modes of engagement makes it easier to imagine and package humanities infrastructure.

Having a multiple-mode engagement between the humanities and the digital is an important and nontrivial premise of big digital humanities. The modes should be seen not as distinct or mutually exclusive but rather as codependent. It is, however, still fruitful to analyze these modes individually as part of understanding the digital humanities and the building blocks required to make big digital humanities.

The Digital as a Tool

In a much-discussed *Science* paper on culturomics from 2010, the authors claim that computational analysis of about five million books enables the study of culture in a way that had not previously been possible. According to the article, culturomics "extends the boundaries of rigorous quantitative inquiry to a wide array of new phenomena spanning the social sciences and the humanities."[5] This instrumental use of technology in the service of the humanities, just like corpus tools or geographical information systems, represents a long-standing mode of engagement. Methodologies and toolsets such as culturomics, topic modeling, and timeline tools come with worldviews and assumptions, and the digital humanities needs to engage with such tools both instrumentally and critically. Culturomics, for example, has been heavily critiqued for its hyper-quantitative approach, reliance on Google's Ngram analysis, and for producing "small answers."[6]

The instrumental role of information technology seems rather self-evident. Computers and information technology are very capable of handling an increasing set of tasks. Historically, computers have often been seen only as tools, although that perception has changed over time:

> In its fifty-year history, the computer so far has been a calculating machine, an electronic brain, a filing cabinet, a clerk, and a secretary. . . . In the 1940s, when the brilliant and elegant John von Neumann, the brilliant and eccentric Alan Turing, and many others were designing the first programmable computers, they were not defining a new medium. They were building super-fast calculating engines to solve problems in science and engineering.[7]

Computers in humanities computing often took on the role of "calculating engines," and although the focus was not on science or engineering problems, they often became "textual engines." In contemporary digital humanities, technology is to a large extent still seen as a tool. Massive digitization projects, web-driven applications, online learning projects, and infrastructural efforts tend to have such a focus. Different tool-based efforts are instrumental to dif-

ferent degrees, however, and some tools have a strong interpretative component. Many others seem to be made in the same production house or along the
same kind of conceptual framework. One common model is "retrieval": such
tools tend to be built around a query interface, and many still show a very close
connection to library catalogs or notecards. Similarly, map-based tools have
become increasingly common as the result of a surge of map-based resources,
sensor technologies, and geographically oriented systems.

Also underlying the use of computers as a tool may be an ideology of cog-
nition and functionalism.[8] The instrumental relationship to information technology is nearly a defining property of traditional humanities computing. According to a 2012 *Ars Technica* article, the "digital humanities is, at its simplest,
the use of digital tools and processes in the service of the humanities, those
academic pursuits that focus on understanding the human condition."[9] One
important question is the nature of the connection between the academic pursuits and the tools, and tools at times seem to have a life of their own.

The tools envisioned are different from standard tools such as word processing and web browsers. The challenge, as identified by Andrea Laue and
others, also involves producing a new set of tools that are less machine-like:

> In practice, the symbiotic machine became a problem-solving rather than
> a problem-posing device. For the most part, that is how the computer con-
> tinues to function. Licklider's dream remains largely unfulfilled. Perhaps
> transforming the computer from machine to tool, from a device that au-
> tomates mundane mental tasks to one that augments critical and creative
> thought, is the task now facing computing humanists.[10]

Laue's argument clearly fits within the framework of the computer as machine
or tool. In some other varieties of digital humanities—for example, coming
from media studies—the instrumental use of information technology does
not often extend far beyond standard tools. Here, tools are mainly a means
to an end and do not necessarily carry much prominence. In addition, there is
often limited interest in creating and developing tools, although this may be
changing.

The Web as Platform for Tools

Since the turn of the twenty-first century, a great range of tools and materials have become available over the web, which in many ways has become a

primary platform for digital humanities tools and materials. Digital humanities work has moved away from tool sets and platforms that were more specific and in some cases restricted. The packaging has changed from pieces of software, data files and CD-ROMs to interconnected websites, services, databases and "the cloud." Digital humanities projects have connected to an infrastructure that is much more modular and less built from scratch. The focus on access in humanities computing and the cultural heritage sector has productively coupled with ideas from social media and web technologies to open up archival spaces that have traditionally been seen as unchanging. In addition, crowd-sourcing and other means of digitization and markup work have become possible.

At the same time, the reliance on the web can be seen as imposing restrictions and constraints. Old-time applications could more flexibly employ the resources of the computer (for example, management of multiple windows), whereas web applications are restricted by the materiality of the web platform. Even though web standards have evolved dramatically, a number of basic properties cannot easily be challenged. One example is the reliance on single-screen deployment for web content, which makes tools designed for several screens uncommon. This may sound like a trivial issue, but in essence, the web has become a new standard format for content and interaction. It borrows much from pen-and-paper logic, so there is a sense of familiarity, but a critical question is how the digital humanities is constrained by focusing on the web and how the digital humanities relates critically to the web as a default platform.

For example, the Digital Resource for Palaeography (DigiPal) developed at King's College is a web-based resource designed to develop new methodologies for studying medieval handwriting.[11] One of the three main parts of the project is a "generalized web framework for the delivery of palaeographical content online."[12] The project is an excellent example of the conceptually grounded use of technology in the service of the humanities. It is sensitive to the epistemic tradition of palaeography and stresses the importance of providing material results to the users rather than quantitative "black box" results. Consequently, the project shows actual (digitized) letters on a timeline rather than just a plot of frequency or variation. The tool provides obvious added value and is visually and intellectually sophisticated.

However, DigiPal is keyed to the web as a delivery platform. While this makes sense in many ways, it can also constrain the possible space of the tool, particularly since the project has a material grounding and deals with rich and complicated data. It would make sense for someone interested in looking at individual letters across manuscripts, the development of "hands," forms of a letter over time, or annotated manuscripts to think carefully about the use of windows and screens. A multiple-screen environment or a floor screen might allow the display of letters across manuscripts in different ways, enabling researchers to "see more" at one time and juxtapose different facets of the material (such as letters and manuscripts). And it is not just about quantity. If someone wanted to discuss in detail the relations between ten allographs, access to ten screens would permit the display of ten examples in high quality, using the screen frames as a way of emphasizing the individuality of the examples. An eleventh screen would allow examples to be miniaturized and moved to that screen before a new series is shown on the other screens. Or the eleventh screen could point to parallelisms or allow overlay or juxtaposition of examples. A more complex display environment, fixed or mobile, would also make it easier to provide aggregated values and visualizations without removing the original material.

Data and Tools

A significant development that is partially tied to the web concerns the availability and production of data.[13] A massive infrastructure supports online entities such as map services, social platforms, and different types of databases (e.g., archives and online materials). Data can also be systematically collected from online environments, games (e.g., game metrics), tools and methodologies such as eye-tracking equipment (e.g., for analysis of game play or online newspaper reading), multispectral analysis (e.g., reconstruction of the making of art pieces such as paintings), and fMRI scanning (e.g., tracing brain activity associated with different types of reading strategies). Environmental archaeology data can be used for the large-scale aggregated modeling and visualization of prehistorical environments, and data and material about historical sites can be used to create virtual reconstructions.

Naturally, methodology and the critical assessment of data sources and interpretative processes are central here. The same is true of grand projects such as the culturomics approach and the "cultural analytics" platform developed at the University of California at San Diego, which uses quantitative analysis, interactive visualization, and to some degree qualitative analysis to "begin analyzing patterns in massive cultural data sets."[14] Lev Manovich describes the implications of such an approach:

We believe that a systematic use of large-scale computational analysis and interactive visualization of cultural patterns will become a major trend in cultural criticism and culture industries in the coming decades. What will happen when humanists start using interactive visualizations as a standard tool in their work, the way many scientists do already?[15]

Here, very powerful tools are projected, and the cultural analytics research group has some impressive examples,[16] but any alignment with science methodology in this manner should be critically analyzed, as should the hopes invested in visualization and access to large amounts of data. Rob Kitchin points to the urgent need for critical work in this area and to the importance of avoiding polarization between quantitative and qualitative approaches. He suggests an epistemology that brings together the situatedness, positionality, and politics of the social sciences and humanities with quantitative models and methods such as radical statistics and critical GIS.[17] While it makes sense to be skeptical about some of the ideas associated with big data, access to large materials and datasets is not likely to decrease, and the digital humanities can be useful in aligning data-rich methods with careful humanistic consideration. Thomas LaMarre urges the humanities to become involved in setting agendas for this kind of work to avoid "a massively scientistic attitude" and notes his reservations in terms of methodology:

> For experimenters know that the set-up is directed toward a certain problematic, and if the results are not predictable in advance, they will nonetheless fall in a certain range and register of experience. Without foregrounding some of these issues, I think we risk capitulation to neoliberalism and the university as hedge fund, to put it crudely.[18]

This set of concerns is warranted, given the current fascination with big data and with humanists moving into areas such as digitally supported distant reading, network analysis, functional magnetic resonance imaging brain scans, n-gram based analysis, and cultural heritage visualization. Methodological awareness is critical in all these cases. What does it mean to test brain patterns for leisure versus professional reading in a context where the subjects are placed in a tube in a clinical setting? How representative is the Google Books material used for Ngram analyses, and what does this analysis say about the culture in which these texts were created? What epistemic traditions and aesthetic preferences are built into the visualizations we use and produce? Answering these questions is not a matter simply of maintaining a critical perspective on tools "out there" but of being engaged in critical-creative processes. This is one reason why we need to encourage experimental modalities and critical making.

Designing Tools and Experimental Spaces

A range of digital tools are available for the humanities, and the digital humanities has not yet developed a comprehensive framework, design sensibility, and assessment methodology that allows us to design, critically discuss, and evaluate different kinds of tools in the best possible way.[19] Such a framework may not be possible given the diversity of tools and epistemic traditions, but at the very least we need to foster careful design and the reflective analysis of tools. A consensus seems to exist that the digital humanities has not traditionally focused on design or realized the importance of it, as Johanna Drucker points out:

> Blindness to the rhetorical effects of design *as a form of mediation* (not of transmission or delivery) is an aspect of the cultural authority of mathesis that plagues the digital humanities community.[20]

Earlier work by Drucker and her colleagues at the University of Virginia demonstrates innovation within a conceptual framework, a strong interest in design, and a critical discussion of both the framework and the actual tools. Several of the tools or projects (e.g., Temporal Modeling and Ivanhoe) are situated and carefully described in Drucker's 2009 book, *SpecLab: Digital Aesthetics and Speculative Computing*. But we have not seen many more interpretative tools of this kind following these early experiments, perhaps because of cost, a strong tradition of more established tools, low adaptation, and possibly limited generalizability over curricula and institutions. We need to allow for the specificity of exploratory work, particular infrastructures and intellectual tools, but also accommodate comprehensive infrastructures and support standardized solutions.

Digital tools can facilitate an experimental and predictive space that goes beyond individual instruments in suggesting an experiential and exploratory approach. The humanities is often portrayed as not having a predictive or intervening role, whereas the sciences are said to attempt to both explain and predict natural phenomena. In looking at the primary interests of natural scientists, social scientists, and humanists, Jerome Kagan distinguishes between prediction and explanation of all natural phenomena (natural scientists), prediction and explanation of human behaviors and psychological states (social scientists), and "an understanding of human reactions to events and the meanings humans impose on experience as a function of culture, historical era, and life history" (humanists).[21] The use of *understanding* in relation to the humanities does not necessarily indicate a passive role but certainly does not indicate an active one.

Partly in reaction to this view of the humanities, Lars-Erik Janlert and Kjell Jonsson explore the possibility of a cultural laboratory.[22] Their vision clearly challenges the understanding of "tool" as a distinct category. They argue in favor of an active, experimental humanities. Dynamic visualization can offer a window to large datasets and possibilities to visualize or enact complex objects of analysis. Interactive tools can help the researcher get an intuitive sense of the models and objects of analysis and allow fast what-if analyses. On a more profound level, researcher interaction can change the models themselves or their parameters, data, and relations, thereby allowing the study of hypothetical correlations or the comparison of outcomes from different models applied to the same object or situations. "Thick," qualitative models—of detailed environments, objects, processes, and correlations or of unstructured information—can be handled through the use of technology, and complex qualitative correlations can be modeled by massive simulations. Digital, controlled spaces—such as virtual worlds—can be used to facilitate cultural laboratory work. Participants in simulations could be humans or computer-run entities. Real-time interactive data can feed into digitally enhanced research spaces. This is a thought-provoking vision that seems to respond to the call for tools that are interpretative and scholarly as well as to the increasing humanistic interest in engaging with very large datasets.

There is power in imagining new tools, whether they are actually implemented or not. A very useful example is Catherine D'Ignazio's reflections on feminist data visualization, where she engages conceptually and materially with critical perspectives on visualization.[23] She suggests that we need to find new ways of representing uncertainty, missed data, and data provenance. Furthermore, she argues that we should refer to and represent the material economy associated with data. She asks, "What if we visually problematized the provenance of the data? The interests behind the data? The stakeholders in the data?" D'Ignazio also calls for ways to destabilize visualizations and make dissent possible: "Could we effect visualization collectively, inclusively, with dissent and contestation, at scale?" Through throwing out these ideas and provocations, D'Ignazio opens up a conceptual and material space that is valuable regardless of whether it results in actual tool building or not at this point. It would seem very worthwhile, however, to take these ideas to prototype or full-on implementations.

In their construction and contextual use, tools reproduce certain assumptions. While generic tools such as word processing programs are more easily construed as neutral, the subjective and epistemic nature of tools is more apparent with interpretative and experimental tools. This does not mean that the epistemic commitments associated with digital tools and their use are well understood or receives enough attention. As Matt Ratto shows, these commitments are particularly relevant when different disciplines and epistemic traditions deal with the same digital objects.[24] Epistemic commitments may influence and determine identification of study objects, methodological procedures leading to results, representative practices, and interpretative frameworks. Consequently, specific tools cannot easily be separated from their epistemic context, including research materials and research questions. This contextual view of tools is a central tenet of big digital humanities.

The Digital as a Study Object

The digital is unsurprisingly an object of analysis for the humanities. Linguists, for example, may be interested in the details of taking turns in a specific digital platform or across communication media. Cultural anthropologists with an interest in how we create and sustain identities may want to study these processes in different types of digital environments. Someone in literature may do work on how our brains are affected by online reading on a neural-cognitive level. Robots and drones give rise to philosophical questions about what makes us human and how we regulate nonhuman behavior. A book history scholar may want to investigate attempts at re-creating physical materiality in relation to electronic books.

As these examples show, study objects are not likely to be entirely digital. Indeed, we cannot possibly separate digital manifestations, perspectives, and materials from the human condition that humanists explore. In other words, such study objects and research issues are digitally inflected. For some fields, such as media studies and history of technology, this is a fairly common inflection. The digital as a study object is a very different mode of engagement than is interacting with technology primarily as a tool.

Digital tools can nevertheless shed light on such research issues and materials. The conflation of these modes of engagement—tool and study object—is an important argument for seeing the digital humanities as a multiple-mode meeting place—big digital humanities—instead of a mostly technological or a mostly critical discipline. Furthermore, because such research issues tend to be interdisciplinary and require a technological sensibility, they are likely to benefit from being approached from a position that combines intersectionality and disciplinary depth. And in cases when there is hesitancy toward digitally inflected research problems or methodologies in the disciplines, the digital humanities as a meeting place and infrastructure can empower both individuals and departments.

As the humanities became institutionalized in the late nineteenth and early 20th centuries, links formed between certain objects of study or facets of those objects and certain disciplines. Julie Klein discusses how this process related to development of the relationships between knowledge and science and between amateur and professional as well as the development of often-minute methodologies to handle humanistic objects.[25] A single object could be analyzed using the different methodologies strongly associated with the disciplines, but this growth of disciplinary focus and specialization meant that a great deal of synthesis would not necessarily occur.

How does the epistemic ontology of established disciplines relate to today's digitally inflected world? The disciplinary model has faced pressure from an increased interest in interdisciplinary studies and different types of thematically organized research agendas, and according to Cathy Davidson and David Goldberg,

> It is easy to see, in hindsight, how disciplines professionalized and specialized objects of analysis. To say that such objects were (under the older regime) disciplinarily driven is to say that disciplinary demands—historical and textual, institutional and official, methodological and epistemological—determined which were legitimate for analysis.[26]

Interdisciplinary practice calls for objects of analysis that are more diffuse and multifaceted than those disciplinarily conceived. As Drucker points out, a tension exists between this type of object and the established sense of what normally constitutes a valid object of analysis in the traditional humanities: "Traditional humanistic work assumes its object. A book, poem, text, image, or artifact, no matter how embedded in social production or psychoanalytic tangles, is usually assumed to have a discrete, bounded identity."[27]

Drucker emphasizes the codependent nature of that identity. One interesting question is whether these codependent identities and diffused objects of analysis are manifested in digital humanities work that primarily sees the digital as a study object. The problem is not necessarily the investment in particular epistemic traditions but rather the gatekeeping and inability to operate deeply across disciplinary boundaries. For the digital humanities, gatekeeping often occurs on behalf of both the humanities disciplines and the digital humanities itself.

This is one reason why it may be advantageous to work with other areas, such as gender studies, that are typically less institutionalized than traditional disciplines, and such areas at times appear to have more energy and willingness to engage. The most important reason, however, is that it is an intellectually productive connection. Working more with areas such gender studies, ethnicity studies, dis/ability studies, queer studies, environmental humanities, urban humanities, and neurohumanities would thus seem to possess intellectual and strategic potential. While these fields are not fully comparable, they all bring research questions and perspectives that align well with big digital humanities. From the point of view of the digital as a study object, questions of gender, ethnicity, and environment have a very direct bearing. How can we engage with the digital in any capacity as humanists without thinking about environmental perspectives or gendered structures? It is much easier for a broadly conceived digital humanities to do this convincingly, as these perspectives penetrate tools, platforms, and research questions as well as our practice. Consequently, big digital humanities is well placed to engage in some of these collaborative possibilities.

Environmental humanities, for example, engages with technology and mediation in many different ways. The questioning of the commonplace photographic representation of the earth from the outside is a deeply humanistic, digitally inflected matter:

Remote sensing technology does not "see" but perceive the Earth in complicated ways. The resulting images convey the coherence and completeness of photographic pictures but they only emerge through intricate processes of translating large sets of discrete data into consistent visual formats. The processes of generating, aggregating and translating data points into a visual whole are imbued with the ambitions, interpretations and applications of different actors in international and transnational settings.[28]

This type of research is part of infrastructure studies as well as emerging critical work on digitally driven visualization. The institutional home for such work can be intellectual history, media studies, environmental studies, or science and technology studies, and there are many examples of this line of research. Critique of and reflection on visualization would seem to be a humanistic matter and an area to which the digital humanities could contribute significantly. From the point of view of big digital humanities, such engagement constitutes a necessary component of the making carried out in the field. In other words, the humanities must be critical about its own practices as well as those of others. Traditional science and technology studies can benefit from the material sensitivity and infrastructural know-how (ideally) associated with the digital humanities.

This example also points to parallels with other emerging areas such as software studies, critical code studies, and platform studies that are mostly framed in terms of introducing new or understudied objects of inquiry. Platform studies is described as "a new focus for the study of digital media, a set of approaches which investigate the underlying computer systems that support creative work."[29] Software (in software studies) can be seen as "an object of study and an area of practice for art and design theory and the humanities, for cultural studies and science and technology studies and for an emerging reflexive strand of computer science."[30] Critical code studies "explores the rhetoric, material history, style, and culture of code—aspects that have previously been only marginally discussed in computer science courses and scholarship."[31] While all these (and other partly overlapping) areas are concerned with digitally inflected objects, they also engage with the making of software to some degree (although critical code studies arguably does so most strongly). There is potential in invoking the digital humanities to introduce a stronger presence of making and technological engagement in relation to these areas (especially software studies).

The humanities (and the digital humanities) ideally can also bring an increased sense of the broader political and critical context that sometimes seems to be underemphasized in work carried out in these fields. Jussi Parrika, for example, points to the lack of political attention in some work in software studies,[32] while Dale Leorke has critiqued platform studies for being constrained by the notion of platform and failing to offer a deep enough theoretical perspective on the platform as a concept and framing.[33] At the same time, the digital humanities can learn from the interest in the "metal" (hardware, code, interfaces) that often characterizes these areas. On a similar note, David Berry suggests that the digital humanities can benefit from incorporating the medium specificity that is often part of platform and critical code studies and that although these fields are currently fairly separate, they could be more closely aligned.[34]

Along the same lines, Laine Nooney investigates the social and cultural construction of "gamer" in relation to the computer game industry of the 1980s, looking particularly at gendered notions and using Sierra On-Line and its products as an example. Her object of inquiry is clearly digitally inflected, although she is not primarily focusing on creating computer games or creating academic installations. Her work sits within media studies but relates to digital humanities, software studies, and gender studies. Jennie Olofsson looks at what happens with screens once they are discarded. What is the ontological status of screens? When do screens cease to be screens? How can we engage with and theorize electronic waste? Again, the study object is digitally inflected, and we are not primarily concerned with digital tools or expressions, although her work relates to artwork. Olofsson is a cultural anthropologist, and her work seems located somewhere between digital humanities and environmental humanities. The work of both these researchers has an activist element. In addition, Olofsson is interested in making an academic installation (enacting and problematizing the death of screens), while Nooney has expressed interest in using complex display infrastructure for critical readings of games. This shows that the step from one mode of engagement to another is not so large, and given the right opportunities, new types of work may emerge.

Humanities-based engagement with information technology as an object of analysis is obviously multifaceted and complex, but looking at the digital humanities in a broad sense, this mode of engagement seems quite prevalent. The digital does not have to be the main focus: the study objects can be phenomena, cultural artifacts, and processes that are digitally inflected in various ways. Initiatives with a significant investment in this mode often seem fairly discrete in the landscape of the digital humanities but are rarely recognized as digital humanities. Big digital humanities includes humanities-based critical work on the digital.

The Digital as an Expressive Medium

Higher education incorporates a number of modalities and expressions at any time, but broadly speaking, the humanities and many other areas are very text-centric, especially in such important areas as degree papers, scientific publications, and tenure portfolios. According to the website of the Stanford Humanities Center,

> Humanities research often involves an individual professor researching in a library in order to write a book. The books that result from this study are part of an ongoing dialogue about the meaning and possibilities of human existence that reaches back to ancient times and looks forward to our common future.[35]

While this is a traditional view of the humanities and the situation is changing, this statement remains largely true. Print publishing has been around for a long time and is part of institutional, academic, and sociological structures. The Stanford Humanities Center is a good example of such structures. Humanities centers typically expect fellows to work on individual book projects.

The academy faces increased pressure from a digitized and multimodal world and to some extent from artistic practice and research. Digital modalities are increasingly intertwined in scholarly processes, and the systematic efforts to create platforms for alternative scholarly work play an important role, as do efforts to create systems for accreditation (such as the Modern Language Association guidelines for evaluating work in the digital humanities and digital media).[36] All of these are still fairly marginal phenomena in the humanities, but a combination of bottom-up and top-down work is starting to yield substantial results. This development means not that the monograph or print will disappear but that a broader ecology of institutionally possible scholarly modalities will develop.

Indeed, such ecological thinking will make it easier to create both experimental modalities with or without a credentialing function and formats that unapologetically build on established modes of scholarly expression and on a solid understanding of the situational factors at play. The online journal *Digital Humanities Quarterly* has established itself as an important publishing venue for digital humanities scholarship without engaging a great deal with the first commitment listed on the website for the journal—"experimenting with publication formats and the rhetoric of digital authoring"—and without publishing many (if any) examples of "experiments in interactive media" (listed as a possible publication type).[37] DHQ is an excellent journal with a stronger multimodal component (mostly images) than earlier, but is not experimental in this sense, and does not really need to be in my mind. Similarly, recent publishing initiatives such as Luminos (University of California Press) place the monograph, as traditionally conceived, within an open access digital distribution system without seeking to upend the format. Scalar (Alliance for Networking Visual Culture) is also usefully situated within an institutional structure, but is much more experimental in terms of narrative and multimodal capabilities without challenging existing forms of scholarly expression radically.

Scalar is a scholarly publishing platform, and such platforms allow users to produce content, incorporate and organize materials, enable interaction and create narratives. These narratives are constrained and enabled by the systems used to make and deliver them. Such platforms are often attempts at creating new templates for scholarly knowledge production. And since content delivery is an institutional, infrastructural, and cultural process, any system will also have to relate to standards, status, merit systems, longevity, market shares, and many other parameters. Delivery and publishing systems such as Omeka, Drupal, and Scalar manifest certain values and suggest specific modes of organization and ways of making arguments. This epistemic embedding is probably why these systems are rarely revolutionary in terms of structuring content or suggesting expressive modalities.

An important consequence of increased digitization and particularly of the web is dramatically increased access to and availability of different types of content and media as well as production methods and distribution channels. Some of this content analog-created, but much of it digitally born. Increasingly, but not necessarily, these expressions are media-rich, polytextual, and mixed. Jeffrey Schnapp and Michael Shanks discuss "fungibility"—the gathering of many types of content (moving image, text, music, 3-D design, database, graphical detail, virtual walk-through, and so forth) into a single environment—as the core of digital mediation.[38] Content can accordingly be infinitely manipulated and remobilized without loss.

A significant point, however, is that this fungibility is shaped by the tools used to produce that content, and the resultant expressions and environments are constrained in different ways. This is particularly obvious with different kinds of authoring tools. PowerPoint and similar presentation tools would be a very simple example of this lock-in effect in imposing a serial slide perspective on the world, certain templates, a specific type of aesthetics, a set range of expressive modalities, and file-delivery mechanisms. Also, such tools structure the presentation situation through the materiality of the interface, including the reliance on one screen and one presenter, one-by-one delivery of slides, and the way the presenter gets or does not get notes on his or her own screen.[39]

Manovich shows that another fairly generic tool for digital production, Photoshop, is heavily based on an analog logic. For example, he finds that all the seemingly digital filters have direct physical predecessors.[40] Just as with presentation software, a very clear connection exists to predigital processes and logic. Manovich also discusses how the introduction of layers in the software marked a significant change in how the tool is used and hence influences how much of digital visual imagery is engineered and produced.[41] Manovich's study essentially explores how digital production tools shape work processes, how the underlying logic and surface materiality of production tools structure our expressiveness, and how such logics often have a clear analog lineage. A reader of Manovich's online book, published via Issuu, encounters reproduced pages, simulated page turning, and many other "paper" features.[42]

While we can tweak platforms such as PowerPoint and Photoshop to break out of the templates and inscribed ways of using them, there is a basic logic that we cannot really escape. Similarly, the universal appeal of the web as a platform imposes a number of constraints and predispositions for much digitally enabled content. Academic authoring and commenting tools are no exceptions, and platforms such as Scalar and MediaCommons Press both enable and constrain us. The digital humanities needs to have an in-depth discussion of conceptual principles for designing tools and platforms, and this work is clearly relevant to all of the humanities.

Expressive Modalities

A range of alternative expressive modalities is available. Online video is an important genre, used, for example, by sociologist Simon Lindgren in a series of "Social Science in 60 Seconds" short clips and by media scholar Jonathan Sterne in "Footnotes to a Manifesto for Diminished Voices," which is a largely silent textual commentary on the neglect of studying and acknowledging voice (privileging text) in academic work.[43] History of ideas scholar Linn Holmberg made a "trailer" of her dissertation work on a "forgotten encyclopedia" (the Maurists' dictionary of arts, crafts, and sciences).[44] She also made a replica (in wood) of the monastery where much of this intellectual work took place, and while this was not part of her official doctoral work, it helped her in the research process.[45] Another example of explorative doctoral work is provided by Nick Sousanis's work on education articulated through a comic book.[46] In all these examples, the mode of expression seems deliberately to carry considerable weight. What is being said is entangled with the medium used. There is also an awareness of stepping away from the traditional scholarly format, which is probably not surprising, given the privileging and "templating" of mostly textual modalities in the humanities.

The level of interaction and performativity suggested by most scholarly work seems to have a limit. True, some scholars present their work in a more expressive way than do others, and different scholars have different strategies for engaging with participants, but such presentations often operate within the established framework. This framework no doubt offers a great deal of expressive potential, but even small steps away from what we expect are unusual and at times worrying. For example, Micha Cárdenas starts her talks by asking participants to breathe together (as a synchronizing exercise). Similarly, Sterne sometimes asks audience members to read quotes aloud. I use our eleven-screen landscape for talking about HUMlab (or other topics) by walking from screen to screen instead of seating everyone and showing a slideshow. Again, this is a simple idea, but the difference can be substantial. For one thing, people standing close to the speaker interact with that speaker differently than when they are seated as a group. Also, having all the images visible at the same time rather than one at a time (seated slideware presentation) creates other narrative potential and retains the story in the space.

However, more artistic modalities are rarely employed for humanistic research unless a researcher-artist collaboration is taking place (often resulting in an exhibition). Indeed, it would be hard to imagine a humanistic scholarly presentation as raw and expressive as Kelly Dobson's "Blendie," where the viewer must speak with a blender in its own language to make it do its work, or as embodied and expressive as a dance performance.[47] The point here is not that we should necessarily dance our work but that we should think about boundaries and possibilities and step outside of our comfort zone. Doing so is not easy given the institutional, epistemic, and cultural embeddedness of knowledge production. One way of approaching this problem might be to introduce "academic installations," which would not claim to be artistic and would not be have templates related to specific platforms or spaces. Another possibility is to engage in critical discussion through the material manifestations (academic installations, digital projects, presentations) in a manner reminiscent to critique (or crit) sessions in art and design education.

Some disciplines in the humanities, including visual and media studies, have been affected more significantly than others by new expressive modalities. This engagement has typically occurred on the level of object of study rather than the production of expressive, creative media. Tara McPherson critiques this imbalance:

> We have been slow to explore the potential of interactive, immersive, and multimedia expression for our own thinking and scholarship, even as we dabble with such forms in our teaching. With a few exceptions, we remain content to comment about technology and media, rather than to participate more actively in constructing knowledge in and through our objects of study.[48]

This argument concerns not only the importance of carrying out both critical and expressive work but also the ways in which knowledge can be made through expressive media, which necessarily requires the integration of the critical and expressive aspects of humanistic scholarship. This integration or entanglement is an important part of big digital humanities.

Expressive Conditioning in Different Academic Contexts

As McPherson also indicates, it is easier to find experimentation with digital media in undergraduate education than in research or doctoral-level education. Graduate education tends to be much more traditional than undergraduate education for several reasons. There is more epistemic and social control at this level as Ph.D. education essentially produces new peers. There is also typically less focus on employability and digital literacy. Furthermore, graduate education is relatively privileged compared to most other types of education.

In faculty research and education, increased accountability and the expansion of so-called quality-based systems make experimenting more difficult. In Sweden, university education is now evaluated mainly on degree papers or projects, and the right to give an educational program can be revoked based on these evaluations.[49] An economic incentive also exists to score highly on these evaluations. Such a system would not seem to encourage risk or an expansion of the expressive repertoire.

As with the evaluation of educational programs, scholarly work tends to rely on assessments of quality. The reward structures of academe have a significant impact on how scholars choose to publish and express themselves. And again, systems such as the United Kingdom Research Assessment Framework are not likely to encourage untraditional forms of scholarly expression.[50] Although Andrew Prescott is right when he points to the obsession with U.S.-style tenure-track assessment in the digital humanities,[51] tenure-track systems are a relevant reward structure to look at in this context. Such systems are common in North America and are based on an initial time-limited employment as assistant professor that can be made into a permanent position. Tenure-track scholars often have a sense that digital modes of representation may place them at a relative disadvantage and in fact may receive explicit advice to that end from senior faculty and administrators. These reward structures may be changing, but it is at a very slow pace, and there is no simple path forward, although work such as "New Criteria for New Media" is part of a lively and important discussion.[52]

The reward structures, however, do not always stop doctoral researchers from expressing themselves alternatively, but such efforts are often seen as "extra" undertakings that do not replace the traditional work needed to qualify academically. This pressure sometimes induces researchers to secure very strong academic merits as well as engage in alternative practices and modes of production. Some of the discourse surrounding this issue (often produced by senior, well-established, and "safe" scholars) seems to imply that every digital humanist would have an interest in alternative, nontraditional production, but such is obviously not the case. Monographs and in some disciplines peer-reviewed articles are not just tied to a traditional reward system but may represent a rightful dream of academic expression and a distinct scholarly identity for early-career researchers. This sentiment may be difficult to disentangle from the fact that publishing presses and venues are invested with respect and value. McPherson points to the importance of working with academic presses to form new kinds of partnerships and platforms for digitally rich publication.[53]

A range of possible digitally inflected modes of expression exists, and they are situated within different disciplinary, institutional, and personal contexts and consequently come with different implications and degrees of risk taking. A humanities dissertation presented as a floor screen installation would naturally be much more challenging to the established system than using a personal research blog or a research-oriented Twitter feed as a supportive device. The situation is slowly changing, however, and it now seems easier to do an academic doctoral dissertation as some kind of multimodal online presentation than would previously have been the case. The emergence of guidelines for digital content probably plays an important factor here, as does a more general acceptance of the web as a platform for academic content.

Even more is at stake in the artistic realm. Can a history or communication doctoral project be manifested through something that looks like an artistic installation? While most history and communication departments likely would find such a proposal challenging, this distinction is breaking down somewhat in at least some contexts. For example, in Sweden, the introduction of practice-based doctoral dissertations has changed the landscape, and on the Umeå Arts Campus and elsewhere, both kinds of work happen at the same time, blurring lines. Sousanis's comics work is a recent example of alternative modalities in doctoral work.[54] At the same time, we are essentially concerned with two different worlds and territories. Scholarly works can draw on expressive modalities taken from art and can have artistic components, but they will usually not be art pieces.

Activism as a stance and practice is a related perspective that can blur the distinctions among art, artistic practice, and the humanities. Sharon Daniel's Vectors project, Public Secrets, which addresses the prison system in Central California, is an example of activism in an academic setting, arguably within the digital humanities.[55] The project features a strong sense of intervention that resonates with the idea of "active" humanities. Daniel was admitted to the Central California Women's Facility as a legal advocate, and her recorded interviews with the women there play a very important part in the Vectors piece. Work such as Public Secrets brings together an artistic and activist installation and academic expression in a single frame that serves both as a cultural critique and as an activist call for change.

Connecting "tinkering, playing, and visualization" and the academic criticism and cultural critique of her own kind of work, Rita Raley discusses the aesthetic strategies of artists and activists as using hybrid forms of academic criticism.[56] According to Drucker, "making things, as a thinking practice, is not only formative but transformative," and she includes aesthetic provocation as part of the practice of speculative computing as opposed to traditional digital humanities.[57] Much digital humanities work seems a bit tame in this regard, and there is a great deal to learn from such practices. The influx of digital humanists from areas such as queer studies and ethnicity studies will likely make the digital humanities more active in this sense. An example is the work by Roopika Risam and Adeline Koh (and many others) to rewrite Wikipedia from a postcolonial and gender perspective:

Thus, Postcolonial Digital Humanists have an obligation to engage with Wikipedia editing. Postcolonial studies has prided itself on challenging paradigms that perpetuate social inequality in terms of "who" and "what" is worthy of representation. Through Wikipedia editing, Postcolonial Digital Humanists have the opportunity to intervene in what postcolonial studies critics have termed colonial paradigms of knowledge production and imperialist hierarchies of information.[58]

The digital humanities could have a great deal to contribute in terms of engaging with the digital as an expressive, scholarly, artistic, provocative, and activist medium. As the conditions and platforms for scholarly work are shifting, there is also a growing emphasis on the role of the medium and the material manifestation in humanistic knowledge production. Critical attention is given to issues such as search engine algorithms, our dependency on enterprise-level platforms for online learning, and gaps and biases in library classification systems that hinder access, data ownership, and open access as a way of enabling public scholarship.[59] A key challenge is to connect these and other critical perspectives to our own knowledge production and expressive practice. Humanistic creative engagement with existing and new expressive technologies must be critically informed. Furthermore, as intellectual questions, scholarly materials, expressive modalities, and work processes increasingly come together in digitally inflected platforms or installations, it is not really possible to separate expression, communication, or presentation from interpretation, analysis, and enactment.

Premise: The Digital Humanities as a Meeting Place

To engage with the digital across several modes of engagement, the digital humanities requires an institutional position, a breadth of epistemic traditions, methodological competence, and material resources. The second premise of big digital humanities suggests that seeing the field as a meeting place can help meet these requirements. The digital humanities constitutes a curatorial and catalytic enterprise involved in shaping intellectual agendas, infrastructure, and intersectional activity.

Given strong and flexible connections to all the humanities disciplines as well as to other areas, the digital humanities can be seen as a relatively discipline-neutral field. The digital serves as a kind of material and boundary object, a concept that is also important to the idea of digital humanities as a meeting place and trading zone. Matt Ratto and Robert Ree argue that the digital media is not a sector, and a similar argument can be made that "the digital" is not a discipline.[60] The digital cuts across disciplines and modes of engagement, and seeing the digital humanities as a contact zone and meeting place can enable us to take seriously this quality of the digital.

The idea of the digital humanities as an in-between operation is not new. Indeed, much of the struggle of humanities computing and digital humanities has been about managing this liminal position, which has previously made it difficult to employ faculty, gain institutional credibility, and achieve a respectable level of scholarly status. One among many examples of this kind of discussion is a 1999 seminar, Is Humanities Computing an Academic Discipline?, organized by the Institute of Advanced Technology in the Humanities at the University of Virginia.[61] The digital humanities has often been more practice-based than theoretically oriented, at times leading to a sense of difference or even stigmatization. Many humanities computing centers have been closed or restructured over the years,[62] a common fate among academic enterprises seen as service units. At least from a historical point of view, therefore, association with humanities computing or a digital humanities center brings a fair degree of risk.

At the same time, this position has allowed the digital humanities to work outside established structures and to gain leverage from its difference and from its status as not competing directly (or as obviously) with other departments and disciplines. An entity that exists somewhat outside of traditional structures can more easily take on a catalyst and intermediary role and work with a range of disciplines. This is not to suggest that the traditional digital humanities has been positioned between in all respects. In particular, the intersectional position has been restricted to certain types of areas (notably methodology development) and has often been embedded in a service framework (of one kind or another). One key question, in any case, is whether the digital humanities prefers a liminal position, or whether there is a push toward a more independent role and a more disciplinary, departmental structure.

Meeting Places, Trading Zones, and Boundary Objects

On a general level, higher education would benefit from more strongly supporting what happens between disciplines. While the university can be seen as a meeting of minds, ideas, and perspectives in the context of knowledge production, most universities and other educational institutions are highly structured organizations characterized by specialization, professionalization, credentialing and accountability. Disciplines have a long history, and the establishment of new disciplines is a very rare occurrence. Many of our current disciplines were established in the latter of part of the nineteenth century and beginning of the twentieth century. New centers and various interdisciplinary formations emerge more frequently but normally exist somewhat outside the main structures of a university.

What does liminal, in-between work look like? It can certainly be carried out in distributed ways or without access to costly local infrastructure, but advantages can accrue when different types of meeting places help facilitate this kind of work. This is particularly true if it is seen as important to bring together a varying range of epistemic traditions and modes of engagement. In the humanities, such platforms include libraries or more commonly humanities centers or advanced institutes. Other examples include campus-wide or cross-campus networks, research groups, seminar series, collaborative writing platforms, and lab environments.

Many intersectional platforms in the academy are exclusive in that they do not necessarily include students of all levels or people from other schools. Such platforms can seem open but in practice typically impose restrictions through the way people are invited and greeted and through intimidating settings. The argument is not that higher education does not need to be specialized but that few open and accessible places exist for such meetings across areas and disciplines that are not overly predetermined in terms of content, form, and ideational direction. The digital humanities has a role here.

Peter Galison's work has been important to our understanding of how different epistemic traditions can meet and work productively together. Primarily analyzing the collaboration between physicists of different paradigms, he has developed the concept of trading zones as a way of understanding how scientists can communicate and collaborate even if they come from different paradigms in the Kuhnian sense and even if there is incommensurability between experimentalists and theorists.[63] While digital humanities as a field may lack such incommensurability, a parallel certainly exists in terms of the need to support work across epistemic traditions that in some ways are quite distinct. Another connection is the need to connect local practices with what Galison calls a global language of science. In the case of digital humanities, the global language would presumably be international-level discourse about the field and the way it is conceptualized and written.

The concept of trading zones applies more broadly to interdisciplinary work and demonstrates the possibility of maintaining disciplinary depth and focus (expertise) as well as meaningfully engaging in intersectional work. Galison describes the "thinness of interpretation" in trade rather than the "thickness of consensus."[64] This is another point at which we may want to problematize the discourse around niceness in the digital humanities. The goal may not be to reach consensus, and while being nice is naturally fundamental to any field, talking about being nice can sometimes be a way of hiding, of avoiding in-group critiques, and of failing to engage in a real way with groups outside one's own tradition and group. Trading zones are about brokering cultural exchange, and while they operate on an institutional level, they can never succeed without cultural performance and individual enactments. Indeed, individual enactment and engagement are critical to well-functioning meeting places.

On a critical note, the concept of trading zones comes from work on science (not the humanities), is obviously based on trading as a structuring metaphor (which may be questioned and seen in neoliberal or postcolonial terms), and consequently has a functional focus. Part of the beauty of "free" academic work is that it is not fully transactional but emergent and unpredictable. Galison shows, however, that it is possible to maintain disciplinary depth and focus while meaningfully engaging in intersectional work.

The digital humanities can be seen as a trading zone, contact zone, and meeting place, and this approach is compatible with digital humanities as a humanities project. I see trading zones and meeting places as partially overlapping concepts, where the latter is more general and less instrumental. A related and useful notion is that of contact zones, as developed by Mary Louise Pratt. She emphasized the often asymmetrical relations of power in "social spaces where cultures meet, clash, and grapple with each other."[65] This sensitivity to power relations is highly relevant to any liminal operation, especially one that claims to be open and inclusive, as big digital humanities does.

Another relevant concept is that of temporary autonomous zones, which describes the strategy of creating temporary spaces on the boundary lines of established region that elude formal structures of control.[66] The open and dynamic sensibility associated with temporary autonomous zones contrasts with the instrumentalism associated with trading zones. Arguably, big digital humanities needs to incorporate elements from both. The tension between liminal experiences and the establishment of permanent structures is a well-known issue in work on liminality.[67] For example, an important question concerns how a liminal operation learns over time if there are few structural properties and a constant influx of new people. Big digital humanities needs to be open enough to allow for unexpected outcomes and unforeseen pursuits. It also needs to be structured and have an agenda to prevent it from becoming a fairly bland place without sharpness or memory. There is probably no point in trying to institutionalize liminal spaces or operations across the board, because their relative unstructuredness is an important property. However, higher education generally needs to support more such initiatives and be sensitive to the usefulness of unstructured in-between spaces such as coffee shops and even hallways.

In an illuminating study of multidisciplinary health care as carried out in an Australian teaching hospital, Rick Iedema and his collaborators analyzed how a clinical team used the corridor as a liminal space using video-based ethnography. Corridors are important because they allow unstructured and unplanned communication, they are places for informal teaching, and they escape the hierarchies built into many other medical spaces. Because corridors have a marginal status in the organization of care, they become "central to the dynamic unfolding and heedful managing of complex and highly patient-centred care processes."[68] But what would happen if the liminal space became fully institutionalized and structured? Again, the power of open meeting places and trading zones such as big digital humanities lies both in structuring exchange and allowing the unexpected, unplanned, and controversial. In addition, intersectional meeting places are not homogeneous, and it is quite useful if they have a hallway outside them or a coffee shop nearby.

No institutional structure exists outside its institutional context, of course, and the role of intersectional operations is not stable over time. The work of Harry Collins, Robert Evans, and Mike Gorman is useful in suggesting a model based on two dimensions: the extent to which power is used to enforce trade, and the extent to which trade leads to a homogeneous new culture. Furthermore, they propose an evolution of trading zones, where one starting point can be when a university encourages faculty from different disciplines to collaborate to formulate a new initiative or proposal.[69] In the case of digital humanities, a fair amount of such encouragement currently occurs. Under this reading, such situations contain some degree of coercion, which would presumably also be the case when a funding agency launches a new program for an area such as the digital humanities. If scholars decide to work together, the trading zone would become more collaborative and voluntary, and Collins, Evans, and Gorman propose that this may lead to a fractioned trading zone with shared boundary objects or interactional expertise emerging from deeper interest in others' work.[70] Further development according to this model might include the trading zone and cultures becoming more homogeneous, leading to an interlanguage trading zone that might ultimately turn into a new disciplinary formation and the loss of the actual trading zone.

To avoid becoming totally generic, trading zones and meeting places, require something that attracts people to gather there and interact around ideas and projects. Indeed, this has to be the starting point, and if there is no strong motivation and no dedicated scholars and students, there is little sense in establishing meeting places. However, building such operations takes time, and the digital allows for a range of interaction points, meaning that many different sets of shared interests come together under the umbrella of digital humanities. One way of describing the digital and the shared interests is in terms of boundary objects.

Susan Leigh Star and James R. Griesemer develop the idea of boundary objects primarily based on studies of the historical development of natural history research museums.[71] In this world, boundary objects are said to be created when different parties (mainly researchers, sponsors, and amateurs) work together to produce representations of nature. There is a shared common goal and shared objects such as field notes, maps, specimens, and museums.

> Their boundary nature is reflected by the fact that they are simultaneously concrete and abstract, specific and abstract, specific and general, conventionalized and customized. They are often internally heterogeneous.[72]

The digital has a boundary quality in that it brings together a number of actors with different perspectives and epistemic positions. This certainly applies to the digital in relation to digital humanities. According to Star and Griesemer, boundary objects are "both adaptable to different viewpoints and robust enough to maintain identity across them."[73] The authors also stress the heterogeneity of boundary objects, which would seem congruent with the multiple modes of engagement and different perspectives associated with the digital humanities.

Star and Griesemer's framework emphasizes making, and representations created together (for example, in a museum) are thought to contain and resolve the different commitments and views of the actors involved. This relates to the discussion of making in the digital humanities and is indeed an argument for including making or building as part of an epistemic basis. Multiple perspectives and viewpoints can be contrasted, negotiated, and perhaps resolved in processes focused on shared making and creating. Ratto makes a similar point in relation to "critical making," where critical thinking and physical making are connected.[74] Shared making is seen as supporting the formation of a collective frame, which enables epistemic differences to be demonstrated as well as possibly resolved. This model contrasts with the argument for building in the digital humanities made by Stephen Ramsay and Geoffrey Rockwell, who attempt to establish a materialist epistemology.[75] Ramsay and Rockwell focus more on the resultant artifacts and individual production than does Ratto, who stresses the collective process. Ramsay and Rockwell also suggest a more distinct shift from traditional scholarly modalities to "building," whereas Ratto stresses the importance of closely relating the two:

> However, the ability of the participants to engage with the social theories presented to them and to develop and share new understandings was intimately related to the joint conceptual and materially productive work.[76]

The question of making, particularly when exemplified through coding, also illustrates the digital humanities' tendency to become stuck in epistemic conflicts, which can be productive to a certain degree but rarely resolve anything. Many of the current tensions in digital humanities seem to be tied to establishing the territory of the field. One possible solution is not to claim institutional territory as a department or discipline does but rather to establish the field as a meeting place.

Developing Digital Humanities as a Meeting Place

Digital humanities as a meeting place should have its own integrity and appropriate organizational status, but the idea would be to work with the rest of the humanities and what is outside. This may not be a new proposal, but this meeting place must support many modes of engagement with the digital and must both engage in tool building and connect with the future of the humanities. This key premise of big digital humanities offers a way to engage with the digital broadly and richly in relation to humanities-based questions and issues—essentially the human condition. Such a meeting place should have technological engagement and an acceptance for different epistemic traditions.

The sentiment and engagement associated with the digital humanities as a meeting place are central to the field as a whole, but every institution does not necessarily have to do everything. A large digital humanities center, a distributed network, a working group or a research group within a traditional discipline (whether English, media studies, or something else) can all fit into this model. While this book emphasizes physical digital meeting places, most of the reasoning applies to the whole range of possible enterprises. In fact, commonalities are accentuated by seeing the digital humanities as a liminal operation, including the processes and practices required to make and sustain meeting places. Among other things, keeping such operations relevant, stable, and vibrant requires good curatorship.

The digital humanities as a contact zone is congruent with a view of the interrelation between the humanities and the digital as rich and multifaceted. If the digital humanities is about engaging with technology as tool, object of inquiry, and medium of expression, and if we regard these modes as intrinsically interconnected, we need to see the field as a place where these perspectives and epistemic traditions come together. In terms of structural integrity and sustainability, it may be more advantageous to construe the digital humanities as a meeting place, innovation hub, and trading zone than as a distinct discipline. This would clearly give the field reach across the humanities.

Viewing the field as a meeting place emphasizes certain qualities that are present in almost all varieties of the digital humanities, such as the relative openness to working with other disciplines and areas and the facilitating or intermediary function. However, digital humanities as a meeting place and trading zone presumes profound openness to a number of different epistemic traditions and a facilitating role that is not strictly instrumental or service minded but multifaceted and dynamic.

There are several rationales for framing the field as a contact zone. First, a multiple-mode engagement with the digital across the humanities benefits from or may even require the digital humanities to be a meeting place. This is also a way of expanding the territory and reach of the field considerably without raising tents. A trading zone implies respecting (but not necessarily adopting) other epistemic traditions and a shared interest in boundary objects. Furthermore, considerable potential gains across the territory may not currently be fully exploited, such as an increased use of digital research tools and rigorous data management in media studies or a stronger theoretical anchoring of some more tool-based work. Opening up the digital humanities in this way would ease the process of incorporating the various traditions and newcomers. In many cases, this engagement will also extend outside the humanities to include, for example, science, engineering, and design.

Second, the coming together of disciplines and competencies is necessary to tackle the scholarly, technical, and structural questions associated with the digital humanities. What does it mean to be human in a digital age? Can media be thought of in terms of architectural representation? How do we build robust metadata schemes for cultural heritage materials and humanities research? What kind of interpretative power can a temporal-geographical system with faceted browsing access to cultural heritage possibly give? What is the future of academic publishing? How can students, faculty, and the public benefit from different types of multimodal representation to depict and explore key issues in, for example, history, philosophy, or comparative literature? How can we examine the interrelations among media, place, and technology? Most of these issues are complex and require collaboration across disciplines and scholarly as well as technological competence. Collaboration in this context requires more than simply working together on projects; it requires sharing an intellectual and material environment.

The digital humanities as a meeting place—reaching across the humanities and outside—can also be seen as a powerful way of channeling dispersed staff, technology, and faculty resources, which can be pooled as part of a humanities-wide initiative. Perhaps more important, a large enough reach and mass facilitate arguments in favor of infrastructure in terms of space, people, and technology. This can probably not be done in all institutional contexts as a consequence of resources, leverage, and priorities, but infrastructure can also be small and cheap. Relatively few digital humanities (and humanities) environments have strong spaces and innovative technology setups. If we see knowledge production as spatially and materially situated,[77] the digital humanities as a humanities project offers an opportunity to acquire and design space (physical and digital). This idea speaks to many humanities scholars and students and can be instrumental in making the contact zone come to life.[78] Such a development holds the potential for synergy and unexpected connections. Also, if we believe that situated and embodied practice is important, humanities laboratories provide one place for such work.[79]

Finally, universities and institutions of higher education often lack intersectional meeting places and contact zones.[80] Many institutions of higher education have failed to fill this niche, but opportunity exists and need is increasing. The digital has the intersectional power required, while the humanities possesses the awareness and potential legitimacy to be that place. So rather than disregarding the digital, interpreting it as purely technical, or seeing it as an uncomfortable denomination, it can be used as a means of making the humanities a catalyst for interchange, development and envisioning the future of the academy.[81]

Interlude 5: The Challenges of Living in-Between

Institutional meeting places and platforms are often presented or proposed through narratives filled with bustling activities, creative energy, and visionary projects. Rarely do we get to see or experience empty lab spaces, failed projects, institutional frustration, or collaborative online platforms devoid of participation. A good example is Neil Freistat's spatial walkthrough of the premises of the Maryland Institute for Technology in the Humanities or my description of HUMlab in Interlude 7.[82]

This pattern is not surprising. First, it is rather natural to show and narrate what is most interesting and successful. This is normally what is expected or what representatives of such operations believe is expected of them. Institutional hardships and problems are rarely the focus. Second, we tend to remember what works well and what is exciting. This tendency may be more pronounced with intersectional platforms, which usually have more variety in terms of intensity and engagement over time. The high points stick to institutional memory and as work on organizational memory shows, may also be part of what we are expected and institutionalized to remember.[83] Third, in contrast to many other institutional formations, such platforms often have a pronounced interest in envisioning their own future. Such visions easily become intertwined with the current implementation, and they become difficult to untangle.

So for a moment, let's consider the other side of the digital humanities as a meeting place. Some aspects of such meeting places are not necessarily so visible, apparent, or immediate.

Meeting places normally depend on other people for much of their core operation. A coffee shop or a library would not function without patrons, and most humanities centers without resident fellows would be as uninteresting as online collaboratories without participation. Any host of an event at which attendance has not been mandatory will probably know the fear that no one will show up. Hosting comes with responsibility, and orchestrating meetings and intersectional activities on a large scale takes time and effort.

I once presented HUMlab to the leadership of a Swedish innovation agency, Vinnova, and was surprised when the first comments were not so much about the actual setup or core ideas but rather about how we had managed to create what to them seemed an active and sustainable meeting place or innovation hub. They knew that creating such intersectional operations can be quite difficult and thought that our experiences might transfer to other domains. On the one hand, being in-between institutionally can be quite advantageous in terms of visibility, the ability to present visions and ongoing work, and channeling energy. On the other hand, it takes a great deal of work to make a meeting place work in an institutional context where everyone is busy and where the traditional institutional structures are very strong.

Bringing people together is difficult and requires an engaged and skillful team as well as the ability to find boundary objects and common interests. Digital humanities as a meeting place would seem to come with expectations of external engagement and bringing people together. Since big digital humanities largely exists outside disciplinary structures, much of this engagement must be built on scholarly and methodological interest in the digital (broadly speaking) and a willingness to participate in something outside the discipline or the department. This interest and buy-in will vary among projects, activities, and groups, which means that the meeting place itself becomes quite dynamic and undetermined. Having this kind of flux is quite important to the core operation and ideally allows for overlap and connection points among simultaneous activities. Such overlap can be random and emergent as well as orchestrated. Activities in adjoining spaces are more likely to influence each other than the same activities in different buildings. Can institutional memory grow in an operation characterized by flux and unpredictability? Major benefits no doubt accrue from a broad, open, and emergent engagement rather than from a more closed, traditional institutional model.

Persistence is critical for implementing big digital humanities and probably for most other types of institutional endeavors as well. For the digital humanities as a meeting place, there will be many occasions when very promising conditions for fruitful exchange have been created but the expected audience and spark do not materialize. There have been many times when HUMlab had first-rate international scholars visit, but no one participated from the humanities disciplines that would have gained the most from such an engagement. I used to think and say that activities we host should be so exciting and important that people would be sorry if they did not attend. I think this may still be a worthwhile approach, but it is of course better to have people come to an event than for them to be sorry they missed it.

Developing operations outside the established structures of higher education can be very rewarding but typically comes with challenges. As Julie Klein emphasizes, fit is a key problem for interdisciplinary efforts.[84] If the digital humanities could easily be placed within existing institutional structures, there would probably be no need for extended debates about the place and role of the field. But would any field be in such a situation? The digital humanities would likely either be absorbed into a discipline or be evenly distributed across disciplines with a good enough fit to avoid upsetting prevailing ways of organizing knowledge and work. But if a poor fit exists between the intersectional operation and institutional structures, we should try to create new structures or change existing ones. Such structures push back against established formations, and even if big digital humanities does not necessarily strongly challenge established departments and disciplines, a competition essentially takes place for funding, recognition, and ownership of certain fields of knowledge. As a result, new initiatives almost certainly will meet resistance, even if questions of digital tools, literacy, and reward systems would seem highly relevant.

Resistance is not necessarily an unnatural or counterproductive thing but can be expected and logical. It would be strange if the tradition of organizing knowledge and work in the humanities did not resist change to a certain degree. But a readiness to change must also exist. In 1998, when HUMlab was still mostly a sketch, a very important board meeting of the Faculty of Arts at Umeå University took place. HUMlab had received a major external grant for equipment from the Kempe Foundation, and board members discussed whether to allocate funding for running costs for this new enterprise. The vote ended in a tie, meaning that the chair of the faculty board had the decisive vote: the running cost funding was approved. I do not see the board's initial resistance as surprising or wrong. It is a matter of the distribution of resources and long-term financial and strategic commitments. HUMlab was quite likely to be a long-term undertaking, and lab environments are not necessarily easily dismantled. But this example also demonstrates the fragility of the birth process for such institutions as well as the critical role that external funding agencies can play. Without the external grant, HUMlab would likely not exist. Such foundations are often willing to take risks in a way that universities and mainstream funding agencies are not.

Persistence is a critical quality, as is working with faculty and others to show that the platform is well worth the investment. Intersectional operations at times have strong support from university leaders because they encourage work outside the traditional structures of the university. But even with good support, institutional fights and hardships are likely to arise along the way, but with a strong idea and institutional willpower, most obstacles can be overcome. It is also advisable not to stress an outsider sentiment too much and to frame the digital humanities as always opposing established structures. Big digital humanities emphasizes working with the departments and disciplines, and providing much more scalability and long-term growth.

However, existing outside those structures and having the power to do things that others also has benefits. Big digital humanities work requires a good ability to tweak and push existing structures. Such work will meet resistance, but it is not necessarily insurmountable. Resistance may come from faculty and leaders as well as from the administrative level. Administrative templates are typically very fitted, and institutionally difference can significantly challenge the system. While HUMlab has always had a close and productive collaboration with university administrators, opinions have certainly diverged at some points. When HUMlab had received the grant from the Kempe Foundation in 1998, one administrator argued that the funding should be transferred and managed by this unit rather than being managed by a *humanities* lab. Fortunately, the cowboy in charge of HUMlab at that point just told off the administrator.

Despite the potential challenges of living outside traditional departments and disciplines, a very strong case can be made for seeing the digital humanities as a meeting place. An alternative way of putting it is to say that a strong case can be made partly because of these very difficulties: these challenges would not exist if we were concerned with something already thought out, institutionally anchored, and safe.

Premise: The Digital Humanities as a Humanities Project

The third premise of big digital humanities is intimately related to the role of the digital humanities as a meeting place. It describes the digital humanities as a humanities project and place to configure, develop, and channel the humanities. This is an important part of big digital humanities: the humanities needs an intersectional place or laboratory for thinking about, rethinking, and renewing itself. A potential and a responsibility exist here that cannot be achieved from the position of a traditional department or discipline. This potential draws on the tension between the humanities and the digital humanities.

In some ways, the digital humanities appears to be everything that the humanities has resisted: a seemingly technocentric, neoliberal, noncritical, practical, collaborative, "nice," and outwardly successful enterprise modeled on science and engineering and overtly invested in presentation, outreach, and visibility. It could be argued that the digital humanities has occupied a place that could have been engineered and manifested by the traditional humanities had they taken the opportunity. The digital humanities thus becomes a missed opportunity as well as an image of what the humanities could become if they ever succumbed to outside pressures. Somewhat similarly, the traditional humanities sometimes seems to serve as a reminder of what the digital humanities does not want to be: resistant to innovation, disciplinary, focused on individual work, invested in traditional forms of knowledge production, technophobic, unwilling to acknowledge nonacademic forms of expertise, hierarchical, and slow to change. Of course, many digital humanists come from or are still affiliated with humanities disciplines, so a multilayered and historically laden connection exists. And many (if not most) of the projects in the field have been carried out with the humanities disciplines.

There can be no doubt, however, that the place of the digital humanities will always be understood in relation to the humanities at large. And increasingly, the rest of the humanities will have to think about how their disciplines and questions relate to the digital, broadly speaking. Indeed, the somewhat dogmatic mapping of positions in the preceding paragraph can be turned around. Much of what the humanities may be skeptical about in the digital humanities are also things that that the disciplines need to tackle. For example, engaging with alternative models of knowledge production, adopting a more active relation to the world outside the university, learning from science and engineering models, and being demonstratively and passionately proud of your work. And the digital humanities would be well served by drawing on the disciplines' traditions and intellectual history, their intellectual curiosity and sense of accountability, and the sheer range and volume of work, ideas, and networks available in the whole of the humanities.

In this way, the field can be a site of engagement in relation to the current status and future of the humanities, as it already is to some extent. This is less about individual disciplines or individual modes of engagement and more about seeing the digital humanities as a humanities project. With the

4humanities initiative, Alan Liu and his collaborators link the digital humanities to the cause of the humanities. In addition, the #transformDH initiative discussed in chapter 2 is not just about changing the digital humanities but about creating a new kind of humanities. Many white papers and descriptions of the digital humanities feature rhetoric about developing and transforming the humanities, arguing that the reach and visionary capacity of the digital humanities must be part of the field's texture.

Seeing the digital humanities as a humanities project can be problematic in some respects. From an internal point of view, not all members of the field would agree that serving as a humanities project is the job of the digital humanities. Those outside the field might ask what gives the digital humanities the right to represent and envision the humanities. This question is linked to the overall conception of the field. The benefits of big digital humanities are many, and the role of the field described here follows from this model.

This does not mean that big digital humanities should be infused with vague visionary speak or that everyone in the field must be engaged with the future of the academy on a daily basis; rather, the realization that the digital humanities is essentially a humanities project means that a connection exists with all of the humanities as well as with the outside and that the field is a place for engaging with the future of the humanities, pushing structural change, and facilitating intersectional discussion. Such a position necessarily resonates with technological, methodological, and disciplinary work carried out in the area.

The notion of the digital humanities as a humanities project draws on the reach of the humanities and the digital. The digital humanities operates across the humanities (or at least has the potential to do so). Many possible interaction points exist between the various humanities disciplines and the digital humanities. Information technology provides powerful tools for the humanities, and the digital constitutes an integral part of our culture. These actualities affect all the humanities disciplines on a fundamental level. Traditionally, digital humanities centers and initiatives have also been institutionalized differently than regular departments, helping to explain this in-between position.

Furthermore, the digital humanities represents the humanities in different contexts, in part because of the current interest in the digital humanities but more fundamentally because the intermediate position of the digital humanities makes the field a useful one-stop manifestation of the humanities. External funding agencies and institutions can sometimes perceive the digital humanities as a part of the humanities that is easier to understand or target. The discourse on humanities research infrastructure exemplifies this process.[85] Funding agencies, such as the U.S. Office of Digital Humanities at the National Endowment of the Humanities, can serve an important function in reaching across the humanities and speaking both to the broader funding agency ecology and to the humanities at large. Representing the humanities also means engaging with academic partners outside the humanities proper. The digital humanities can help create connections with science, medicine, engineering, and the arts through intellectually and technologically driven collaboration building on respect and mutual interest.

A strong historical and contemporary link exists between visionary discourse and technology,[86] and the digital humanities clearly has a strong investment in technology, technological infrastructure, and the digital more generally. For example, visions that draw directly on existing or future technological innovation are common in the discourse of research infrastructure and traditional humanities computing.[87] Such discursive potential can be recruited to imagine the future of the humanities, refined digital publication systems, humanities-based infrastructure, or new research projects.

There seems to be a sense that doing digital humanities work requires pushing against established traditions and structures. For example, a one-week online and print book project, *Hacking the Academy*, declared, "Today serious scholars are asking whether the institutions of the academy as they have existed for decades, even centuries, aren't becoming obsolete. Every aspect of scholarly infrastructure is being questioned, and even more importantly, being hacked."[88] While it would not seem that scholarly infrastructure is questioned as profoundly as this citation suggests, the challenging potential of the digital humanities is important. This is probably one of the principal reasons why the field attracts people interested in thinking about and reconfiguring the humanities. The tension between the digital humanities and the academic establishment is multifaceted and involves institutional hurdles to doing interdisciplinary and collaborative work, a need for space and technological infrastructure, tenure systems not adapted to digital production and publications, and the need for nonfaculty experts and corresponding career paths. Based on these and other factors, a strong sense exists that the university and the humanities need to change to accommodate this type of work, and all of these phenomena feed into a vision of a transformed humanities.

On a more general level, a strong visionary and transformative sentiment goes beyond these intermediate-level issues. This is where we find intense, sweeping statements, as when David Parry proclaims, "I don't want a digital facelift for the humanities, I want the digital to completely change what it means to be a humanities scholar."[89] This discourse seems grounded in the issues discussed previously (coming from the practical work of the field) as well as in discontent with the current situation for the humanities, the academe, and to some extent society at large.

This sentiment arises from a strong sense that the humanities is in a precarious situation in terms of funding and recognition and that higher education as a whole is facing a series of major challenges.[90] The current financially dire times in countries such as the United States and United Kingdom are part of this scenario, but according to many observers, higher education is also threatened by a lack of flexibility, adaptation of corporate culture, and an increased need to justify the humanities and arts.[91] The recurring discourse regarding the crises of the humanities is not new but remains current.[92] In this light, we see frustration and discontent among both junior and senior faculty. Early-career faculty and graduate students are concerned about the lack of possibilities for the future and the humanities' apparent inward sentiment and structural resistance to new ideas.

A strong connection exists between the digital humanities and the humanities, and it seems reasonable that big digital humanities should have both a responsibility and willingness to engage with the humanities and the academy in terms of tackling substantive challenges and problems, channeling transformative sentiment, attracting disciplinary interest, and imagining a scholarly, technological, and societal future. This is a job for a broadly conceived digital humanities and cannot easily be carried out from a single disciplinary perspective.

Intellectual Middleware

We need digital humanities to be big for many reasons. One issue in particular that requires largeness is the coming together of research questions, data/materials, and material manifestations.

On one level, this would seem to be what the field is about, but in actuality, creating such deep connections presents a major challenge. Much of the work in the digital humanities has focused on the data/material layer and to some degree on material manifestations. In light of the field's history, the reluctance to step into the intellectual territory of the disciplines seems understandable, but this reluctance constrains the methodological and technological work carried out. In this case, stepping in means being involved in shaping the intellectual endeavor, which is more a question of curation than service. And there has been a lack of a developed material aesthetics in the digital humanities on a par with the best work available. For example, interaction designers and digital production experts are rarely involved in the process, meaning that practices such as prototyping and user testing are underutilized. Many projects were produced for a very limited group of people, resulting in little need to tailor interfaces to a large constituency. Also, the work of the digital humanities has focused more on the back end than the front end. This propensity is not just a matter of technology or design but is also part of the field's epistemic tradition.

Scholars from the disciplines, conversely, tend to lack the methodological competence and computational rigor associated with the digital humanities (and areas such as library science) in relation to working with data and materials. Among other things, this can lead to an endless series of "new starts" and to a dearth of systematic approaches. The critical sensibility and imaginary capacity of disciplinary scholars also sometimes seem stifled when engaging with digital environments. Furthermore, people can hesitate to step outside the perimeters of the disciplinary epistemic tradition, as when they engage with alternative expressive modalities such as academic installations.

While this description certainly stereotypes and simplifies complex interrelations and overlooks numerous exceptions and much excellent work on various levels, it addresses weaknesses both in the digital humanities and in the humanities at large. The digital humanities suffers from the overall lack of scholarly impact, which means that there are very few examples of achievements that have had a substantial impact on other fields or that have been intellectually remarkable on the level of the most significant work in other fields. And for a field whose foundational narrative typically refers back to the late 1940s, its supposedly emergent nature may not suffice to explain the lack of substantial intellectual impact. Work in the humanities disciplines has not engaged strongly with the levels of data structures and material manifestations where such an engagement could be intellectually rewarding. Furthermore, much expertise in design, information science, publishing, cultural heritage, and other domains is not yet optimally or systematically integrated in these processes. Big digital humanities emphasizes the potential of closer intellectual and material ties between the humanities and the digital humanities.

Johanna Drucker's notion of intellectual middleware points to one of missing elements: a space where these different levels, competencies, and intellectual drive come together.[93] According to Drucker, "Designing the intellectual 'middleware' that frames artifacts with interpretation requires substantive engagement with the field and discipline."[94] The notion foregrounds intellectual work but does not disassociate it from the technological, systemic, and material levels. On the contrary, all of these competencies and perspectives are needed to create intellectual middleware. In addition, the concept recognizes that such a middle space exists and is important. However, this recognition does not automatically mean that intellectually/materially significant and innovative work will happen. Through digital humanities, we can create conditions, processes, and environments that make such work easier and that serve as a place for meaningful and sharp intellectual and technological exchange. Such a place also needs to acknowledge the importance of the institutional, cultural, and social situation.

The particulars of intellectual middleware may be difficult to conceive because it sits between different levels and because it is conceptually challenging to entangle (and disentangle) complex research questions, data, and material manifestations. We need a language for articulating and critiquing middleware that is intellectually and materially sophisticated enough to be useful.

One way to develop this language is to ask questions in relation to existing platforms. Omeka is an "open source web-publishing platform for the display of library, museum, archives, and scholarly collections and exhibitions."[95] But what notions of cultural heritage and associated institutions are built into the platform? And why does it *display* rather than *interpret* or *enact*? Do problems arise because the Dublin Core scheme must be used for items and collections? What role do the template designs play in the deployment of materials? What does it mean that the platform has an ontology based on items and collections? How does the browsing modality (as the primary way to explore the material) built into the platform affect the material structure of sites? What narrative structures are supported (and not supported) by the exhibit function? What kind of arguments are supported? Does it matter that the platform operates through a one-window interface? Why do most Omeka sites look so similar?

Discussions of intellectual middleware across platforms share some recurring parameters. One parameter is the operationalization of argumentative structures—that is, how scholarly arguments are made in different platforms. Arguments are neither consequences of their manifestation nor independent abstractions. They conform to certain patterns, and it seems likely that parameters such as "comparing" and "calling forth evidence," part of classical rhetoric, have a life across different platforms. A regular search interface based on the Dublin Core enables certain types of comparison and typically results in a list of isolated items that conform to the search query. It is much rarer that such juxtaposition is demonstrated visually (through visual overlay or other means), although geographical distribution has become a common way of representing search results. How can one make queries that allow for complex and interpretative searches? One model is faceted browsing, where many facets (variables) can be shown and selected and where filtering is typically direct, meaning that live interaction with the dataset is carried out.

A number of processes are commonly used to enact and understand complex relations and materials and operate on a more material level than high-level parameters such as "comparing." Examples include scaling, focusing, overlaying, layering, juxtaposing, and framing. These parameters do not apply solely to the visual domain, although a visual bias exists here. Just like the parameters discussed previously, such processes can be useful both when comparing different middleware platforms and when thinking about what resources may be used to approach different intellectually driven issues. In most Omeka applications, items—an ontologically encoded entity in the platform—are represented in their own visual frames (one per item). The platform thus imposes cultural heritage as a list of decontextualized artifacts, although some of the intertextuality and connectivity is available in the Dublin Core data associated with the item.

An alternative entry point would be to start from the ontology laid out visually and stacking items that overlap ontologically. Such an ontological visual map would allow us to explore what parts of the ontology are not active in relation to the material or zooming in on ontological hotspots. Another approach would be to provide an alternative framing through a multiple-screen setup. One screen could hold the geographical information (showing the positioning of artifacts and allowing zooming), another one could show the ontological structure (where multiple categories and relations could be selected), and a third screen could show the five most similar or dissimilar items within the geographical and ontological focus. These images would be overlaid and shifted dynamically (five at a time). In addition, turning off parts of the ontological structure would enable us to see resulting changes in the visual landscape.

Intellectual middleware attaches to different types of infrastructures. Omeka is primarily associated with the web as a delivery platform. Other platforms have a much stronger relation to physical materiality. Shannon Mattern's work on intellectual furnishings, for example, discusses the role of furniture for knowledge work and how space articulates ideas or how ideas can be articulated by space. Mattern's project suggests "that we think about the literal furniture of our knowledge institutions—and how those material objects inform how we organize our media, structure our thoughts, and cultivate our values."⁹⁶ The use of the term *furnishings* instead of *furniture* in the title of her work seems to indicate a more abstract, middle layer, similar to the notion of intellectual middleware developed here, placed between the thoughts and the physical furniture. Mattern's work demonstrates the importance of remaining materially sensitive in this type of work. At the same time, we also must be careful not to be deterministic about the relation between the material and idealistic levels. Furniture does not condition us but creates conditions and to some degree structures our work.

Some infrastructure exists somewhere between Omeka and furniture, clearly engaging with structuring data and physical manifestations. A display system developed in HUMlab exemplifies the physical-digital infrastructure associated with intellectual middleware. This system was created for a HUMlab's December 2014 conference on knowledge production. One challenge of a multiple-screen setup such as HUMlab's (see chapter 4) is allowing the making of arguments across screens. This can be accomplished infrastructurally by having clusters of separate computers, working with very large desktops, or doing media signal-level processing, but ultimately, it requires a platform that can serve as a materially grounded "thought tool." The web system developed gives the user a schematic view of the space in question, facilitates upload of content, and deploys a simulation of the content and infrastructure in an interactive 3-D model. This tool allows arguments to be tested and shaped in a way that was practically impossible before. We need to be able quickly to explore different argumentative and experiential scenarios. The structuring provided by version 1 of the software imposes a number of constraints: it specifies two types of presentations (lightning talk and stepped talk) and does not allow web content or use of sensor technology. The whole platform is fairly visual-centric, and while it departs from the single-screen paradigm of most presentation software, it is still based on a notion of sequences (of decks of slides/content). These and other constraints and biases need to be discussed critically as part of reflecting on the tool and associated middleware, which in turn feeds into continuing development of this sketching tool for making multimodal scholarly arguments in a multiplex screen context.

Intellectual middleware often emerges in contact zones, and the final example comes from the productive intersection of environmental humanities and digital humanities. The example relates to a planned project, where the intention is to challenge the predominant narrative of nature and the environment. This discussion was originally more instrumental, as a grant proposal necessitated outreach and some multimodal expressions. Over time, however, it became clear that the intellectual questions integral to the project had a considerable digital and medial inflection. What emerged was an understanding that creating alternative narratives of nature is intimately tied to knowledge production, expressive modalities, and infrastructural resources. Indeed, environment's predominant narrative is intertwined with the research infrastructures that created it and with the expressions that manifest it. Challenging such narratives is also a question of infrastructure, in the sense both of critically engaging with the infrastructural level of these narratives and of employing infrastructure and expressive modalities to enact humanities- and arts-based narratives. This matter involves not merely presentation or representation but also ontological, interpretative, and creative processes that are critical to the understanding, creation, and sociopolitical enactment of natural knowledge.[97]

Conclusion

A big, inclusive notion of the digital humanities can solve many of the problems the field currently faces and can provide a sustainable and inviting model for the future. This notion takes into account many scholarly, educational, and technical challenges; the multiple epistemic traditions linked to the digital humanities; intersectionality through categories such as gender and race; the field's potential reach across and outside the humanities; and the digital as a boundary object. The liminal position of big digital humanities can meet these challenges and give it strong connections to the rest of the humanities, the academy, and the outside world. As the concept of intellectual middleware emphasizes, such work has to be intellectually driven, materially sensitive, and critically aware.

// FOUR //

Humanities Infrastructure

We are now in a position to consider what types of infrastructure may be useful in facilitating big digital humanities and more broadly in supporting the humanities. Shared, humanistic infrastructure is critical to the big digital humanities as it can support the three premises discussed in chapter 3: the digital humanities as a meeting place, multiple modes of engagement, and the field as a place to engage with the situation and future of the humanities.

It is not possible to imagine digital humanities—or any kind of humanities—without infrastructure. However, most of the humanities may not think of itself in terms of infrastructure, and the digital humanities must engage with infrastructure not just where doing so may come most naturally, such as language technology and archaeology, but wherever there is a need. Engagement is required not just in terms of building and using infrastructure but also in terms of conceptualizing and critiquing infrastructure. Moreover, we need to relate to existing infrastructures such as libraries, digital publishing platforms, and humanities centers and reflect on their conditioning and potential in terms of infrastructural imagination. These humanities infrastructures can provide valuable partners for the digital humanities.

While discussions of infrastructure may not immediately attract considerable scholarly excitement, infrastructure can be seen both as an enabler, facilitating and supporting academic work, and as a relevant object of critical study. Indeed, infrastructure involves using imagination to connect conceptual ideas with material manifestations. In this sense, thinking about an infrastructural agenda for the humanities equates to shaping the future of the humanities and the academy. At the same time, infrastructure is institutionally, culturally, and politically laden, and humanists need to bring their critical awareness to it. Emerging work in infrastructure studies is important here, although such work mostly addresses other domains than the humanities and rarely our own knowledge production. Not all humanities infrastructure can

131

be subsumed under the digital humanities, but there is potential in seeing the field as an infrastructural platform for the humanities. Big digital humanities, positioned as a meeting place with a broad technological and critical engagement, is a strong platform for articulating the need for humanities infrastructure and perspectives.

This chapter opens with some observations on infrastructure and research infrastructure before describing and critiquing three common models of humanities infrastructure: extending existing infrastructure such as libraries, the notion that the humanities has no infrastructure, and science and technology as a template for how to create humanities infrastructure. The second part of the chapter proposes a framework for research infrastructure—in particular, humanities infrastructure—based on three levels of analysis: conceptual infrastructure, design principles, and actual infrastructure. The level of conceptual infrastructure provides an ideational grounding, and the set of design principles offers a way to connect this conceptual level with the material level. HUMlab at Umeå University offers a detailed case study of how this framework can be used, so digital humanities labs receive particular consideration. The chapter ends with a suggested infrastructural agenda for the humanities.

Approaching Infrastructure

In some ways, infrastructure is pervasive and transparent.[1] It is a texture that provides electricity, phone services, roads, and many other seemingly basic things, and at least in some parts of the world, we can expect this infrastructure to be there and be reasonably reliable. Infrastructures are interdependent in different ways and often part of very complex systems. For example, in an article critiquing a planned national investment in high-speed trains in Sweden, the authors argue that people travel mostly regionally, that high-speed trains are mostly beneficial for privileged groups of people, that the long-term environmental gain is questionable given the environmental cost of construction, that commercial actors running the trains have other goals than the state, and that any such major investment will decrease infrastructural maneuverability over the next few decades.[2] They also acknowledge that the decision is ultimately a political one. There is certainly complexity here, and increasingly digital technologies play an important role in enabling, expressing and connecting infrastructures. Just think about how cars, road infrastructure, geographical positioning systems, visual map displays, live traffic feeds, automatic reading of traffic signs, parking apps, Über and new driver-less vehicles interact. Infrastructural systems are not and have never been one thing, but are rather situated socially, culturally, economically, environmentally and materially. Infrastructure is also about creating monuments, enacting dreams and packaging things that would not always seem to belong together.

There is a sense of infrastructure that primarily refers to research, cyber, or academic infrastructure,[3] much of which is less pervasive. It is typically costly equipment associated with the sciences, engineering, and medicine—for example, microscopes, biomedical imaging, high-performance computing, and synchrotron radiation facilities. Other kinds of infrastructure, such as libraries, are much less likely to be seen as relevant in relation to recent investments in research infrastructures. According to the Swedish Research Council,

> For an infrastructure to be considered a national infrastructure, it should be freely accessible for researchers within the area and be of national interest, as well as have an independent board with a national perspective and responsibility. There should be a process for prioritising utilisation of the infrastructure, using scientific excellence as the criterion.[4]

Would even a national library qualify as research infrastructure in this sense? Probably not, as libraries are not really part of the framework of research infrastructure and are normally funded in a different way. Most research councils advertising resources for research infrastructure would be perplexed if libraries applied for core funding for themselves. And while prioritizing utilization of resources based on scientific excellence works better for supercomputer centers than for libraries, it would not be impossible to frame libraries in such a way. But is this really what we want to do?

Language plays an important role here, and it is safe to say that there was no real attempt to include the humanities in this text. I am arguing not that the needs of the humanities in this respect are as large as those of science, engineering, and medicine but rather that there is no point in talking about including all areas and fields if that inclusion does not even affect the language and framing of such authoritative descriptions. Furthermore, the text excerpt also makes it clear that we are concerned with facilities or resources that are used primarily for research. The humanities could choose to think differently and more broadly about infrastructure.

Given this discursive framing of research infrastructure, it is not very surprising that the humanities are generally not privileged in the allocation of infrastructural funding. For example, none of the twenty projects that received grants from the Swedish Research Council in 2014 involved humanities-based infrastructure; the preceding year, only one of the twenty-seven funded projects was humanistic, and somewhat predictably, it was a grant for a language technology work within a European initiative (CLARIN).[5] The situation is similar almost everywhere; moreover, even recent initiatives that sought to articulate a humanities infrastructure have tended to focus on data and access rather than on actual humanistic research questions and the overall mission of the humanities.[6]

Nevertheless, research infrastructure, while traditionally not associated with the humanities, has become a topic of conversation on faculty boards and among humanities researchers. And regardless of the actual allocation of funding, at least nominal humanistic interest comes from funding agencies, councils, and various organizations under rubrics such as cyberinfrastructure, e-science, and knowledge infrastructure. While all of these terms appear in this chapter, I prefer *academic infrastructure* because it does not focus on research only and has fewer connotations than *knowledge infrastructure*. In any case, work is being done to secure funding, define key questions, and align the humanities with an epistemic framework that bears a strong science and engineering legacy. Many opportunities exist, particularly for a field such as the digital humanities, but there are also real risks and important considerations.

Particular attention needs to go to the assumed epistemic and ontological neutrality of the "infrastructure move" and its assumed broad applicability for everything from geology to cultural studies. I therefore consider the risks associated with modeling humanities infrastructure on existing infrastructure, such as libraries, or on a technology- and science-driven paradigm. The humanities should engage profoundly, critically, and unapologetically with their own infrastructural needs. The stakes are high, and the infrastructure movement as a whole can be seen as an epistemic power play, but it has very real implications and possibilities for the humanities and the digital humanities.

Interlude 6: Framing Infrastructure and a Call for Leadership

As the ex-director of HUMlab and someone involved in building material environments, part of my job is to think about our work in infrastructural terms. This strategy is not just pragmatic but comes from a belief that the material level of infrastructure can articulate deep conceptual foundations and that the interplay between the conceptual and material levels can be very productive.

Infrastructure may seem solid and not particularly subjective, but it is the result of institutional, cultural, political, and conceptual processes. An excellent example of this embeddedness is Nicole Starosielski's work on the infrastructure of undersea cables, which investigates how infrastructure for the "immaterial" Internet is very material, situated, and a result of cultural production.[7] Such knowledge can and should inform our thinking about infrastructure, particularly since funding schemes and ideas of infrastructure are typically not based on humanistic or cultural challenges but rather on those of science, engineering and technology.

When HUMlab applied for infrastructural funding from the Swedish Research Council in the early 2000s, what we imagined clearly did not fit the template offered by the funding agency. In particular, we envisioned a disparate set of technologies in relation to an idea about how that infrastructure could further humanities research. Such funding is often keyed to the idea of expensive scientific apparatuses, and the call explicitly mentioned "functional units." For all kinds of reasons, we did not receive funding, but the process helped us to think about the framing of infrastructure. Such framing must clearly draw on humanities-based notions of infrastructure but also must take cues from areas with a stronger infrastructural engagement to strengthen the argument for humanistic infrastructure.

In the spring of 2012, I had talked with scholars and research leaders from the sciences and medicine at Umeå University. At the same time, various schools at the university, including the arts and humanities, had been asked to identify and articulate their infrastructural needs as a result of a decrease in the national funding for infrastructure and a corresponding increase in the need for universities to fund more of their infrastructure.

My discussions with chemists, biologists, and plant science physicists showed that their operations already had a clear infrastructural framing. Again, this may not be surprising, but I was struck by how this was not just a strategic sentiment: individual scholars saw it as key to their work and a reason for being at Umeå University. They often used the word *platform*, and such a notion can be quite useful (and critiqued, see Interlude 2 in chapter 1). For example, a range of science and medicine disciplines at the university are oriented around a number of key platforms (such as proteomics and metabolomics) that are sets of infrastructures or specific, costly apparatuses and associated methodological competence. These platforms possess a sense of sharing, both in the sense of use and accessibility and in the sense of (external) funding. In practice, however, not all platforms are equally accessible, and problems may arise when some stakeholders do not know enough to use these devices. However, a story and basic idea matches director-level and researcher-level interest with an infrastructural layer. Furthermore, infrastructure is seen as an instrumental way of connecting different fields and groups. According to the Umeå University Chemical Biological Centre website,

> Although the departments are administratively independent, they have the ambition to share resources (technical platforms) and build up tight networks between the departments to overcome the borders of faculties and universities.[8]

This statement makes assumptions regarding the intersectional capacity of infrastructure. Sharing does not necessarily mean working together closely, but shared infrastructure can undoubtedly help create possibilities. Perhaps just as important as the actual infrastructure is the idea of having common platforms and the idea that individual researchers and groups simply cannot fund or motivate such infrastructure for themselves. Similarly, libraries provide a model for access to materials that is much more cost-effective and structured than large individual or group collections. A parallel argument can be made for resources associated with the digital humanities. This is a matter not just of infrastructure and people but also of ideational and conceptual framing and articulation. This conceptual framing of infrastructure in the humanities should go beyond access to digitized cultural heritage and managing large datasets. At this point, we need to articulate a set of intellectual arguments for humanities infrastructure. Furthermore, we must possess technological vision and an unapologetic attitude toward the humanities' need for infrastructural investments.

In 2006, I took part in a workshop on cyberinfrastructure at the University of California at Irvine along with some key humanities scholars and other interested parties. Dan Atkins, then head of the Office of Cyberinfrastructure at the National Science Foundation (NSF), showed considerable interest in our work, and he asked the humanists present to show leadership in terms of cyberinfrastructure. When I met him again in the spring of 2013 in Ann Arbor, he repeated this sentiment and showed considerable personal engagement in humanities infrastructure at the University of Michigan.

The humanities can and should imagine its own infrastructure, but must also engage in collaborative efforts. I prepared a project proposal about critical visualization together with a group of scholars in 2014 and one of the key partners was a physicist and visualization expert. The physicist, who runs a large visualization facility, and I had been working together for some time, and we soon realized that our respective visualization infrastructures were very different, but with many links, common challenges, and considerable complementarity. When I sent him a first draft of the project proposal he distinctly critiqued the way I had portrayed science-driven visualization (as largely positivistic). I already knew that science visualization is not necessarily positivistic—in fact humanities visualization often comes across as quite positivistic—but somehow I let a traditional humanities framing of STEM influence my writing. I was wrong and changed the narrative as a consequence.

Our collaboration later led to HUMlab participating in a multiple-site national bid for visualization infrastructure (to the Swedish Research Council). Most of the nodes in this collaboration were science-based and they found our humanities-based infrastructure important since it provided a different, materially manifested model of what visualization and scholarly enactment can be. This type of collaboration can be an important way forward for the humanities, but it requires the humanities to first imagine and build its own infrastructure.

The humanities needs to articulate and argue in favor of humanities infrastructure not to maximize funding but as a way of making strong visions come true. And if the infrastructural engagement results in the humanities declaring that we do not need additional infrastructure, this is obviously also acceptable. The most important factor is intellectual and material engagement.

Research Infrastructure

According to the *European Roadmap for Research Infrastructures Report* 2010,

> Research Infrastructures are facilities, resources or services of a unique nature that have been identified by European research communities to conduct top-level activities in all fields. This definition of Research Infrastructures, including the associated human resources, covers major equipment or sets of instruments, in addition to knowledge-containing resources such as collections, archives and databanks. Research Infrastructures may be "single-sited," "distributed," or "virtual" (the service being provided electronically). They often require structured information systems related

to data management, enabling information and communication. These include technology based infrastructures such as Grid, computing, software and middleware.[9]

This definition is fairly typical of the discourse of research infrastructure through its focus on data, instruments, and excellence in research. Another typical feature is the listing of different types of technologies and research infrastructure (which is clearer in the full report). There is no simple way of defining *research infrastructure(s)* or *cyberinfrastructure* since the terms are part of a social, institutional, and political context. Indeed, *infrastructure* broadly refers to "the resources (as personnel, buildings, or equipment) required for an activity" as well as "the underlying foundation or basic framework (of a system or organization)."[10] According to Paul Edwards and his coauthors, the term often "connotes big, durable, well-functioning systems and services, from railroads and highways to telephone, electric power, and the Internet."[11]

In practice, the notion of research infrastructure carries a number of assumptions linked to funding structures and to the idea of a resource of national or international interest. Research infrastructure is typically taken to be advanced and costly, to require national or international funding, to be associated with leading research and researchers, to be part of a system, to extend beyond single research groups or disciplines, to have longevity, and to add significant new research possibilities.

In general, much discussion of academic infrastructure is driven by technology and data and takes place at the structural level. This is partly a result of the selling, reselling, and packaging of new generations of research infrastructure and partly a result of the emphasis on the traditional infrastructural needs of science, engineering, and technology.[12] As with *digital humanities*, the relatively high level of abstraction of a term such as *cyberinfrastructure* allows for descriptions grounded less in specific disciplines and more in a set of high-level epistemic and technological commitments:

> The Advanced Cyberinfrastructure (ACI) Division supports and coordinates the development, acquisition, and provision of state-of-the-art cyberinfrastructure resources, tools and services essential to the advancement and transformation of science and engineering.[13]

As Christine Borgman observes, *cyberinfrastructure* is often defined through example, typically emphasizing the "integrative, collaborative, and distributed nature of new forms of research."[14] In addition, there is frequently an assumption of very large and complex datasets, currently fueled by interest in big data. While we do not necessarily need to question these assertions, we are concerned with a particular type of discourse and epistemic framework. This implies that a possible humanities alignment with cyberinfrastructure in this sense is, in fact, also an alignment with this discourse and associated assumptions. For example, distributedness in the sense of optiputers or grid computing is far more likely to be seen as research infrastructure than multimodal communication, data exchange, and analysis through small-scale qualitative databases, Twitter, and tools for online ethnography. The emphasis on big data shadows the importance of small data, and a positivistic data and research regime (whether enacted by humanists or others) can lack the critical sentiment central to the humanities.[15]

Another assumption is that research infrastructure is quite costly. Small-scale installations are less likely to receive external funding. The packaging of infrastructure becomes an important issue. Humanities infrastructure is likely to be more multiplex and cheaper than traditional science infrastructure. Here platforms such as labs are useful in the sense that they can frame multiple pieces of technology, a range of expertise and other resources. The humanities needs to both resist and engage with the high-cost assumptions of infrastructure, avoiding expensive solutions for the sake of hitting a high price point and preventing infrastructural and intellectual imagination from being curtailed by a low-cost humanistic sensibility.

It is striking that discourse on academic infrastructure tends to have very little obvious critical inflection. For example, the aforementioned *European Roadmap for Research Infrastructures Report 2010* does not contain a single instance of "gender" or "race." The same is true for many other reports and white papers on research infrastructure. There is also very little political, societal, or environmental concern in such documents. It would clearly be useful to engage more strongly with such perspectives when imagining and articulating academic infrastructure. What critical perspectives could inform the building of new infrastructure? How can our current knowledge infrastructure be critically analyzed? How can such critical inflections be addressed and explored through the infrastructure itself? We need to bring critical sensitivity to academic infrastructure while also engaging with the making of new infrastructure.

In addition, most notions of infrastructure for the academy are very focused on research. If we believe that education and research are intrinsically connected, we need to think about how infrastructure can serve both needs. This does not apply equally for all infrastructure, but it is an important overall sentiment that the humanities should take care to point out when discussing infrastructure. After all, a key example of humanities infrastructure, the library, serves both education and research. This is one of the reasons why *academic infrastructure* seems like a more useful term than *research infrastructure*.

Academic infrastructure intended for research seems to easily acquire a status and life beyond merely supporting or facilitating research. Research infrastructure is not research or independent of research challenges, and it seems appropriate for research needs and challenges to shape the establishment of new infrastructure.[16] The humanities is thus primarily concerned with research challenges and infrastructural needs identified by the humanities, particularly humanities researchers. A few examples of these needs and challenges include looking at older materials and aesthetics through a digital lens, understanding the dynamics of "Twitter activism" through network analysis, studying the transformation of urban spaces through media technology, tracing narrative structures in computer games, studying the notion of "frames" through working with multiple screen sites, using map-based visualization to find patterns in large sets of archival information, applying text-mining technologies for literary and linguistic analysis, and investigating reading comprehension with the help of eye-tracking equipment.

However, the nature of infrastructure and funding mechanisms normally makes the process more complicated than matching a single research challenge with an appropriate piece of infrastructure. In practice, infrastructure often must be abstractly framed and typically must serve more than one specific research need to qualify as infrastructure. Technologies such as visualization and grid computing fulfill this requirement, and they often come across as black boxes rather than sites of situated research facilitation. Furthermore, funding is much more likely if the infrastructure is associated with "new" research and "major" potential advances. There is also a push for interdisciplinary research endeavors. What I have described here is in fact an infrastructural template with which the humanities needs to engage.

Academic Infrastructure for the Humanities

The discourses and practices of research infrastructure are strongly situated in science and engineering. While many funding sources are in principle open to all areas of research (including the humanities), they have a strong tendency to fund science, engineering, and medical research. The humanities has not been seen as a significant player in these kinds of funding schemes apart from certain areas such as computational linguistics and digital libraries; consequently, observers rarely elaborate on the specifics of humanities infrastructures and engage in relatively little discussion of what humanities infrastructure could actually be.

However, the humanities in general and the digital humanities in particular have begun to acknowledge the importance of and push for a better research infrastructure. This process is strongly linked to a realization that material, tools, and culture are becoming increasingly digitized and that academic work is more likely than before to be carried out in a distributed and digitally supported fashion. Unfortunately, this realization often merely results in a transfer from known infrastructure, typically cultural heritage institutions, to the digital realm.

> The digital age is compelling us to introduce such physical collections onto the digital plane by digitisation and/or to construct new collections of digital objects as subjects of research in Humanities today.[17]

This European Science Foundation statement represents a fairly expected stance based largely on an analog mind-set. The risk may even be that such digital collections become decontextualized and that not enough resources are put into the interpretative layer. Moreover, while digitizing existing infrastructure is important, humanities infrastructure involves much more than this.

The background to the current interest in infrastructure is a relatively recent "infrastructure turn" (in the words of Geoffrey Rockwell) or even a revolution (a term often used by funding agency reports and other sources).[18] At least in terms of how it is presented, infrastructure in this sense is more likely to include human resources and other nontechnical aspects than were earlier generations of infrastructure. Nevertheless, the movement is essentially a science- and engineering-driven enterprise:

> The Panel's overarching finding is that a new age has dawned in scientific and engineering research, pushed by continuing progress in computing, information, and communication technology; and pulled by the expanding complexity, scope, and scale of today's research challenges.[19]

The use of *new* in this influential NSF Blue Ribbon Report is not accidental: the discourse of academic infrastructure prominently features *new*, *emerging*, and *expanding*. According to Christine Borgman, *new* appears 133 times in this report, and similar documents have similar language.[20] *New* appears 89 times in the 64 pages of the American Council of Learned Societies (ACLS) Report on Cyberinfrastructure for the Humanities and Social Sciences.[21] These figures suggest that "newness" may be a useful prerequisite for research infrastructure. It is not problematic or surprising that infrastructure discourse emphasizes what is new and what can be imagined, but these documents are often set in an overly positivistic and rigid infrastructural framework with limited connection to the subject matter.

This NSF report explicitly mentions the humanities only once (in relation to digital libraries), but there is evidently an interest in engaging with the humanities and social sciences despite the NSF's primary focus on science and engineering.[22] Similarly, many accounts of cyberinfrastructure include a note about the impact on these "nonprimary" areas:

> Although our focus is on e-Science, other research fields such as the social sciences, arts, and humanities will also require and benefit from this emerging cyberinfrastructure.[23]

Such statements are external to the humanities in that they often make outside assumptions about the field's needs, requirements, and priorities. For the humanities to control its own academic infrastructure, it needs to express humanities-driven needs and engage in constructive dialogue about our current and future infrastructure. As Andrew Prescott points out, infrastructure in science is often tied to specific research questions, while in the humanities, "our thinking about infrastructure is too often disconnected from research issues."[24] Prescott's statement may well be true, but it also exemplifies a tendency to take for granted the often implicit rationale for science infrastructure.

The close and complex connection between research issues, materials and tools discussed under the rubric of intellectual middleware in chapter 3 is highly relevant in relation to humanities infrastructure. There is no such thing as neutral access to content and the design of research tools encapsulates interpretative frameworks. Infrastructure projects should take this into account as there is considerable academic potential in allowing infrastructure to be inflected, integrative and intellectual.

Risks, Strategies, and Models

Some risks of conceptualizing and building infrastructure for the humanities must be addressed. First, there is a danger that existing humanities infrastructure might be disregarded since we have no tradition of thinking about libraries, seminar rooms, and databases in terms of infrastructural framing. Second, the science-based and data-driven model might be imposed on the humanities (sometimes by humanists themselves) without careful discussion of its premises and consequences. Third, infrastructural needs or agendas most compatible with a largely science-based model might be inappropriately prioritized. Finally, new humanities infrastructure may be uncritically based on existing infrastructure, such as libraries, and associated epistemic commitments.

The current interest and investments in academic infrastructure for the humanities present an opportunity to think carefully about what the humanities may or may not need in terms of infrastructure. We cannot do so, however, without maintaining a critical stance and advocating a truly humanities-based approach to academic infrastructure. At the same time, we do not necessarily know what kind of infrastructure we will need, and we must simultaneously explore humanities-based research issues and challenges and technology and different kinds of infrastructure, including infrastructure that is part of what is seen as science and engineering infrastructure. Consequently, we must allow for combinations of technology- and humanities-induced visions and implementations.

Furthermore, we must be aware that any investment in academic infrastructure prioritizes resources and that certain parts of the humanities are more likely than others to be good candidates for such investments. We need to question such prioritizations, which are likely to privilege humanistic infrastructure based on a predominantly science and engineering template or on existing infrastructural traditions (such as libraries). Academic infrastructure is not neutral, as illustrated by the omission out of the humanities from much of the policy and practice on infrastructure.

In fact, the humanities has long used academic infrastructure in scholarly practice. Libraries and archives, for example, are often cited as an essential and historically important infrastructure to the humanities. Indeed, some writers claim that the humanities itself makes up vital infrastructure or that elements of cultural infrastructure can function as trading zones for technological, artistic, and humanities practitioners.[25] Humanities infrastructure can also be tied to science models of infrastructure or to a sense that there is not much infrastructure. Three models for humanities academic infrastructure exemplify the nonneutrality of academic infrastructure: existing infrastructure, the lack of a humanities infrastructure, and a technology- and science-driven infrastructure.

Model I: Extending Existing Infrastructure

One model of humanities infrastructure is based on the assumption that considerable humanities academic infrastructure is already in place and that this infrastructure is a very good candidate for becoming cyberinfrastructure or being digitized. The European Science Foundation's 2011 report, "Research Infrastructures in the Digital Humanities," traces humanities research infrastructures (RIs) back to the Musaeum in Alexandria, medieval libraries, and art collections—early databases that "provided material for subsequent phases of RIs in the Humanities."[26] Although the report calls for a move beyond the current model, a sense exists that the current infrastructural needs of the humanities primarily relate to this heritage.[27] This picture is also evident in a report by the American Council of Learned Societies:

> The infrastructure of scholarship was built over centuries. It includes diverse collections of primary sources in libraries, archives, and museums; the bibliographies, searching aids, citation systems, and concordances that make that information retrievable; the standards that are embodied in cataloging and classification systems; the journals and university presses that distribute the information; and the editors, librarians, archivists, and curators who link the operation of this structure to the scholars who use it. All of these elements have extensions or analogues in cyberinfrastructure, at least in the cyberinfrastructure that is required for humanities and social sciences.[28]

This fairly accurate description of existing infrastructure largely omits infrastructures outside of libraries, archives, museums, and publication systems and accentuates only some aspects of such institutions and systems—for example, by overlooking the idea of the library as a social infrastructure and a place for knowledge production.

We are thus concerned with a library- and collection-based model. Such a model accords well with a large part of the humanities but also brings a set of epistemic commitments pertaining to structure, delivery, material types, retrieval systems, selection procedures, the relationship between researchers and library institutions, and other issues basic to the humanities. Any major new investment in academic infrastructure should therefore not be uncritically based on these existing structures and descriptions. This model distinguishes fairly strongly between the collections (institutions, distribution systems, professional functions involved, and so forth) and the researchers and research community. But as Johanna Drucker notes,

> The design of new environments for performing scholarly work cannot be left to the technical staff and to library professionals. The library is a crucial partner in planning and envisioning the future of preserving, using, even creating scholarly resources. So are the technology professionals. But in an analogy with building construction, they are the architect and contractor. The creation of archives, analytic tools, statistical analyses of aggregate data in humanities and social sciences is work only possible with the combined expertise of technical, professional, and scholarly personnel. . . . Modelling scholarship is an intellectual challenge, not a technical one. I cannot say this strongly or clearly enough.[29]

In contrast to much of the discourse of academic infrastructure and digital humanities, Drucker focuses on the scholarly challenge rather than on the technology or technology-induced visions. However, the terms on which this analogy is constructed reinforce specific roles, and the terms *contractor* and *architect* mark clear institutional positions. Will new institutional roles develop, and if so, will they blur the roles described by Drucker and the ACLS report? Along these lines, Christopher Blackwell and Gregory Crane call for institutional change:

> We need new institutions to provide access to the results of our work. Neither the libraries nor the publishers of the early twenty-first century serve the needs that emerge in this collection. While libraries may survive and indeed flourish as an institution, they will do so by subsuming and transforming the functions that we entrusted to publishers in print culture.[30]

It is true that both publishers and cultural heritage institutions are under considerable pressure and that functions will shift and develop over time, although often in directions we might not anticipate. When new generations of infrastructure are based on traditional infrastructures, we have to be sensitive to the complexities and changing dynamics of those traditional infrastructures. For example, there is an assumption in the above quote that providing access has been and remains a primary and unchanging need not only for libraries and publishers, but for any new institutions in this domain. But is access really the most productive or interesting way to think about the future of these institutions and contemporary stakeholder needs? Cultural heritage institutions as a model is thus not static, and if we are going to model tomorrow's research infrastructure on past or current infrastructure, we must do so critically and with a mind to what tomorrow's intellectual-material needs will be.

Model II: The Lack of a Humanities Infrastructure

The sense that traditional humanities has very little need of academic infrastructure is illustrated by the way funding is allocated for students in higher education in Sweden, where the price tag for humanities students is much lower than that for students in most other areas. Similarly, the humanities receives little funding for research infrastructure in most countries. In some cases, the humanities does not see itself as technological and retains a "pen and paper" conception of itself. At the same time, some members of the (digital) humanities community realize that needs may be changing:

> Despite a slow and uneven uptake of digital technology in some areas of the Arts and Humanities research, the discipline is no longer based on pen and paper. Specific individual needs of research that relies on the use of advanced technologies must be better understood and matched by a level of support that is already enjoyed by the scientists.[31]

Such reasoning to some extent reinforces the sense that basic humanities relies primarily on technologies such as pen and paper, which is by no means a new argument.[32] This construction shows the humanities as not only relatively free of technology but also hesitant about it or even Luddite.[33] This account also connects to the overall tendency of mainstream humanities to engage with the digital as a study object rather than as an interpretative tool or an expressive medium.

Given this view, the digital humanities often takes on the role of helping or educating the humanities, thus reinforcing the view of the humanities as nontechnological. Emphasizing slow uptake is a rhetorical strategy for demonstrating the infrastructural needs of the humanities and is commonly used by representatives of digital humanities centers:

> Equally important, digital humanities centers are key sites for bridging the daunting gap between new technology and humanities scholars, serving as the crosswalks between cyberinfrastructure and users, where scholars learn how to introduce into their research computational methods, encoding practices, and tools and where users of digital resources can be transformed into producers.[34]

Such rhetoric plays up the gap between humanists and technology, creating a problematic frame by discursively depicting humanists as technology novices and technology as something very complex. It implies that humanists need to learn and will have to be changed from users to producers, and that teaching them is the job of the digital humanities. Similarly, according to a website for a digital-humanities-related organization, "We show researchers and students with little knowledge of advanced computing how to use new technologies in their work."[35] These statements increase the gap between the humanists and technologies and impose an instrumental connection that does not acknowledge digital humanities work as an iterative intellectual and technological process.

More broadly, the view of basic humanities as having little or no significant infrastructure not only assumes a science- and technology-based idea of what makes up infrastructure but also imposes a pen-and-paper construction of the humanities. Pen and paper, while inherently communicative and collaborative, is also linked to the assumption that humanities scholarship is to a large extent a solitary endeavor (the individual scholar in his or her study):

> Humanities scholars often work alone without collaborators or assistants. In contrast to the cooperative efforts common in the sciences and social sciences, humanities scholarship is the result of solitary research and thought.[36]

As Anthony Grafton points out, most humanities research is not at all solitary, even though authorship is often attributed to one person.[37] One possible consequence of construing the humanities as lacking infrastructure and being a solitary enterprise is a greater tendency to adopt science and engineering models of academic infrastructure simply because there is nothing already there.

Model III: STEM Notions of Infrastructure

When a science, technology, engineering, and mathematics (STEM) framework is transferred to the humanities and social sciences, attempts occur to align specific STEM tool sets and technologies with the subject areas in question. The starting point is often the research material or the technology rather than the research question. We also need to distinguish between STEM-based infrastructure and STEM-based infrastructure as it is understood by the humanities. In particular, the humanities does not always seem to see the complexity or layering of STEM infrastructure and therefore runs the risk of basing infrastructural efforts on simplified models.

Big data is an example of such a domain being tackled by the humanities. Because of the assumed access to big data, humanists are expected to engage with it, as exemplified by a 2013 call for project proposals issued by the United Kingdom's Arts and Humanities Research Council.[38] Projects under the more costly funding strand

> would need to take a more in-depth approach to their proposed research. They could possibly include visualisations and analysis of big data, creation of new tools and workflows for big data, the assessment of use of high performance computers, creation of artworks and other objects with big data, and may generate new big data. These projects may involve greater collaboration with both academic and non-academic partners and within or between disciplines.
>
> [More generally, proposals should] produce innovative, collaborative projects that add value to the Digital Transformations theme, can potentially have a big impact in the Arts and Humanities, and also raise enthusiasm about the potential of big data to facilitate and support innovative research in the Arts and Humanities.[39]

On the one hand, this call is quite attractive in that it is open-ended, encourages exploratory work, and seeks innovative research in the arts and humanities. I would be delighted if the Swedish Research Council dared to propose calls of this type. On the other hand, though, there seems to be little substance to the conceptual foundation articulated in the call and the guidance document. The documents offer little intellectual rationale for why this investment would lead to innovative research or even why it is important. Why might such projects have a big impact? The expectations in relation to the more expensive projects (up to £600,000) seem almost naive, and there is little focus on the scholarly challenges or on a deep conceptual rationale.

Furthermore, the call is clearly based on a science model: the first paragraph of the guidance document states that some of the best-known examples of use of big data come from the sciences. The document gives statistics from the Large Hadron Collider, which is said to produce 15 petabytes of data every year and points out that a grid consisting of 140 centers in more than 35 countries analyzes these data.[40] The call, however, contains very little discussion of what the collider does in terms of facilitating research or tackling research challenges. It gives corresponding numbers for other humanities-like datasets: the George W. Bush e-mail archive, for example, consists of 200 million e-mails (80 terabytes).[41] But what, if anything, do these statistics mean?

The call also fails to discuss the perceived objectivity of data or relevant work done in science and technology studies on data. Lisa Gitelman and Virginia Jackson remind us that objectivity, as situated and historically specific, is the result of "conditions of inquiry, conditions that are at once material, social, and ethical."[42] Despite the importance of encouraging exploratory work and engagement with technology, the call has significant weaknesses that come from a combination of starting out with the material, assuming a science model (through a humanities lens), failing to focus on research challenges, and failing to incorporate the critical modality that we associate with the humanities. This is where the digital humanities and the humanities more generally should be involved in discussions with funding agencies, making sure to connect scholarly needs with infrastructure.

Grid computing exemplifies starting from technology rather than the material or data.[43] Questions asked in this context may include: What can grid computing do for the humanities? What large humanities datasets are particularly suitable for grid computing applications? The gap between high-performance computing (HPC) perspectives on grid computing and humanities-based research issues and questions can be very large, and facilitating meetings between the two requires creating a common discursive space and allowing time for dialogue. A good example of deep thinking about this process is provided by "Mind the Gap," a report arguing that the main gap between HPC and research in the humanities relates to research culture and support:

> On the one hand we have to find ways of training and preparing humanities research teams to be able to imagine using existing HPC facilities, and on the other we have to develop the ability of HPC consortia to be able to reach out and support.[44]

The report recommends that humanists become involved early in the process (as well as in management and decision making). A balance must clearly be struck between discipline- and technology-driven issues and questions, and finding this common ground is not trivial. We also need to acknowledge that technology competence can be very diverse, research-intensive, and complex. Since the discourse of research infrastructure tends to take place at an aggregate level in relation to complex and internally diverse entities such as the humanities or science and engineering, real, grounded encounters can be particularly valuable.

On a more abstract level, concerns arise about aligning academic infrastructure as a project with the humanities and social sciences, as the ACLS report outlines:

> Humanities scholars and social scientists will require similar facilities but, obviously, not exactly the same ones: "grids of computational centers" are needed in the humanities and social sciences, but they will have to be staffed with different kinds of subject-area experts; comprehensive and well-curated libraries of digital objects will certainly be needed, but the objects themselves will be different from those used in the sciences; software toolkits for projects involving data-mining and data-visualization could be shared across the sciences, humanities, and social sciences, but only up to the point where the nature of the data begins to shape the nature of the tools. Science and engineering have made great strides in using information technology to understand and shape the world around us. This report is focused on how these same technologies could help advance the study and interpretation of the vastly more messy and idiosyncratic realm of human experience.[45]

Again here, there is a risk of adopting a science- and engineering-based model for humanities infrastructure in such a way that it significantly constrains and shapes possible research enterprises and directions. Is it possible to discern "the point where the nature of the data begins to shape the nature of the tools"? If so, that point might occur very early, and more may be at play here than the nature of the data. The alignment described in the ACLS report is simply not feasible. As Jonathan Sterne notes, "Disciplines never fully constitute their objects; they fight over them."[46] He argues that these fights are partly what make disciplines maintain their intellectual vibrancy. If the range of data and the study objects are in question, it may be difficult to "process" data up to a certain point and to use generic tools without early involvement from researchers. Furthermore, as Geoffrey Bowker contends, any data would already be part of the information and knowledge infrastructure that is relevant to knowledge production and the creation of tools and technology:

> Information infrastructures such as databases should be read both discursively and materially; they are a site of political and ethical as well as technical work; and . . . there can be no a priori attribution of a given question to the technical or the political realms.[47]

Moreover, the ACLS report seems to advocate a notion of infrastructure very much concerned with incorporating as much data (basically the entirety of our cultural heritage) as possible. Asks Andrew Prescott,

> Is the vision of large quantities of university-created digital content requiring central curation still the most pressing issue? Isn't this a vision more appropriate to 1995?[48]

Academic infrastructure is intertwined with various institutional, social, cultural, and historical layers inside and outside the disciplines themselves. This is the realpolitik of digital humanities. Because research infrastructure often but not necessarily supports interdisciplinary work, it seems particularly important to situate data structures, standards, technologies, knowledge structures, and tools in a broad epistemological context. This is even more important given that infrastructures have a tendency to become invisible over time and that scalability is a commonly assigned property of research infrastructure.[49]

There is a risk that external pressure on the humanities, including the digital humanities, will lead to a positivist, results-driven approach. Here the need to provide motivation for funding agencies and university administration unsurprisingly plays an important role, as Melissa Terras points out:

> I'd just like to chip in and say this is what the funding councils are calling "Evidence of Value"—and are asking us to show evidence for the value of digital humanities research. Its important, as funding cuts in this area (such as the withdrawal of funds for the AHDS) are based on the perceived lack of evidence of value. Unless we can articulate, as a community, the better/faster/more nature of digital, we will struggle even harder for funding in years to come.[50]

Terras's use of *better/faster/more* suggests a view of the digital humanities and associated infrastructure that is in line with the positivist discourse of science and technology-driven research infrastructure. Terras's short, informal statement does not provide arguments that bring in research issues or current disciplinary challenges, which would seem indicative of the methodological and technological focus of traditional humanities computing. A tendency exists to fail to connect humanities infrastructure to research issues, and there is a substantial risk that humanities infrastructure becomes an issue of data and funding rather than research and conceptual grounding.

Implications

At the same time that external pressures push us to specify infrastructural needs for the humanities, humanities-based interest in academic infrastructure and the digital is growing. Furthermore, the ways that we articulate and implement academic infrastructure for the humanities have strong implications. What happens if we fail to explore multiple visions, focus only on digitizing existing infrastructure, or let the agenda be set through a technological focus or a model strongly based in the sciences?

An overly narrow vision of academic infrastructure will limit the players and participants to those who match the epistemologies embedded in the new infrastructures. Similarly, a singular focus on extending current infrastructure may result in a kind of epistemological conservatism that would foreclose potential new ways of knowing and legitimizing knowledge. And allowing a science- and technology-inspired model to drive the agenda could result in academic infrastructure for the humanities without a strong grounding in the disciplines, humanistic knowledge production, or the needs and interests of the humanities.

There is also the risk of "epistemic double-binds,"[51] where humanities researchers who want to use the new technologies are caught between the commitments of their academic disciplines and those of engineering, computer science, and science more broadly. Matt Ratto cites an example from computer-supported visualization and modeling in classical archaeology: three groups of scholars and scientists—for different reasons grounded in different epistemic commitments—rejected a project where an immersive 3-D environment was used to question the traditional understanding of the use of terra-cotta materials in a particular form of pre-Roman temple.

> Acknowledging these commitments can help us develop appropriate technologies that help rather than hinder existing research practice, add a layer of reflexivity to researchers' choices and decisions, and ultimately, facilitate productive cross-disciplinary collaboration.[52]

Acknowledging and managing different sets of epistemic commitments is important to big digital humanities, and Ratto's work more generally helps explain why certain practices and modes of expressions meet with resistance in different disciplinary contexts.

Given the infrastructural push and the considerable interest in establishing new initiatives for the digital humanities, a window of opportunity is currently open for articulating and implementing a humanities-based notion of infrastructure. This opportunity needs to be combined with a critical engagement to establish good practice, explore possible models, and have an infrastructural dialogue across the humanities. Building infrastructural platforms is partly a matter of creating alliances and working with other institutions. Libraries and humanities centers would seem to constitute important potential partners. Another possibility is work between other intersectional areas within or outside the humanities, such as environmental humanities, ethnic studies, and urban humanities. The only way such alliances can work over time is if the fields in question share a sentiment, a conceptual grounding, and a willingness to negotiate.

Sketching Out an Alternative Model

A critical factor for creating humanities infrastructure involves connecting the conceptual level of infrastructures—the underlying ideas—with actual infrastructure in a way that is not too reductive. Doing so can be accomplished using a framework that incorporates three levels of description and analysis. This model draws on existing infrastructure and sees STEM as a possible infrastructural partner, but in contrast to the models discussed earlier, it acknowledges the need for a new conception of humanities infrastructure and the importance of connecting humanistic thinking to material configurations. The model presented here partly overlaps with the notion of intellectual middleware (chapter 3), but is focused on infrastructure and a design perspective.

The first level in this model, conceptual infrastructure, refers to the underlying ideas and visions behind an infrastructural project. Above this conceptual level is the level of design principles, which connect the ideational level with material academic infrastructure. The design principles provide a means of discussing and articulating infrastructural projects without getting caught up in only detailed infrastructure or the abstract visions typical of the discourse on academic infrastructure. The third level is the surface—the actual, material infrastructure.

In this way, actual infrastructure—including space, technology, digital platforms, encoding systems, support and expert functions, research facilities, and low-level material installations—can be implemented with the support of the immediate level of design principles, which, in turn, draw on the level of conceptual infrastructure below. While this model may seem overly ambitious for small installations and for conventionalized infrastructure, such as a traditional classroom intended to be used in a default way or a standard query system for a research database, it can be quite useful when thinking about learning platforms, research spaces, or new ideas for access to digital materials. It encourages us to be clear about the conceptual underpinnings and epistemic scope and to think carefully about how they can be translated into design principles and operationalized in relation to existing infrastructure and planned academic infrastructure.

If successful, such a process would help us articulate our requirements, visions, and ideas in a broad, contextualized sense as well as in relation to conceptual issues and physical and digital implementation. Furthermore, it may help us create an interaction point for people from the enterprise (department, university administration, users) and for people involved in the creation of new infrastructure and space (architects, hardware and software specialists, contractors, property owners, and sometimes also funding agencies).

Arriving at a conceptual foundation and implementation is often a complex and exploratory process, and it can take many possible paths. In practice, the flow will be iterative, new space and infrastructure can never be built without constraints imposed by existing systems, architecture, and infrastructure as well as existing funding regimes and policies at the administrative level. Such constraints and possibilities need to be presented and negotiated throughout the process. To illustrate this three-layered structure, I use HUMlab at Umeå University as a case study. This is a lab-based example, which means that material space is more important than would be the case for a digital platform and that we are concerned with a specific institutional setup and context (a relatively well-funded comprehensive university in the North of Sweden). However, much of the principal thinking would apply across different types of infrastructures.

HUMlab is a meeting place for the humanities, culture, and information technology and came into being the late 1990s. This meeting place is enacted through physical and digital spaces, technology, and programming as well as through people and through collaborating extensively inside and outside the university. The operation currently incorporates a series of joined lab spaces on the main campus of Umeå University as well as a newer lab space (HUMlab-X) on the Umeå Arts Campus. HUMlab has had a long engagement with virtual worlds, social media, and different kinds of digital environments, including a series of digital platforms built on a concept called faceted browsing. Activist engagement and regional outreach have always been important, but the Arts Campus location has made it possible to scale up this broader engagement.

Conceptual Infrastructure

A set of conceptual underpinnings has shaped HUMlab's emerging infrastructure from the beginning, although some of them may not have been articulated until quite late in the process. Other parts of the conceptual foundation have developed and changed over the years.

Meeting place. The notion of a meeting place is central to HUMlab as an idea and space and was clearly articulated in early vision documents as well as in practice. The design principles included translucence (encouraging contact and having a sense of what other people are working on), flexibility (supporting many different kinds of meetings and technological platforms), and intensity (a space and endeavor that attracts engagement and interest). HUMlab has plenty of social spaces (both inside and outside the labs proper), meeting tables, an "outward" design that makes many computer screens visible to others, many large screens, coffee (often free), and a range of software, hardware, expertise, and activities that attract people from different parts of the university and from outside it. The lab is also available to users twenty-four hours a day every day.

A well-functioning lab space can help create a platform for managing and supporting academic infrastructure in that a range of competencies and skill sets is always available, as is (ideally) a willingness to help and share knowledge. The sense of meeting place extends outside the physical lab space, and there are a strong dispersed community, ongoing distributed work, and shared datasets, materials, and tool development. Practices such as curatorship and empowerment channel the power of this infrastructure.

Multiple modes of engagement. Another conceptual and epistemic baseline for HUMlab is the interest in multiple modes of engagement with information technology and the digital. The lab has been set up to support work with technology as a tool, an object of study, and an expressive medium—essentially the description of big digital humanities laid out in chapter 3. Although there was no early explicit commitment to these particular modes of engagement when HUMlab was started, there was an openness and flexibility (both in terms of technology and content) that allowed for very different kinds of projects and activities. Much of the early inspiration came from open-ended educational projects. Over the years, cumulative practice and reflection on this practice—also in relation to other international initiatives—resulted in a model of modes of engagement that is part of the conceptual infrastructure of the lab.

This commitment to a range of different kinds of engagement has very direct implications for design and infrastructure. For example, a multiple-mode focus is not compatible with a traditionally instrumental computer lab setup because the space needs to work for activities such as seminars and meetings and must relate to various study objects (digital and nondigital). These elements are also important to bring in researchers and students from different disciplines, not only because familiar elements may be attractive but also because they perform basic epistemic functions such as allowing intellectual exchange and visual enactment of materials.

A commitment to multiple modes of engagement also calls for a varied technological setup, and HUMlab offers a wide range of technologies for analytical work, visualization, creative work, screenings, and physical computing. The downside may be that it becomes more difficult to allocate substantial resources to single areas (as in a specialized lab environment). More generally, the humanities often seems to need a more diversified and multiplex infrastructure than the kind of science and engineering infrastructure described in policy and vision documents. This a necessity for big digital humanities.

Multiple perspectives and rich context. The humanities provides rich cultural and historical context as well as multiple viewpoints and critical perspectives. But visualization technologies and setups often are not designed for such richness, and the humanities needs infrastructure that does not promote only single viewpoints. A simple example would be the single-screen model that prevails in most university spaces. Here the primary associated design principle is multiplexity, and the most obvious implementation would be the screenscape in one part of HUMlab and the underlying technological infrastructure. This screen and interaction space (with eleven screens) has different functions in relation to different projects, activities, and modes of engagement, but the underlying principle is to support critical discussion based on heterogeneity and contextual depth. Another relevant installation consists of an angled screen setup (two screens set at an angle) in what could have been a traditional cinematic setup with a single screen, but is now an environment where one screen can be used to "speak to" or critique the content on the other screen. Imagine for example an immersive 3-D installation being flanked by a critical analysis of the underlying ontology. More generally, the mixed setup of the lab caters to multiple perspectives and epistemic traditions (for example, through different screen configurations, a range of software and digital platforms, artistic installations, physical making stations, tables, and integrated performance space). The implemented infrastructure is intended to stimulate ideas, experiments, and uses, and in this sense the infrastructure is just the beginning.

Design Principles

One way of approaching an infrastructure such as HUMlab in a more structural and systemic manner is to look at how the infrastructure has been designed and implemented in relation to the ideational underpinning and to identify overarching design principles. A number of central design principles emerged in the course of the development of HUMlab. While these principles are situated in a specific context, they also have some more general applicability. These design principles can, in turn, be related to the level of conceptual infrastructure.

Design principles are a way of connecting the ideational level with material infrastructure and of facilitating a means of discussing and articulating infrastructural projects without getting caught up in only detailed infrastructure or the abstract visions typical of the discourse on academic infrastructure. The principles are anchored on both these levels. Design principles can be seen as a design-driven operationalization of intellectual middleware as discussed in chapter 3.

Here I discuss four suggested design principles for HUMlab as an infrastructural project: translucence, flexibility, multiplexity, and intensity. While HUMlab had other design principles as well and while these have changed over time, they suggest an anchored and systemic-level foundation for HUMlab as infrastructure and illustrate how infrastructure for big digital humanities can be conceived and implemented. All the design principles discussed below also relate to distributed environments.

Translucence

Translucence has been an important principle in designing the space and operation of HUMlab. This principle relates directly to the digital humanities as a meeting place (conceptual infrastructure), and the basic idea is that it is important to see what is going on in the lab while not resorting to having one large and totally open space. In optics, translucent materials allow light to pass through them diffusely. The constraints and affordances are not only visual, of course: for example, an awareness of whether one can be overheard by other people is an important factor. In a studio (or other) environment, this translates to having a space that that has divisions and separations that allow subspaces to maintain spatial, auditory, and conceptual integrity (to different degrees) at the same time that a sense of what is going on in other parts of the space is retained. This affects possible interactions in several ways.[53] One of these ways is that participants have access to concurrent activities, processes, and dialogues. For example, when the lab or a project is presented to a visiting delegation in the inner glass room, there is a good visual sense of activities and people outside the room. Similarly, people outside this room have a sense of what goes on inside (and will, for example, be prepared to act when the delegation prepares to leave the inner room). Paul Dourish and Sara Bly's notion of awareness and their porthole system are based on a similar idea, although they emphasize the distributed nature of the system:

> Awareness involves knowing who is "around," what activities are occurring, who is talking with whom; it provides a view of one another in the daily work environments. Awareness may lead to informal interactions, spontaneous connections, and the development of shared cultures—all important aspects of maintaining working relationships which are denied to groups distributed across multiple sites.[54]

HUMlab takes as its point of departure the organization of collaborations across physical-digital boundaries. Seminars, for example, primarily take place in the physical space, but they are almost always streamed live, and there is often a Twitter channel for questions. HUMlab-tagged tweets appear on a secondary screen in the physical space. For workshops and conferences, remote participants are often "beamed in" on separate large screens, giving them individual presence. A more recent development has been to think carefully about the feedback given to remote participants and about their perspective. We therefore use extra cameras to give them multiple points of view and to allow them to see themselves and other remote participants. Designing for awareness and translucence is also quite important in physical space, and many current spaces are "mixed."

In the physical lab, screens (both public and semiprivate) play an important role in representing ongoing work and in bringing in external worlds and materials (portholes). Both HUMlab on the main campus and HUMlab-X on the Arts Campus have large display walls, and they can be connected via cameras, thus creating human-sized digital portholes between the labs. In both labs, many simultaneous activities can take place in such a way that there is a sense of what is going on in other parts of the lab, but there is also separation, thus enabling a sense of copresence and collocation without unnecessary disturbance. Moreover, this arrangement opens up space more generally and helps coordinate collaboration. Translucence is supported through many separate, semiprivate sections as well as through the way screens are positioned to allow a sense of ongoing work. The translucent nature of dividers (e.g., half-height bookcases, hanging absorbents, pillars, screens, and an aquarium) allows dialogue, copresence and some overhearing between sections.

Done correctly, an appropriate balance can be maintained between seeing and not seeing, between collaborations and individual work, and between mutual engagement and individual intensity. With a platform such as HUMlab, it has been critical to create opportunities for continuously connecting these extremes.

Flexibility

Flexibility is connected to the digital humanities as a meeting place and to a multiple-mode engagement with the digital (conceptual infrastructure). A wider range of activities and initiatives can be supported by allowing flexible use of an infrastructural resource such as HUMlab. Work on the design of learning environments and studio spaces often emphasizes flexibility.[55] Simple examples would include the ease of reconfiguring the space and changing furniture around, allowing many different kinds of activities, flexible distribution of media, and a multiplex technical implementation. In short, a flexible setup allows more change in pedagogical, scholarly, and technological practices.

A fixed setup, conversely, has a stronger investment in a particular model or framework.[56] A tension arises between what is flexible and what is fixed, and total flexibility is probably not possible because decisions will always constrain the level of flexibility. A totally flexible space would probably have to be a compromise. Also, some degree of fixedness can be part of good design practice and of deliberate choices to encourage certain kinds of use and activities. In the case of HUMlab and probably many other similar environments, a rather delicate balance exists between flexibility and fixedness. Some of the fixedness comes from a set of basic underlying ideas about what a space is and how it should be used and can be seen as part of the conceptual infrastructure.

In some of the virtual spaces associated with HUMlab, similar tensions can be observed. For example, an art installation and artist (with assumptions of exhibition and controlled space) coexisted in the same Second Life space as people who are continuously doing experimental building, and who fly through the asserted space of the exhibition with, for example, spaceships. Negotiation and curation are often needed to resolve these clashes. More generally, flexibility is a relevant category for analyzing and creating digital environments. Maximum configurability and general access are often thought-after properties in digital humanities systems and tools. However, superficial flexibility can conceal the hard-coded epistemic, aesthetic, and technological fixity that is often part of such systems. Furthermore, interpretative tools often need to be specific as well as flexible.

Multiplexity

Multiplexity is a parameter that interrelates with translucence and flexibility and that goes back to the investment in multiplex perspectives and rich context (conceptual infrastructure). The humanities, richly engaged with a multiperspective, complex, and multilevel subject matter, needs an academic infrastructure that supports these multiple perspectives, complex datasets, and heterogeneous contexts. In HUMlab, multiplexity in this sense is facilitated in particular through the screenscape in one part of the lab. It allows simultaneous engagement with many types of materials, ideas, and perspectives through the screens, interaction technology, sensor technology, and audio. Furthermore, multiple screens can have a more empowering function than single screens. Where there is just one main screen, it is traditionally controlled by a teacher, who thus holds all power over how that screen is used. With many screens, as in HUMlab's screenscape, that control can be held by a single user or by many, and in either case, many screens can be used at the same time. A fundamental difference exists between, one the hand, having eleven slides presented on eleven screens in the space and moving among these slides (and screens) physically in the lab and, on the other hand, doing a series of eleven slides on one screen. The multiplexity of this system is not only dependent on the physical screens, but also on the software layer and on digitally based content.

Other related infrastructural projects in HUMlab are more wholly software-based. Multiplexity is a central design principle for the faceted browsing system developed in HUMlab, which enables navigation of complex data sets. This web-based system allows users to select and show many facets (variables) at the same time. The resultant view or views depends on the selection of facets. The facets are displayed in the web interface, which makes live interaction with complex data sets possible without losing track of the complexity and heterogeneity of the material.

HUMlab also supports multiplexity through the many different kinds of meeting spaces, technological implements, and workplaces in the studio space and through digitally supported spaces. The mix of workstation setups, couches, private nooks, glassed rooms, almost insular furniture, and different types of studio spaces is a critical component for the operation. The fact that the two main labs are quite different (although built using similar design principles and conceptual foundations) is a clear asset. However, they have also been shaped and inflected by the hyperlocal context and conditioning. Another factor that plays into the difference between HUMlab and HUMlab-X is the historicity of the spaces. HUMlab was built in the early 2000s in an old exam hall below the university library, quite literally shaped by the rotunda outside the library, with alcoves adding to the complexity of the space. HUMlab-X, in contrast, was built around 2012 in a complex where new structures were juxtaposed with repurposed industrial space. In some ways, allowing multiplexity in the new space, which had to be created from scratch, proved more difficult than in the old one.

In addition, the technology setup is multiplex in that it includes a variety of technologies, systems, and software. Students commonly give this varied setup as an important reason for working and studying in HUMlab. Most technology-rich labs at the university are either generic (basically providing browsing, word processing, and printing) or program- or department-specific (and highly restricted, such as 3-D–modeling labs in the computer science department). One idea underlying HUMlab is that a varied technological setup can facilitate exploration and many different types of activities and crossover effects.

Intensity

Intensity involves the importance of having infrastructure that is not too linear, orderly, or sterile—that is, academic infrastructure that stimulates engagement. This is an important property of digital humanities as a meeting place (conceptual infrastructure).

William Mitchell has discussed the importance of supporting intense and exciting experiences through designing appropriate spaces. One key parameter mentioned by Mitchell is variation and diversity (which basically relates to all the design principles discussed earlier).[57] It is, of course, impossible to pinpoint exactly what combination of features gives a space such qualities, but nonsterile and heterogeneous spaces seem more likely to evoke this kind of sentiment, and a sense of energy can be derived from having many (different) people share the same space, from ongoing creative work, from a sense of process, and from a culture that supports collaboration, community, and dialogue. Although I focus on physical space, intensity is also a property of distributed environments and media ecologies.

Architecture is set up around a typology of spaces, and a standard type for higher education is the classroom. Traditional classrooms tend to have a fairly low degree of intensity. They do not normally reflect ongoing work to a large degree and tend to be nondescript and standard. When the class is over, the norm is typically and understandably that the room should be left tidy and organized (and thus fairly devoid of rich context). Traditional learning spaces are also often horizontal in the sense that floors and ceilings are rarely used beyond their obvious core functions; they are not seen as important design elements in a nonlinear space.

Another architectural type of space is the lab, which can have many different configurations. Labs associated with the domains of digital media, visualization, and associated methodology tend to appear somewhat sterile, particularly because they are large, rectangular, and fairly monofunctional. They are often organized around specific sets of equipment such as visualization walls. Studio spaces, conversely, typically reflect ongoing processes and are hence more contextual and untidy. As Daniel Fällman stresses,

> While each and every piece of among the multitude of material objects that appear in a progressive design studio seldom by itself has a strong or even explicit link to an aspect of the project at hand, they as a collection seem to conspire to create the rich environment needed to stimulate creativity and create novel ideas.[58]

Design studios often contain sketches and prototypes that provide a sense of process as well as points of display and discussion. Daniel Buren similarly emphasizes how artistic studio spaces can contain a collection of visible materials that creates a sense and understanding of process.[59] As a set of disciplines, the humanities are much concerned with rich historical and cultural context, which would seem to be well in line with a highly contextual space. If this space is also flexible, it may allow for shifting contextual landscapes (for example, through dynamic screens) as well as a more static or semistatic context.[60]

People are the most important reason why any space or digital platform is experienced as being intense and engaging—for example, through flows of people gathering for project meetings and other activities or for doing their own work as well as through a constant influx of new people such as visiting postdoctoral fellows and guest speakers. Most digital humanities operations and spaces will benefit from including undergraduate and graduate students, which is probably one of the best ways to enable intense and productive work.

Exciting exchanges of ideas also come from careful programming, which often both depends on and enables active space. Programming for intensity can involve facilitating many simultaneous activities, or condensing time by asking everyone interested to be present for a couple of hours every week on a given day. Intensity is not a constant and it is important to give time and space for different paces, processes, and work practices.

Furthermore, integration of external materials and distributed presence is important in this context. Physical elements can clearly play a significant role here—HUMlab has a neon sign outside the lab, beanbags, inviting couches and tables for meetings and coffee drinking, tall immersive couches for individual work, pictorial mats, an oriental rug, a pink lamp, designer wallpaper, whiteboards, plants and a plant wall, and a large aquarium. These elements can be just as critical as computer workstations and visualization walls in supporting a collaborative, engaging technology-rich environment, but their meaningfulness is also contextual and situational. Beanbags and designer couches will not automatically produce an attractive studio space.

Material Infrastructure: A Screenscape Further Explored

Lev Manovich has explained how having access to the visualization environment HIperSpace at CALIT2 at the University of California at San Diego has made new ideas or directions possible:

> HIperSpace is the reason why I am able to think of being able to map and analyze global cultural patterns in detail. I would not ever think about it if I just worked on my laptop screen.[61]

While facilities such as HIperSpace and HUMlab are very flexible and generate ideas, uses, and experiments beyond what could be envisioned at the start, users and uses are also constrained by the way these infrastructures have been conceived and implemented. That is part of the conceptual infrastructure. HIperSpace is a very large tiled display made up of many small screens—basically a large rectangular screen with internal boundaries caused by the frames of the individual screens. It is the front end of a large computer resource, an optiputer, and the main overarching goal is to "examine a 'future' in which networking is no longer a bottleneck to local, regional, national and international computing."[62] The boundaries are seen as eventually becoming reduced and perhaps disappearing altogether, thus creating one large seamless display. This is not just a technological development but an aesthetic-technological ideal that strongly suggests that one screen is better than many frames making up a large screen.

HUMlab, conversely, has invested in allowing both big display walls and smaller visually distinct screens. The frames of the screens are thus quite important, as is the positioning of individual screens at the periphery of a large space. On a very large screen, such as the HIperSpace installation, a number of different materials, sources, and windows can be displayed, so the individual bits will be framed on the screen, but this framing is internal to the screen. This relates to what Anne Friedberg calls "multiplex frames" and Manovich's earlier discussion of computer windows and is rather different from having separate screens with "heavy" frames.[63] This difference is equivalent to someone working on a laptop screen showing a word processor window and a web browser window (showing a secondary source) versus someone working on a laptop showing only a word processing document while a web browser appears on a separate tablet computer. This change is more significant than just organizing the "same" content differently; it is about the two arrangements affording different kinds of interactions regarding and relations to what is inside the computer/s.

A somewhat related paradigm for visualization is virtual reality (an earlier generation of privileged infrastructure), which often tries to remove the frame altogether:

> The visual (and aural and haptic) displays that immerse the user in the virtual world and that block out contradictory sensory impressions from the real world.[64]

In some ways, the distributed screenscape of HUMlab is the opposite of such virtual reality manifestations. In HUMlab, sensory impressions from the "real" world are quite important, and the screens are integrated in a lively studio environment, potentially making the screens less "aggressive" than in many other visualization environments.[65]

This part of HUMlab borrows elements from visualization spaces as well as from traditional seminar, studio, and exhibition spaces, and the collaborative affordances (whether or not in relation to technology) are quite important. In addition, the screens have their own identity and framing. The epistemological stance thus differs radically from that of many virtual reality environments where the users, as Dan Sandin, coinventor of the CAVE (Cave

Automatic Virtual Environment), points out, "in a sense, view things from inside the scene."[66] In other words, there is arguably no frame:

> There would be no screen between the user and the information and no way for the user to step back and contemplate the screen at a distance, because she would be wearing the screens as eyepieces that completely covered her field of view.[67]

This is reminiscent of the discourse surrounding recent products such as 3-D TV sets and the Oculus Rift headset, which is said to allow one to "seamlessly look around the virtual world just as you would in real life."[68] In contrast, HUMlab's screenscape installation seeks to bring together multiplex frames (digital screens that contain separate elements such as windows) and multiple digital screens in a held-together screenscape. Each screen can be run individually in the screenscape, be part of a large "computer desktop," or be part of a video-signal level desktop or extended space (which can include video, computer, and other sources). The screenscape as a whole is situated in a large studio space with a seminar table in the middle of the room, supporting a range of practices and uses—traditional seminars (using no or little technology), individual researchers using their workstations with one or several screens, research groups using the large high-resolution touch screen collaboratively and in a distributed fashion with remote datasets and researchers, students using three screens to discuss different solutions to an assigned problem, and even large interactive art installations using screens, sensor technology, and spatial audio.

As digitized material becomes increasingly available, a screenscape can help philologists and art historians display and interact with manuscript pages or pictures. Researchers in environmental archeology can pull together large datasets, diverse materials, and visualized data models and use a large, high-resolution screen to work with the data model (zooming, modifying, interrelating the model with data sources), locally or together with remote research centers. Site-specific art installations can be created in the space. Students who have built virtual exhibitions in Unity can show their individual or their group's slices of their virtual world on screens. Events such as indie game evenings can use the screens to allow people to interact with a range of games, and in an associated presentation, individual games can be moved to the large screen and juxtaposed as part of a comparative and analytical process. Other events may bring in remote researchers through different types of virtual environments, Skype sessions, and visualized datasets. Thematic screenings of films can be facilitated. An upcoming seminar with an international guest speaker can be contextualized through a curated selection of images, video clips, texts, and web pages.

More generally, complex scholarly environments for humanistic research can bring together analytical tools, distributed materials, representations, and ways to tackle central research challenges in a studio space as well as in associated online environments. One example is a research project that explores the Virgin Mary as a role model in medieval Sweden through a multiple-place installation built on experience and a preromantic sense of aesthetics.[69]

An interesting interrelation exists between the humanities and technology-supported visualization and representation, and the associated academic infrastructure comes with certain epistemic commitments. However, uses also grow from implementation and experimentation. Multiplexity and framing are critical factors in the conceptual infrastructure associated with the screenscape installation in HUMlab. HUMlab differs from virtual reality manifestations where there is ideally no frame (from the inside) and from installations such as the HIperWall (basically very large multiplex frames). Friedberg suggests a taxonomy of variables based mainly on a cinematic perspective, but her examples are limited to cinematic representations (such as Charles and Ray Eames's *Glimpses of the USA* exhibition at the 1959 Moscow World's Fair). Friedberg's discussion of computer screens seems to suggest a one-screen (multiplex frame) paradigm:

> The Windows interface is a postcinematic visual system, but the viewer-turned-user remains in front of (vorstellen) a perpendicular frame.[70]

This view is challenged by the increased use of many linked but individual screens (available on Macintoshes from the late 1980s and on Windows since the mid-1990s). Beatriz Colomina's analysis of the Eameses' multimedia architecture shows how separate video screens, although not one screenscape in a technical sense, can create a thematic and performative whole.[71] With seven enormous screens and seven individual images per screen plus one final image, *Glimpses of the USA* included a total of fifty images. They were presented in thematic bursts in a highly coordinated and very carefully planned installation. Although this arrangement does not make the individual frames visually multiplex at any given time, frame-internal multiplexity is achieved temporally.

The HUMlab setup explores the importance of having multiple screens and multiplex frames at the same time and how it relates to the essence of the humanities: rich cultural and historical context, heterogeneous qualitative and quantitative materials, different modes of representation and presentation, shared presence, and multiplex perspectives. Multiple screen environments of this type are rare, and HUMlab exemplifies how the humanities can marry a conceptual foundation (an idea) with a technological implementation in a way that is not very likely to happen elsewhere.

Nevertheless, while screens can be seen as interactive surfaces that serve as interfaces to computational worlds and bring in nonvisual modalities such as audio and touch, these display solutions exemplify a visual bias that is common in the digital humanities and research infrastructure. One way of counteracting this bias is to actively engage infrastructurally with other modalities. HUMlab is also investing in new screen- and performance-based experiments, partly because of ongoing research on screen infrastructure, including a tripartite display wall that shares space with a church organ.

This installation draws on much of the rationale for multiplex screens, but it is one screen (built by modules), and the three parts are demarcated by the shape of the display. The screen's triangular shape is partly inspired by the triptych form commonly associated with early Christian art and altarpieces as well as with Northern Renaissance painting.[72] A triptych screen allows experimentation with center and periphery in a way that cannot be done on a regular rectangular screen. When bringing in remote participants, for example, active speakers can appear on the main part of the screen while "silent" speakers can appear on the side parts. Also, the setup supports three-part storytelling, with, for example, the side parts supporting the main narrative.[73] If immersive virtual environments were the antithesis of the eleven-screen screenscape, the corresponding frame of reference for the triptych screen would probably be large-scale cinematic display walls.

An Infrastructural Agenda for Big Digital Humanities

Big digital humanities, with its multiple-mode engagement with the digital and interest in serving as a meeting place, seems to align well with the infrastructure turn. Building academic infrastructure is partly a matter of channeling resources, and the digital humanities can offer a platform for pulling together technological, intellectual, and personnel resources. Such platforms are material, whether mostly physical or mostly digital, and their materiality matters. If they start out from a humanistic sensibility and intellectual challenges as well as from technological engagement, then they can enable, stimulate, and enact the humanities as a scholarly and educational endeavor. They have to be critical in the sense of embedding critical perspectives and interpretative capacity, but also in the sense of enacting critical perspectives on themselves, including environmental and equality dimensions.

This endeavor obviously cannot succeed without people, and infrastructure constitutes more than just devices and cables. Postdoctoral programs, residency programs, technological expertise, methodology workshops, teams of doctoral students, and high-quality support can be as important as technology. Whether such human infrastructure can be packaged together with the technology is a matter of the framing of infrastructure and funding agency constraints. However, provisions must be made for such costs within a given initiative or project. In some cases, universities can provide such resources as matching funding. In other cases, it might be worthwhile to package infrastructure as one part of a larger bid that includes, for example, residency programs and high-level technology support as well as the infrastructure proper.

Since infrastructure is so institutionally, culturally, and politically embedded, discussions of academic infrastructure necessarily tend to be fairly strategic. But offering a more nuanced and multilevel argument for infrastructure enables us both to engage with building infrastructure and to think carefully about the conceptual underpinnings. What is the intellectual rationale for having this type of infrastructure? Why should proposed infrastructures make us excited as scholars, educators, and students? Do we even need such infrastructure? What is the environmental impact? Does humanities infrastructure only relate to humanities, or would it make sense to think about infrastructural platforms more broadly and work with other areas?

One advantage of thinking of digital humanities labs as infrastructural platforms instead of focusing on more specific instrumentation or operations is that labs can be more versatile and can accommodate a range of technologies, groups, and uses. This strategy also makes it easier to include components that can be important to the humanities but that may be difficult to immediately classify as infrastructure. Simple examples include a seminar table, cheap technology, flexible workshop space, or new methodologies for digitization. It is increasingly likely that the diverse infrastructural repertoire of the humanities will include layers of distributed resources, physical computing devices, and material sites for the purpose of play, learning, research, collaborative work, individual projects, and exchange within and outside the humanities. Such infrastructure must have an ideational grounding, be maximally available, and support education and research in the humanities. In some cases, it might be advantageous to also have strategic collaboration with existing infrastructure such as libraries and humanities centers or with platforms such as environmental humanities and urban humanities.

Academic infrastructure is about material installations, people, staffing, programming, and ideas. Material infrastructure ranges from mostly physical to mostly digital and will almost inevitably play out in digital and physical spheres at the same time. This said, we need to acknowledge the considerable difference between a digital humanities operation centered around a lab or center and an infrastructure that consists mostly of databases, digital tools, and web services. Digital humanities labs can be very useful as an infrastructural platform, particularly if they are broadly conceived, technologically experimental, and intellectually heterogeneous. They allow integration of many different resources (physical, digital, and intellectual). Labs (or studios) do not have to be large, heavily technological spaces, and some of the most convincing operations, like the Transcriptions Center at University of California at Santa Barbara, are fairly small-scale with high intensity. This does not mean, of course, that the physical lab or studio is the only possible model.

Alternative models include EU-funded infrastructures such as Dariah and Clarin, the thematic humanities laboratory model employed at Duke University, authoring platforms such as Scalar, and online publishing initiatives such as *Debates in the Digital Humanities* and HASTAC, a very powerful, distributed network for intellectual discussion and work.[74] The key factor is to link ideas and a conceptual foundation to material infrastructure. Doing so is not as easy as it may seem, but it is crucial.

Humanities infrastructure includes labs, libraries, software systems, networks, academic programs and projects, publishing and distribution systems, humanities centers, staff, faculty, and students. The humanities has been unwilling to see itself as infrastructural for several reasons. First, infrastructure is assigned to the domain of science, technology, and engineering both in the sense of being located there and as an object of critical inquiry separate from the humanities. Second, the humanities has been reluctant to engage with its own modes of knowledge production critically, which has contributed to inscribing it as a place without infrastructure. Third, the humanities is locked into a construal of itself as institutionally underprivileged and threatened, which is not compatible with acknowledgment of existing infrastructure.

Finally, it can be argued that the humanities as a whole lacks the capacity to imagine and implement intellectually driven infrastructure.

The landscape is changing, however, and institutional actors such as the digital humanities and humanities centers can be transformative agents. There is an opportunity for the humanities to think about infrastructure as an opportunity to create intellectual agendas, a multivalent humanistic platform, grounded outreach, and new modes of material engagement and interpretative frameworks. Making academic infrastructure is ultimately an intellectual challenge.

Conclusion

Academic infrastructure is culturally, institutionally, and technologically situated. The humanities needs to shape not only its own infrastructure but also the frames and discourses associated with it. Neither existing humanities infrastructure nor science and technology may be a useful model.

It would be sensible to think carefully about the ideational underpinning for the humanities in relation to what may be subsumed under the rubric "infrastructure." Such conceptual infrastructure can be related to design principles that in turn can be translated into actual built infrastructure. The humanities must engage critically with academic infrastructure while being involved in conceptualizing and building infrastructure. This is a key challenge for the digital humanities, and big digital humanities is well placed to serve as a powerful and suggestive infrastructural platform. This challenge cannot be met, however, without intellectual drive, scholarly and educational interest, and a multilevel investment in making the digital humanities.

// FIVE //

Making Digital Humanities

This chapter outlines a set of strategies and parameters relevant to implementing the digital humanities—in particular, big digital humanities. In doing so, it builds on the notion of big digital humanities developed in chapter 3 and the infrastructural thinking discussed in chapter 4, but this chapter also draws together many threads running throughout the book and connects them to the implementation of the digital humanities.

I use *making* in the chapter title to accentuate the idea that implementing the digital humanities must be grounded in down-to-earth practice, material-intellectual engagement, and institutional strategy. Making happens on many levels at the same time, and the digital humanities needs to convincingly address these multiple levels. Scholarly motivation cannot really be separated from institutional structures, and the development of a field cannot occur in isolation from the rest of the university and the outside world. While the digital humanities is not a panacea, we should not underestimate the field's capacity to imagine futures and to give scholars, teachers, students, technologists, librarians, and other experts an opportunity to make a difference and be seen as important.

This chapter discusses factors relevant to the making of the digital humanities: building institutions, curatorial work, empowering individuals and groups, and making spaces and infrastructure. These factors can help create conditions for the digital humanities as a site for learning and knowledge building and for critically interweaving conceptual and technological making on a deep level.

Big Digital Humanities

Big digital humanities is a project with considerable potential and range. It

- engages deeply with the humanities disciplines;
- has a multifaceted engagement with the digital;
- intertwines the intellectual and the material;
- contributes to high-quality scholarship and methodological innovation;
- provides humanistic infrastructure;
- reaches out to the rest of the university and the world;
- serves as a model for a proactive humanities; and
- functions as a meeting place and contact zone.

It is also a day-to-day business, characterized not so much by big words as by individual work as well as collaboration, technical development, long-term research processes, institutional politics, and administration. In this sense, *making* is everyday engagement with technology, production of tools, building of databases, thesis work, application writing, dialogue, seminars, courses, and many other activities.

Making as a practice has a special significance for the digital humanities and is a much-discussed issue. Big digital humanities has no expectation that everyone must be a coder or builder of infrastructure, even if being interested and willing to try are important qualities. However, the digital humanities would not exist unless we had those competencies and interests. There must be interactional expertise and an interest in learning from each other. We need to incorporate different kinds of technological engagement, digital production, competencies, and practices of making.

Traditional critical work (itself an example of making) produced in such a context will also necessarily be affected by the conditions of production. Equally important, the making of technology and digital systems will benefit from being carried out in an environment where traditional critical work takes place. This is particularly important for an interdisciplinary meeting place such as big digital humanities, and the various modalities of making likely will also externalize some of the critical and creative processes at play. A framework such as critical making offers structured ways of thinking about how making can help facilitate critical work.

One of the most important functions of the digital humanities is to empower individuals and groups whether they are based in a department, a digital humanities lab, or elsewhere. The daily business of the digital humanities relies on individuals interested in the enterprise, and making the digital humanities is about empowering these individuals and finding ways of supporting a range of people interested in doing high-quality work at the intersection of humanities and the digital. Contemporary academia arguably lacks empowerment, particularly outside the structures of existing reward systems and disciplinary frameworks, and the return on investment for giving people the opportunity to do what they want can consequently be very high.

I draw on the notion of curating and curatorship, taken from the worlds of art and cultural heritage, to propose that making the digital humanities is about curating in several senses of the word: curating data, spaces, infrastructures, events, intellectually driven themes, and intellectual-material projects. Curating is often enacted in an orchestrated space, whether mostly physical or mostly digital, so I also discuss space in terms of making the digital humanities.

Another, more general concern is broader than just the digital humanities or this particular moment in time: the role of the humanities and arts in our society, and making in the sense of innovation and building our own future. Our society needs to incorporate more humanistic and art-based thinking and making to be innovative and sustainable in the long run. Former Rhode Island School of Design president John Maeda and others have articulated this vision under the umbrella of STEAM (Science Technology Engineering Art Mathematics).[1] Artist and engineer Natalie Jeremijenko addresses large-scale challenges such as the our relationship to the environment and to food through promoting agency, systemic understanding and use of technology:

> So I think the cultural challenge is to take these technologies and figure out how to use them to create a desirable future. That's the fundamental participatory demand. We are better than drones make us look, and we have to make them better than that.[2]

The digital humanities can play an important role in activating the humanities and creating a place for such engagement. It is simply not responsible to think about the future of a field that has a certain degree of traction without connecting it to the bigger picture. This sense of responsibility and possibility underscores the fact that the digital humanities cannot easily be confined to a small box in an organization schema and instead exists somewhere in between other boxes, reaching out in different ways. Digital humanities is not a panacea, but it can be a significant player.

Interlude 7: A Day in the Lab

There is pleasure to making. In June 2013, as I was starting off the day in our new lab on the Arts Campus at Umeå University, the installation of a large (five-by-four-meter) interactive floor screen had just been finished. As often happens with conceptually and technologically challenging installations, the path to a finished product was long and iterative. Who can really know how the exact size of the bezels between the eight sheets of glass will affect our subjective perception of the floor? It takes trial and error as well as careful planning. And, on another level, what does it entail to stand on or in the material we are talking about or exploring? What kinds of intellectual engagement can such infrastructure solicit? One underlying notion, coupled with the making, is that we can challenge some of the basic properties of screens through this kind of installation, particularly in terms of orientation, perspective, and the idea of the screen as a flat, unobstructed surface.

Through we sometimes place a large and beautiful oriental rug on top of the screen when it is not in use, the project challenges our sense of the screen as an active surface. Over the next couple of years, we will discover new uses for the floor screen, but now, when the installation has just been finished, we feel a combination of memory of the building process, an almost instantaneous sense of material accomplishment, and the beginnings of a long-term engagement with exploring and using the infrastructure. The process of thinking up the floor screen has generated a broad range of ideas, impressions, and a presence in the lab, almost like a ghost screen. This ghost screen has served as a tool for thinking about what can be done conceptually, concretely, and experimentally, thus generating a good deal of making even before the actual making, so to speak. It has also served as a friendly provocation. When presenting the lab, I have sometimes stated that we do not really know what to do with the screen, and to some extent this is true. This is a provocative statement on several levels. Why should the humanities have this kind of infrastructure? More generally, the experimental and undecided nature of this installation challenges higher education as increasingly concerned with accountability and instrumentalism. Of course, there is and should be a conceptual basis for the interactive floor, but we do not know what it will become. If we already knew that, we probably would not have to build it.

One reason I got to see the interactive floor on this day in June was that I was having meetings and less formal get-togethers in both of our labs, talking to students about their summer projects as well as to faculty and staff involved in various activities. Experiencing and discussing such work creates an instant feeling of joy, and one of the benefits of a lab environment is that it accommodates many such activities and projects at the same time. With the externalization of work processes and an open studio environment, it is quite natural to comment on and discuss ongoing work.[3] A great deal carryover between people and processes also occurs. While much of my own making happens in my office or in meetings around campus or around the world, I need to be grounded in the lab. On a very basic level, the lab, with its people, things, and activities, makes me happy.

We had sponsored a couple of student projects, and I spoke to some of these students that day. One of them had brought a large church organ into the lab, seeking to connect the mechanical and analog with the mechanical and digital. She was working on various physical computing arrangements when I was there, particularly ones based on pressure and air, and her intense connection to the church organ was very apparent. Indeed, the organ had a strong presence in the lab and attracted a stream of walk-in visitors. At the same time, students were working on exploring connections between bodily movement and sound by using Kinect sensors (to track body movements), projection film on glass, and various visualization technologies. In another part of the lab, an interaction-design student presented seven concepts for using the interactive floor in relation to library materials and for discussing the library as idea and infrastructure. What does it mean to give digitally born materials physical materiality via scale and sensory engagement? I realized how different a large floor screen is from other kinds of visualization and interaction platforms, particularly when situated in a highly visible and public place. I also looked at some traces of a project in which an architecture student was using sticky notes as an architectural material. He was waiting for a large shipment of material but had already built a chandelier and another lamp structure using the light from the skylights.

I walked to our other lab on the main campus, where two methodology and programming experts and I discussed the further development of one of our most used digital platforms, faceted browsing. Simply put, our faceted browsing system makes it possible to navigate large and complex datasets by selecting and configuring facets, which in turn serve as the basis for different representations and visualizations. This type of development work is very distinctly linked to research processes, research materials, and user interfaces. The platform contrasts with traditional search query systems because it starts out by offering layered, user-created viewports to the material and its associated context. We had a productive conversation, and after laying out plans for future development of the web platform, I suggested that it might be worthwhile to deploy this web-based application on our eleven-screen screenscape, using the screens to map the facets and layers of visualization often present in such projects and thus challenging the developers to step outside the constraints and benefits of the web as a platform.

Finally, a 3-D artist and programmer showed me some of his work using Unity, a game platform. We had been thinking of ways to explore archives not as static and decontextualized representations (as many web archives are), but as experimental spaces. We had already built a series of prototype applications to explore the representation of the Virgin Mary in medieval Swedish churches, seeking to rethink the medieval relation between word and image through the lens of digital interface.[4] These prototypes, representing a small selection of a large amount of material, were situated in the HUMlab screenscape, and we had been thinking about using a 3-D model of HUMlab to place the prototypes nominally in the virtual space and then to play with the archival material behind the prototypes.

We wanted to draw on the installation as spatially situated but also go beyond the constraints of the model of HUMlab and the reenactment of the installation. One possibility that emerged in the discussion was to change the walls in the virtual model of HUMlab. Many years earlier, I had taken part in a Storefront for Art and Architecture event housed in a temporary plastic conference space in a New York City park. This plastic was semitransparent, and people outside would touch it and even sometimes bounce into it. The idea was to replace the walls in the virtual model of HUMlab with such material, put the full project material (about five thousand images plus video and audio) in the space outside the virtual lab, and have some of the material bounce into the virtual walls. It would make itself known and call for attention, but neither too timidly nor too aggressively. It would also be possible to walk out into the space outside the walls in the 3-D model and encounter the material experientially and maybe even select material there and throw it onto the screens in the virtual model, which could then be mapped onto the screens in the real HUMlab. The screens would then display the archival material as spatially situated in the physical lab.

While these examples may not qualify as curated critical making processes as described by Matt Ratto, they do to some extent combine critical processes and literal making.[5] In addition, they externalize "thinking processes," which is quite useful when working in a contact zone and when engaging with boundary objects. In a big digital humanities context, where technologists, students, digital humanities experts, and scholars from different disciplines often come together in an open environment, work that is primarily critical is likely to be influenced by ongoing making, and the making will ideally be influenced by dialogues with scholars and others who are not primarily invested in producing code, physical computing artifacts, or multimedia. This kind of contact zone thus pressures both practitioners and traditional scholars to engage with others. In an environment such as HUMlab, it should not be possible to maintain a "pure" critical approach; similarly, making will necessarily be critically inflected and enabled.

Making Factors

Many types of making are often at play simultaneously. The interactive floor screen is a very concrete example of material making, but it is naturally also the result of a strong idea. Can we challenge the cinematic and vertical paradigm of screen use? What does it mean to see screen-enabled content from above or to be inside it? How does working around a screen change collaborative possibilities? How can we experiment with layering information and experiences on top of the floor screen? What artifacts and materials were meant to be seen from above or from the inside? It takes institutional work, accumulative building of trust, and a collective culture of technological and intellectual engagement to move from idea to material manifestation. This particular piece of making is situated in relation to layers of previous making and systems. The actual use of the screen relates closely to how the lab is curated, what middleware is built, how experimentation is supported, how individuals and groups are empowered (or not), and how the operation is organized and carried out.

Some perspectives and strategies are particularly relevant to making the digital humanities. They cluster into institutional-level making, curatorship, empowering individuals and supporting collaboration, and making infrastructure and space. All build on a foundation of intellectual and technological engagement and in turn help create conditions for the digital humanities as a site for curiosity-driven learning and knowledge production.

Building Institutions

The digital humanities and earlier humanities computing have had a long-standing preoccupation with their institutional status, which has been contested and undecided. Occupying this uncertain position and facing pressure from conventional academic structures can be frustrating and difficult, but there are also benefits to not having been absorbed fully by those structures. One such benefit is a lively ongoing dialogue about matters that do not seem to be discussed as much in many other fields. Issues often discussed in the history of the digital humanities include: What counts as scholarship? What are viable career paths for digital humanists with a technological or methodological focus? Does the field serve traditional disciplines, or is it autonomous? Who does service to whom? Is the digital humanities a field or a discipline? What is the size of the field? Who is in and who is out? Is making a basic epistemic commitment of the field?

While this discussion is worthwhile, it can lead to the repetition of the same arguments. This long-lasting discussion not only possesses a weariness and staleness but also runs the risk of the obsessive self-examination that Louis Menand identifies in the humanities in the late 1980s and 1990s.[6] Nevertheless, many of these questions remain current, and it is slightly worrying when Sean Gouglas and his coauthors argue that the topic of whether the digital humanities is a discipline is exhausted.[7] This may be true for old-timers, but this reasoning excludes newcomers to the field, many of whom come from lineages other than humanities computing. Some of the new people indeed have a strong institutional interest, and they may well be building institutions, networks, and centers over the coming decades. And the question of whether or not digital humanities is a discipline is both current and critical to the future of the field.

Institution building is in many ways an ideal process through which to address questions of identity and to embody one's answer to the question of what the digital humanities can be. Such incarnations can range from small projects, temporary working groups, urban pop-up labs, and local fellowship programs to regional centers, international networked communities, intrainstitutional centers, digital humanities labs, and departments. There is no single model or solution, and institutional contexts vary considerably. Institution building is always local, which is why digital humanities needs to acknowledge a broad range of initiatives, contexts and strategies.

If the history of mainstream digital humanities is one of partial marginalization and the institutional struggles of centers and initiatives, the situation has clearly changed in the past few years. With increased leverage and interest, the question has arisen of how to operationalize this interest and make the best use of available or potential resources. This is not a simple matter, particularly given the history of the field and the fact that the pressure now comes much more from the outside. And the current relative well-being of the digital humanities does not mean that no problems exist or that higher education has suddenly become perfect. On the contrary, higher education and the humanities in many parts of the world are facing critical challenges, including reduction of base funding, a neoliberal agenda, instrumentalism, and academic isolation of the humanities.[8] From the point of view of big digital humanities, these challenges are not separate from the work of digital humanities, and the field needs to take on at least some of them. It would simply be irresponsible not to use the reach and leverage of the digital and institutional plasticity of the digital humanities to engage with the bigger picture and the bigger world.

The idea of a broadly conceived big digital humanities that has multiple modes of engagement with the digital and the ability to take on major intellectual and technological challenges is highly compatible with the digital humanities as a meeting place and intersectional operation. This type of digital humanities differs from traditional disciplines and departments, which can be useful when arguing in favor of investments in the field. A dean or a university president may be quite happy to see the emergence of a platform that not only will deliver good-quality research and development but also promises to help revitalize the humanities and to create new collaborative networks across and outside the university. And most institutions of higher education are more in need of intersectional centers and initiatives than yet another department or discipline.

There is more to this than simply seeing the digital humanities as a center- or lab-like activity. Indeed, centers may not be the optimal organizational form in all contexts and situations, and in some cases, network models or departments will certainly be a better choice. Implementation and local needs will vary in different settings. But it is important to see the digital humanities as a whole as an intersectional meeting place where a text-encoding initiative, physical computing activities, and media history work can exist simultaneously. Involvement must include the digital humanities platform as well as existing departments and centers. Double affiliation is a useful model, and flexibility and integrity are important. The digital humanities is not a servile function and does not always need to work with others.

Most of these matters have institutional ramifications and will sooner or later have to be addressed in terms of institutional strategy. However, we have to start somewhere, and as long as we have a basic idea, interest, and leadership, most other things can be worked out.

Some Reflections on Doing Institutional Work

While institution making and administrative work combined with an academic career trajectory sometimes can seem unrewarding, distracting, and uninspiring, this is where much of the conditions of academic work are determined. Given the relatively unsettled status of the digital humanities and our current leverage, we have plenty of opportunities for administrative and academic leadership as well as a real need for such leadership. Institutions do not just exist. They are made and remade by people, and the institutional structure seems less fixed and more moldable at certain times and in certain contexts. We now have an opportunity to make ideas come through and to create real change.

Institution building is contextual, situational, and local. There is no standard blueprint that can be employed, and convincing the people in power will likely require us to strike a balance between, on the one hand, the national and international state of affairs (for example, the current interest in digital humanities) and, on the other, the anticipated local contribution and role in relation to this movement. While the local institution as well as funding agencies probably want to see international excellence, they may not be primarily interested in a carbon copy of another institution at another university, no matter how good that model. It is important to demonstrate a good sense of the international situation, but there should be a particular flavor to what is being suggested. This flavor can be carried by a strong idea about something that does not yet exist, but it typically makes sense to connect this idea to what exists in terms of faculty, infrastructure, and regional strengths.

A particular, locally situated, and intersectional framing of the intended operation will also give digital humanities builders the opportunity to frame their own platform. Doing so eases the process of including people from across the local institution rather than from only one school or a department. Looking broadly, talking with people, and making connections simply results in more choices. At the same time, it is important to avoid limiting oneself to the local context. Most initiatives must seek to make substantial international contributions. A junior scholar pushing for a new center or network might want to recruit five leading and up-and-coming international scholars and institutional leaders—people who are passionate and committed about the mission of the new initiative—to serve as part of a distinguished advisory group. And make sure that this group is diverse.

Institution building, like most other forms of making, requires ideas and conviction. Most conventional departments offer limited opportunities for this kind of idea-driven institutional work because much of it is already set, and it is difficult to change large-scale operations that are deeply invested in substantial undertakings, educational or otherwise. The digital humanities benefits from being seen as a relatively new area as well as from being different, fairly small, and comparatively rich in terms of ideas and energy. What gets imagined does not have to be modeled on what is already there or what is expected, but it should be institutionally aware. There is a remarkable power to strong ideas and to people who can manifest and articulate those ideas. Regardless of one's personal persuasive abilities, it is almost always beneficial to let other people see one's interest, drive, and intensity. Such sentiment cannot easily be simulated or constructed. In a meeting with serious academics and administrators, it can be remarkably useful to let some of that energy show and to stress the academic side of things. At the same time, it is advisable to be moderate, not too aggressive, not too opinionated, and scholarly and institutionally anchored.

Such positioning can be achieved by local and international networking, by creating a solid scholarly and educational grounding for the vision, by introducing one's own academic work, and by talking to sympathetic administrators. Formal documents—locally produced white papers and beyond-the-state-of-the-art reports, national strategy documents, and international reports—can be useful for this process. A wide variety of material is available for the digital humanities, and even if only a little can be used, it is good practice to have a profound sense of the national and international context, including the funding landscape. But it is equally important to bring one's own positioning, flavor, and conviction to whatever is being proposed. And why not include a 3-D rendering, a simulation snapshot, or some other kind of digital expression?

While proposals and planning documents often benefit from taking a visionary approach and a long-term perspective, they can also lock the proposer into a "large" mind-set and vision that will at best take a very long time to realize. It is therefore often a good strategy to combine far-reaching goals with a direct line of action. This is why it makes sense to connect to existing faculty, expertise, and resources. At the same time, it may be advantageous to indicate clearly that something new and promising is being created. One possibility is to go for prototype labs, networks, or projects and to use such platforms to test ideas and concepts for a possible full installation. It is often advantageous to have a physical site, even if it is just a small space, that stands out and has clear signage. A strong online presence is useful whether coupled with a physical site or not. Before any of these features are in place, it may be possible to single out a project or a network as a way of initializing or channeling work in the area in question. Doing so can often occur without substantial cost, and for more leverage, flexible and relatively quick seed money is at times available from universities and funding agencies. Seed money is also useful in the sense that it indicates a buy-in from the funder, which can help in the continued process.

Balancing long-, intermediate-, and short-term perspectives in this way is an important part of institution building. Experience shows that building institutions takes more time than one would like to think. Persistence and the ability to overcome temporary (and sometimes long-term) setbacks are important qualifications. And five years can be enough of a window to make a real difference and create real change, so this might serve as an appropriate mental time frame.

Much of this work involves framing and thinking collaboratively about what can be achieved given enough resources. It usually helps to be concrete, listing what might be accomplished within a specific period. It is also useful to have a sense of what will be needed to reach these goals. One of the most difficult questions to answer without preparation is, "How would you make use of a ten-million-dollar donation?" One generic answer would be that over a five-year period, 30 percent of those resources could be spent on infrastructure, while other major investments could include a postdoctoral program, a distinguished visiting researcher program, a fellowship program for the university, and possibly an endowed chair. One might also want to add that the goal of securing additional external funding for research projects and other initiatives. Of course, one would also have to be prepared to answer the same question for a fifty-thousand-dollar donation, academic crowdsourcing, and many other possibilities.[9] The ability to answer such questions requires preparedness, strategic thinking, and on-the-spot making.

Institutional building requires leadership: it involves having a sense of direction, empowering others, inspiring confidence, building trust, and making a difference together with other people. It makes sense to draw on trusted senior advisers and colleagues and to be sensitive to expectations and possibilities, but leadership is ultimately about making choices and daring to be distinct. Over time, the ability to be reasonably true to a basic idea and to avoid unnecessary compromises on core issues is critical to such leadership. Brashness can be a useful quality when doing institutional work but is not recommended on an everyday basis and should be exercised with caution. However, some initiatives—especially in the humanities—suffer when leaders are too timid and unwilling to think and speak big enough. The institutional context and power structures matter here, and it is easier to be brash when one is structurally privileged. In any case, a certain degree of brashness and imagination can help.

One may not want to play by the book in certain situations. If the dean is not supportive, one may have to approach the provost or vice chancellor. Such end runs should not be attempted without very careful consideration but also should not be excluded as an option. If one has a casual encounter with a potential donor, it might be a good idea to strike up a conversation even when a representative of the university's Office of External Relations is not present. If the members of the university board are visiting, one option involves telling them directly what is needed. A brash answer to the question of how to spend ten million dollars would be that a great deal can indeed be done with such generous funding but that fifteen million dollars would enable one to raise another ten million dollars, creating a much stronger and sustainable center of excellence. Sometimes getting what one wants requires pushing the envelope regarding rules and regulations, though not too far. Nevertheless, rules are not set in stone, and personal conviction and warmth can go a long way. Again, it is vital to be cautious and sensible about these things and to protect one's back (make sure to keep a paper trail and do not trust institutions blindly), but one should not accept at face value the statement that something is not possible.

Curating the Digital Humanities

The digital humanities requires more than an ideational underpinning and an institutional platform. These factors create conditions, but hard work and adaptability are needed to move from conditions to long-term implementation. Dynamic and intersectional operations such as big digital humanities particularly require ways of connecting ideas to practice on an everyday basis.

A range of strategies and practices can be adopted to make these connections. While institutional leadership is necessary, it does not quite cover the type of navigation required to manage a big digital humanities operation or many other intersectional collegial operations. Strong leadership is necessary, but such leadership cannot be about control; rather, there must be a constructive space for dialogue, negotiation, knowledge work, and challenging of ideas. The notion of curating, borrowed from the domains of art and cultural heritage, can be instrumental for thinking about the making of the digital humanities.

Curation traditionally incorporates acquiring, classifying, and safeguarding objects. In 1963, zoologist Boyd W. Walker wrote,

> The curator's job is to contribute to knowledge, in the unique way that museums have established for themselves: through the gathering, study, and display of natural objects and the products of men's minds and skills.[10]

The notion of curatorship has long been debated and developed: Walker was worried about curators devoting too much time to research rather than caring for the collections. These debates can partly be explained by the range of responsibilities associated with curatorship as well as the need to balance different interests, a situation that resembles digital humanities. To what extent is curatorial (or digital humanities) practice a theoretical and scholarly endeavor? How is the custodial role upheld? How visible is the curator? What is the relation between the art curator and the artist? What is the relationship between the researcher or artist and the space or infrastructure? How do new forms of art, expression, and technology influence curatorial practice?

One way of looking at curating is to see it as a question of making meaning and creating context in some kind of institutional setting. In the digital humanities, this may translate to the properties of being in between, working with others, and respecting their positions as well as of being instrumental and helpful in shaping patterns and bringing together perspectives. One example could be the intellectual and practical-level steering required to stage an international digital humanities workshop, where new or emergent themes are brought forward and manifested. On an institutional level, curatorial skills may be useful when negotiating digitally inflected faculty lines with departments and disciplines. An important sense of space or infrastructure is also a part of much curatorial work and big digital humanities and is an important facilitator for the digital humanities.

Although digital technology and new orientations have challenged curatorial institutions, they still uphold a traditional sense of curatorship. In particular, such curatorship often focuses on objects. According to the 2007 guidelines of the Association of Art Museum Curators,

> Although curators have many duties and responsibilities, their primary value to the museum lies in their specific expertise. Curators are art historians engaged in scholarship with a special emphasis on physical objects. Many museums provide the necessary resources—library, research time, grant and sabbatical opportunities—for curators to pursue scholarship. This scholarly activity enhances curators' understanding of the works in their care, and redounds to the credit of their museum. Given their unique position as art historians and keepers, curators have particular knowledge of and access to art objects that can generate valuable new insights.[11]

The sense of curatorship presented here is fairly traditional, evidenced, for example, in the emphasis on art history as a disciplinary background and the clear privileging of physical objects. Walker, too, emphasized objects, and this is a clear point of connection with the digital humanities. The curation of digital cultural heritage, as supported by the digital humanities and memory institutions, often has a strong emphasis on objects taken out of their regular context, and sometimes the original museological context is also limited. In this sense, a web-based collection may not necessarily be different substantially from a physical museum, although the digital representation of physical objects may pose a practical challenge. This problem applies both to web-based material and to many traditional museums. Peter Galison and Jeffrey Schnapp suggest that collection-centric museums can learn from science museums, which are better at connecting touch and thinking, albeit in an arcade game format. They claim that traditional museums often use technology to offer the digital equivalents of "wall labels, catalogues, and brochures":

> However well executed and intended, the models of interactivity here employed still tend to reduce the contact of the physical with the digital to the notion of support.[12]

Technology tends to be used either to replicate objects and collections or to create digital wall labels. Not only are individual objects or sets of objects replicated, but ontologies and structures that reinforce certain conceptions and logics are created. What other experiential modalities, contextualization, and conceptual ideas might be possible? Cultural heritage institutions and the digital humanities overlap in this area, and the digital humanities can play an important role.

Cultural heritage institutions and the digital humanities have a common opportunity in the area of creating intellectual middleware.[13] Both the digital humanities and memory institutions need to work harder to connect conceptual ideas to their technologically supported manifestations. For the digital humanities, doing this involves not only cultural heritage contexts but also creating research and educational tools and supporting scholarly expressions and modalities. The production of intellectual middleware, placed somewhere between scholarly issues and technical implementations, is a deeply collaborative, interdisciplinary, and iterative process and requires curatorial expertise. This function comports well with big digital humanities as an intersectional meeting place and trading zone and with curating as a liminal process.[14] Susan Leigh Star and James Griesemer's primary case study for their pioneering work on boundary objects was a museum.[15] The digital humanities can be a laboratory for intellectual middleware and for meaning making between the humanities and the digital. This requires curatorial integrity and the ability to work across professions and disciplines and to develop research and educational infrastructures. This is a key concern for big digital humanities.

Curating is also needed on a more practical level to accommodate such work, and the term *data curation* (or *digital curation*) is often used to cover the more data-centric part of the managing and making of digital resources. Data curation essentially involves the management of data, including methods of data capture, migrating data, and annotation and descriptive and interpretative information.[16] Digital humanities offers a great deal in terms of accumulated experience and long-term investment in cultural heritage materials. Furthermore, almost any kind of data-inflected research in the humanities and the digital humanities could benefit from the methodological rigidity and technological expertise associated with these practices, especially if they are deeply embedded in a critical and material context. The data or digital curation community has to some extent called for such epistemic awareness.[17]

A specific example of such critical work is Emily Drabinski's scholarship on library cataloging. She traces how library classifications have been challenged as objective descriptions through the critical cataloging movement, but also argues that the correctness associated with such movements is problematic and that classificatory decisions "always reflect a particular ideology or approach to understanding the material itself."[18] Most data curation efforts may not engage with queer theory in the way Drabinski suggests, but such critical awareness is useful and, moreover, it would be possible to create experimental platforms and curatorial installations for challenging traditional classificatory thinking in this vein. As the area of data curation exemplifies, however, the most prevalent connections between curatorial work and the digital humanities tend to relate to the custodial and object-based model of curating. And although far-reaching, the description of curation in the book Digital_Humanities also seems focused on cultural heritage rather than active making beyond "organizing and re-presenting":

> To curate is to filter, organize, craft, and, ultimately, care for a story composed out of—even rescued from—the infinite array of potential tales, relics, and voices. In the Digital Humanities, curation refers to a wide range of practices of organizing and re-presenting the cultural record of humankind in order to create value, impact, and quality.[19]

At the same time, technological development puts pressure on curatorial practice more generally. While this applies to most types of curatorial institutions, some seem more susceptible than others. Focusing on art curation, Sarah Cook argues that over the past two to three decades, perception of museums as "storehouses of objects and gatekeepers of the history of art" has shifted in favor of views of museums as "sites of engagement." In particular, new media art or digital art has played a destabilizing role in this process through its tendency to be participatory, time-based, interdisciplinary, and mobile.[20]

The digital humanities would benefit from thinking of itself more as a site of engagement along the lines of Cook's view of museums. Curatorial exhibitions have a natural sense of place, interaction, and situational fixedness that connects usefully to the digital humanities as a project. So while traditional curatorial practices struggle to adapt to distributed media, the digital humanities lacks some of the situational anchorage of curatorial practice. Such situatedness is relevant generally for digital humanities as a meeting place as well as specifically for exploring scholarly modalities outside the conventional ways of making scholarship.

Such work can be carried out through mostly digital platforms. For example, Digital Pedagogy in the Humanities: Concepts, Models, and Experiments[21] is a carefully curated effort to discuss and demonstrate digitally inflected pedagogy through keywords such as 'queer' and 'interface.' In trying to open up student writing to a networked world and reshaping how we conceptualize such writing, the online project Social Paper can be seen as a curatorial task involving a range of communities, identities, structures and tools.[22] Alex Gil's work to establish a framework for creating "low-decay" minimal editions of texts is also curatorial work driven by an interest in going beyond large-scale, high-threshold, expensive editing practices.[23]

Experimental scholarly exhibitions or installations provide another opportunity to explore alternative genres of scholarship. Supporting the development of scholarly installations, whether mostly physical or mostly digital, is clearly a curatorial task. The artists and scholars involved remain the primary agents, helped by the curatorial and collaborative processes that lead to the production of such works. While scholarly installations could not normally be considered to be artistic expressions, overlap exists in terms of expressive modalities and the curatorial process.

The terms *curating* and *curation* have become more widely used in society, and while we may not want to draw on uses such as collecting photos of cookie recipes and organizing them on a Pinterest board, a more inclusive sense of curation can nevertheless be useful when discussing the digital humanities.[24] This looser sense can be exemplified by TED Talks telling us that curation lies at the heart of their mission.[25] In this case, curatorial practice seems to involve programming, selecting speakers, and essentially creating experiences. This ties in with the programming and curation built into museums and art galleries and requires integrity, administrative leadership, and many of the skills associated with curatorial practice.

Such curatorial practice is highly relevant in the context of big digital humanities, a liminal actor with integrity placed between other institutions and groups. Most center-like digital humanities initiatives do some curatorial work in identifying common themes and potential collaborators, organizing activities, offering fellowship opportunities, pushing traditional structures, and creating a common narrative. Curating is thus a key competence and process required for making the digital humanities.

A connection exists here to humanities centers and advanced institutes, which employ similar strategies. Humanities centers have existed in the United States for half a century. Facilitating a semester-long fellowship program at a humanities center in relation to a particular theme and organizing associated activities is curatorial work. At Duke University's John Hope Franklin Humanities Institute,

> The Audiovisualities Lab aims to provide a structure for encouraging teaching and research in the booming field of sound studies, complementing and challenging the existing primacy of visual studies. It offers a privileged space for research gathering of undergraduate and graduate students, and faculty, around a series of topics approached through specific classes, seminars, and workshops.[26]

This institute uses humanities laboratories as a way to package a series of activities and initiatives. And if a digital humanities center works to find faculty across a university interested in multilayered mapping methodology and ends up organizing a series of workshops with those faculty members, this is also an example of curating. Affinities between the digital humanities and humanities centers could develop into more far-reaching partnerships.

On one level, all of these strategies seek to make critical meaning between the humanities and the digital—that is, to make the digital humanities. Doing so requires scholarly, administrative, and technological abilities as well as an honest interest in inspiring other people to grow, take on challenges, and see connections. The role of the curator has been discussed extensively in the literature, and big digital humanities needs neither an invisible, humble curator nor a high priest.[27] The curator in this context is instead a facilitator with integrity, someone who can both steer and stand back and who has respect for the work and ideas of scholars from a range of disciplines as well as of students, technologists, and artists. Curatorial work can be individual and also collaborative (including teams of curators). Curatorial practice in the context of the digital humanities differs substantially from other types of curating work, but many similarities also exist, as is evident in Ceri Hand's description of the relationship between the curator and the artist:

> In my experience a good working relationship with an artist means that you both respect each others strengths & ideas, recognising that together you can make something new & hopefully exciting, that perhaps either one of you wouldn't come to by yourselves or with anybody else. . . . [T]he "power" balance shifts all the time throughout the creative process. . . . [I]f you have set off on the right foot then this is an interesting process.[28]

Managing a digital humanities operation or project similarly often involves working with researchers, teachers, students, and other actors and ideally allowing oneself to be changed as much as the people with whom one engages. An important part of making the digital humanities thus becomes establishing processes and building trust that can support such work. This work is both intellectual and material.

Curatorial Qualities

On a practical level, some qualities are particularly relevant for curating the digital humanities: managing the field's in-between position, tracing and shaping emerging patterns, and combining integrity and respect.

First, since the digital humanities sits in between disciplines, departments, competencies, ideas, and technologies, managing and embracing this liminal position is a critical component. How do we support and facilitate first-rate work between the humanities and the digital? What scholarly, educational, and methodological crossovers can be suggested? How do we integrate critical thinking and making? What might a scholarly exhibition or installation look like? How can intellectually productive meetings be facilitated regardless of whether they occur within a discipline, between disciplines, or with external parties? What intellectual middleware do we need? What infrastructure can meaningfully support the intellectual pursuits that drive some of our best researchers? How can technology and methodology push intellectual agendas? How do we support individuals who want to work outside their disciplines' comfort zones? While no single strategy or response can answer all these questions, the idea of digital humanities as a meeting place contains strategies that can help. This meeting place needs to be dialogic, generous, challenging, and open to renewal. It needs to bridge intellectual and material interests. It needs to encourage risk taking, experimentation, and exploration. These qualities require curatorial work, trust, and curiosity.

Second, the ability to see and sometimes to shape patterns may seem quite abstract, but in part it involves knowing about good scholarship, the direction in which the best research is heading, upcoming interdisciplinary challenges, exciting milieus, technological advances, and emerging areas. An April 2013 symposium at the Maryland Institute of Technology, Shared Horizons: Data, Biomedicine, and the Digital Humanities, sought to create opportunities for disciplinary cross-fertilization through a mix of formal and informal presentations combined with breakout sessions, all designed to promote a rich exchange of ideas about how large-scale quantitative methods can lead to new understandings of human culture. Bringing together researchers from the digital humanities and bioinformatics communities, the symposium will explore ways in which these two communities might fruitfully collaborate on projects that bridge the humanities and medicine around the topics of sequence alignment and network analysis, two modes of analysis that intersect with "big data."[29]

Curatorial work went into this symposium, sponsored by the National Endowment of the Humanities and carried out in collaboration with several other national bodies: choosing the topic, working with the communities, talking to funding agencies, structuring the event, selecting the specific methodologies or modes of analysis, and choosing the keynote speaker and other principal participants. Not every academic event is a massive curatorial effort, but some are, and this kind of work is part of the curatorial profile of big digital humanities.

Such curatorial practice not only involves what is considered new but also involves picking up traditional themes in humanities scholarship. Curators must possess a critical awareness, a sense of what is good work, and the skills needed to collaborate closely with other parties. Furthermore, curatorship in this context requires a good sense of established scholars and their work as well as the ability to identify and sponsor early-career faculty, graduate and undergraduate students, teachers, and technologists as well as nascent themes and ideas.

Mixing junior and senior participants can be a very useful strategy, and it is wise to avoid making junior participants subservient or overly reliant on their more experienced peers. Everyone involved should feel challenged, and in this context, shaping entails listening to key people, identifying themes, recruiting scholars, hosting activities, and building infrastructure. At the same time, curating also includes balance and adaptability and the skills needed to support up-and-coming work and long-term engagement with significant topics. One of the strengths of a big digital humanities framework is the play between the digital humanities and humanities disciplines and that some longer-term work can be absorbed by other disciplines and departments, freeing up the digital humanities to engage with other themes and technologies.

Integrity, the third curatorial quality, is often omitted or discussed only implicitly in the curatorial context. References to integrity often occur only in relation to the integrity of the artist and the artist's vision or of scholarship.[30] Furthermore, when distinctions are made between curators as invisible, humble curators and as high priests, neither archetype necessarily invokes much integrity.[31] Curatorial integrity requires navigating the waters in between many strong actors and certain situational conditions and constraints. Doing so is not necessarily easy. Curators with strong backgrounds in particular disciplines or practices associated with the digital humanities initiative in question may have more success as long as they also have an equally strong investment in the overall goals of the initiative and are institutionally and interpersonally savvy. Without integrity, the digital humanities might well become a service function or a passive onlooker rather than a proactive and inspirational agent in a range of scholarly, educational, and technological processes. Integrity must be combined with humbleness and respect, however, and managing this position is a key challenge for curatorial work in the digital humanities. For example, creating digital artifacts and intellectual middleware might require challenging researchers or educators involved in the process as well as technologists and artists. The curator's primary role here involves facilitating an intellectual direction or argument that is materially enacted in such a way that new knowledge and insights can be produced.

Curators must strike a balance between integrity and respect. Curatorial work involves more than just being nice and genuinely interested—though these are key qualities. It also requires a willingness to point to connections, competencies, and possibilities and sometimes to be clear about which pathways or solutions make the most sense in a particular context or appear most interesting or challenging intellectually, technically, and practically. As result, curators must sometimes say that something is not interesting, worthwhile, or feasible. In most cases, constructive dialogue and suggestions will suffice, and intervention will not be needed. Curators may lack the authority or function to question the premises of individual projects, but being involved and having a milieu that supports dialogue and experimentation is often all that is required.

In other cases, particularly when projects or themes are closely associated with the core operation of a digital humanities initiative, decisions may have to make the preferred choice very clear. Balancing different parts of a digital humanities operation may require preventing one set of interests to control the initiative's direction. Curators may also have to overrule specific expertise, prioritize specific sets of methodologies, or point to missing perspectives.

Maintaining this balance can be tricky, and intuitional-level work often requires simultaneously honoring and resisting academic structures—tweaking but not breaking. It involves gently pushing intellectual, technological, and institutional questions while maintaining a high level of integrity. And it involves having something to offer and on a very simple level supporting and facilitating good work.

Big digital humanities depends on managing the field's liminal position, finding and shaping points of interaction, and combining integrity and respect. Such curatorial work is complex and exciting and always involves dialogue and other people.

Empowering the Humanities

Big digital humanities works to empower people who want to explore questions, perspectives, methodologies, and technologies that would otherwise be difficult to pursue as well as lends support and sanction to people with ideas and drive. The in-between position of digital humanities can be used to empower individuals and groups inside more traditional structures, such as departments, as well as within the digital humanities itself.

Individuals who work within large organizations such as universities are both enabled and restricted by institutional structures. Many things that we take for granted—access to library materials, work space, and largely functioning administrative systems—enable us to do scholarly work. Anyone who has stepped outside such an institutional structure or has not had access to it knows that the lack of such resources can be palpable and disempowering. At the same time, we may feel restricted by the disciplinary structure of academia, territoriality, rigid administrative structures, limited resources, and slow reactions to new ideas and initiatives.[32] Meeting places such as the digital humanities can offer empowerment by breaking up some of these structures, channeling resources, and taking risks. Individuals and groups within institutional structures can thus be helped to do things that might not otherwise be possible. Such benefits can be achieved without taking a confrontational stance toward departments when the digital humanities occupies a different position in an institutional ecology. The advantages of an intermediate position are part of the foundation of big digital humanities, and such a position allows far-reaching collaborations with disciplines, departments, and other actors.

The idea of empowerment in relation to organizations and businesses often presupposes that the candidates for empowerment already occupy a relatively privileged position. One might be disempowered in the context of an organization but privileged to be within that organization. This general position of empowerment comes with responsibility and points to the importance of having a civic and public role in the local community and of working with subjects that are meaningful on a larger scale. HUMlab is in many ways a very privileged platform, and we have a long-standing collaboration with various local and regional community groups (including several activist and comparatively underprivileged groups), and many of the topics around which we orient our work address issues relating to power structures (for example, gender perspectives on computer games and folkloristic perspectives on indigenous storytelling), environmental concerns, and the politics of platforms. The large civic question of societal, political, and cultural empowerment is vital, but the empowering potential of the digital humanities remains important within the context of academe.

What can small-scale empowerment entail on a more practical level? As a junior scholar trying to get traction for the Virtual Wedding project, I benefited greatly from the support of the early organization associated with HUMlab. At this point, we mainly needed infrastructural resources to do work with virtual worlds. I remember the benefits of employing an open, technologically experimental, and malleable lab space instead of an administrative lab with restricted access. I also remember the relief of feeling that we had strong support, that the people behind HUMlab really wanted this, as opposed to the slight resistance or indifference departments often offer despite a basic level of sanction. Out-of-the-ordinary ideas, especially if experimental, do not always sit well within departments, and the support of an intermediary digital humanities platform can help individuals and groups carry out and validate such work. This is often also helpful to the departments.

When I later found myself part of the HUMlab management, I came across a range of individuals and initiatives interested in working with us, and I was sometimes struck with how little we needed to do to make a big difference. When a group of cultural studies and literature students came to us to ask whether they could use the lab to practice "reception talk," we were very happy to oblige. We contributed only the space for a few evening hours and some snacks, but the students put in much work, and the simulated professional reception event was useful even if it was not really digitally inflected.

In another case, a very engaged doctoral student who was researching creative writing websites suggested doing a public panel discussion on the future of literary critique in the digital age. She had already contacted a few possible speakers, and we immediately agreed to sponsor the event. The immediacy of such decisions is significant. We helped to shape the concept, but again, most of the actual cost was the time invested by the junior scholar. Many such activities and projects eventually obtain funding from elsewhere, but it is quite important to have an institution that can offer support and buy-in, take a little bit of risk, and sometimes guarantee the cost, especially as higher education faces increasing economic constraints and administrative control, and becomes ever more compartmentalized. While risk taking can certainly be about money and resources, it also involves taking intellectual and institutional risk through asking difficult questions, challenging established structures, and mobilizing for critically driven action.

This empowering function applies not only to events and activities but also to supporting project work, initiating research strands, offering fellowship and training programs, and supporting different kinds of external funding applications. In many cases, all that is needed is a speaking partner. At other times, we can help to build a simple prototype, involve an international expert, or talk to a game company. The important point is that the digital humanities can be instrumental in enabling people to develop and test their ideas. All ideas or interested parties can probably not receive extensive amounts of time or resources, but there has to be an openness to ideas and willingness to engage. People can help each other, too, and a digital humanities operation can facilitate by forming groups or having open time slots in a physical or virtual space.

One building block of the platform of digital humanities is infrastructure, which can have an empowering function in itself. Access to equipment and associated competencies can help scholars and others to imagine what might be possible at the intersection of the humanities and the digital. Not only is this true of generic and instrumental technology, especially if used in conceptually interesting ways, but there is much to be gained from encouraging experimentation and exploration in relation to less predetermined infrastructure. Encountering conceptually and technologically interesting setups and discussing ideas with people can certainly be empowering, especially with a high degree of accessibility, a low threshold, and a culture that supports play in relation to intellectual and technological engagement. High-quality open access resources and tools can play an important role here, as can open and accessible lab spaces. Empowerment may also be found, however, in not having to rely on others for every move. For example, everyone does not need to be an expert on coding, but scholars can benefit from having a good sense of technological platforms, not only because staff resources are necessarily limited but also because one can learn and imagine through engagement with technology.

Scalar is a multimodal production platform and infrastructure that offers scholars ways of constructing intellectual arguments by drawing on a repertoire of expressive modalities not normally present in most published scholarship. Media theorist Nicholas Mirzoeff, who used the platform for a companion piece to one of his books, *The Right to Look: A Counterhistory of Visuality*, stresses the importance of being able to include nontextual media:

> Scalar allows me to share a wide range of North African and European cinema, newsreel footage, guerrilla documentary and photography with the reader in a way that is obviously not possible in print.

Mirzoeff's companion piece, "We Are All Children of Algeria: Visuality and Countervisuality, 1954–2011," seems a particularly good match for the platform both in terms of the topic and the material. However, using Scalar also allows Mirzoeff

> to explore a more complex form of narrative in which multiple threads (or "paths" as Scalar calls them) can be developed. This opens up a new set of possibilities for comparative and cross-cultural work that have only just begun to explore in digital humanities work but which I think are among its most fruitful possibilities.[33]

This technology is empowering in that it enables the scholar do to work otherwise not possible. Integrating visual materials is empowering on a more direct, instrumental level, while shaping new forms of narratives is empowering on another level. We are more likely to predict the impact of instrumental use of technology, while experimental use is more likely to yield results that we cannot foresee. In addition, results are less likely to be predictable when the technology is present in the digital or physical environment than when the scholar specifically uses the technology. Seeing, experiencing, and discussing technology and the digital in an intellectually rich milieu can stimulate engaged scholarship and education in ways that might not otherwise be possible.

Similarly, a media studies scholar may work in HUMlab on an individual book project with some digital inflection while simultaneously engaging in a dialogue about how that work relates to the infrastructure in which the scholar and the work are embedded. This is not an instrumental or one-way relation but rather a complex, iterative, and (at least ideally) empowering interrelationship among people, ideas, and infrastructure that is central to the digital humanities. The media scholar's work and associated disciplinary traditions influence HUMlab. For instance, being situated in a carefully designed space surrounded by screens may influence how the scholar thinks about material and research questions. This process may lead the scholar to create material installations. In this sense, research is shaped by the infrastructure and the ideas behind it at the same time that the infrastructure is explored, defined, and made by the scholars and technologists involved.

However, platforms such as Scalar and the HUMlab screenscape offer constraints as well as possibilities. They are situated and conditioned in many ways, and the discourse surrounding them does not necessarily bring up these phenomena in any depth. The HUMlab screenscape clearly privileges visually oriented knowledge production and is part of a high-cost, lab-based setup, which comes with certain assumptions. The particular model of knowledge production and representation built into Scalar is not necessarily problematic but is important to bear in mind. And even if the possibilities are channeled through the technical platform, they are really the result of a combination of political, institutional, conceptual, networking, and technological activities. In addition, the platform is situated on multiple levels and points to how empowerment is inflected naturally.

Mirzoeff also touches on collaboration, another type of condition relevant to the digital humanities and empowerment. He argues that collaboration "is built into the platform" since Scalar projects are collaborative efforts involving the authors, designers, and other users of the platform. At the same time, his piece possesses a very individual sensibility, leading to questions about how much collaboration is built into the platform and how much results from the particular process in which Mirzoeff engaged, which among other things included an externally funded summer institute.

From a big digital humanities perspective, empowering different epistemic traditions and working styles is highly relevant and means accepting both more collaborative and more individualistic traditions as well as other modalities. In this light, the emphasis in the digital humanities on collaboration might become problematic, not because collaboration is not important but because a variety of working and organizational styles and strategies are needed.

Individual-Collaborative Empowerment

Constructing the digital humanities as inherently collaborative often depends on seeing other kinds of humanities as inherently individual. According to *Collaborative Research in the Digital Humanities*,

> Collaboration within digital humanities is both a pertinent and a pressing topic as the traditional mode of the humanist, working alone in his or her study, is supplemented by explicitly co-operative, interdependent and collaborative research.[34]

The image of the humanist working alone in his or her office is quite pervasive and persists both within and outside the humanities.[35] In actuality, most humanists are collaboratively minded, even if collaboration is often not manifested in the final scholarly products and even if much of the work process is individual. Seminar culture, scholarly networks, conferences, and collegial engagement are all part of the collaborative texture of humanities work. Nevertheless, the humanities is neither massively collaborative nor structured to meet challenges that require interdisciplinary sentiment, heterogeneous teams, or technological infrastructure. This is where the digital humanities can play an important role in supporting such work, even if digital humanities work is probably not as inherently collaborative as proponents often contend.

How can we empower different work practices within the digital humanities that focus on the individual-collaborative parameter? On a very simple level, drawing on the discussion of translucence as a design principle, the design of scholarly environments (whether mostly physical or mostly digital) can respond both to individual and collaborative sensitivities in a lab environment. For example, the mapping of professional roles and space is not a given. Technical work can be highly individualistic and can require the equivalent of an office or study, although in some cases, the use of headphones in an open office environment or sound-insulated sofas in lab space suffices. And many academics no longer have traditional offices. Accommodating relative privacy in a collaboratively oriented and technologically inflected milieu is a balancing act that embodies the idea that allowing different practices, engagements, and crossovers is necessary to making the digital humanities. Allowing people to see what other people are working on while simultaneously enabling individual separation is important. Semitransparent workplace arrangements as well as the use of headphones can be useful in this context. These ideas apply to digital humanities initiatives without strong physical manifestations, but having a physical space is often helpful and makes some of these connections more obvious.

Translucence as a design principle can also be extended to institutional-level strategies, thus enabling working styles and epistemic traditions to mesh. For example, multiple affiliation—connections to several institutions at the same time—draws on the importance of linking the digital humanities to other departments and disciplines and of creating long-term commitments to such exchanges. People with double affiliations can be involved in changing both worlds (institutions), and individuals not only can help forge strong ties but are empowered by working across boundaries and using both institutional structures to build momentum.

Much potential lies in the spaces between established structures, disciplines, and areas, and big digital humanities draws on this potential. The quality of being in between has an empowering function, as Hakim Bey highlights with his "temporary autonomous zones," which elude formal structures of control and are created on the boundary lines of established regions.[36] Bey's work points to the importance of a dynamic footprint, and even if the digital humanities can be fairly stable in terms of organization, it also must have the ability to shift ground, to approach new areas, and to adapt to the actors involved at any given time. In a fairly static institution such as higher education, such dynamic zones can serve very important functions.

Peter Galison demonstrates the possibilities of combining the identities and practices associated with different epistemic traditions and how this tension offers empowerment:

> Different finite traditions of theorizing, experimenting, instrument making, and engineering meet—even transform one another—but for all that they do not lose their separate identities and practices.[37]

Galison's point echoes the discussion of multiple affiliation as an empowering mechanism as well as the ideas behind big digital humanities more broadly. Empowerment can also be found in low-key work across different disciplines. Supporting collaborative cultures is thus critical to the digital humanities on multiple levels. James Cronin notes the importance of collaboration among actors within the core digital humanities operation and among disciplines:

> While it is understandable to want to reproduce structures institutions are familiar with, nevertheless, no matter what structure institutions may adopt, it is essential, I feel, to foster collaborative cultures between all participants be they academic, technical, or academic-related post-holders. Forming such cultures requires leadership, institutional support and a willingness on the part of all participants, irrespective of their individual disciplinary backgrounds, to engage in dialogue and dissemination.[38]

Deeply collaborative work requires a supportive culture, which, as Cronin suggests, involves a range of factors. Again, engaging in dialogue is important regardless of disciplinary background. In addition, institutional questions and curatorship resonate with Cronin's list of factors.

However, we help to create the conditions for our own empowerment, as Cronin hints when he stresses the importance of a willingness to engage. Such cocreation occurs when people take part in a culture of dialogue and exploration. Mutual respect is an important factor here, as research on interdisciplinary practice points out.[39] This does not mean that there is no productive sharpness or tension. According to Michael Shanks, "Collaboration does not mean consensus—dissent is good. Enable such a diversity of voice."[40] Taking diversity of voice seriously means to be inclusive and incorporating participants beyond traditional patterns of inclusion. Roopika Risam points to the often necessary difficulty of carrying out such intersectional work.[41] Empowerment in this sense can be uncomfortable, and informed and sensible curatorship is important. Élika Ortega importantly asks how we can "foster a true DH ecology of knowledge, that is critical, intersectional, interdisciplinary, and global?"[42]

Empowerment comes into play with the digital humanities in many ways. In an everyday setting, of course, humanities scholars are empowered by access to digital resources and tools. In the context of big digital humanities, the field's intermediate position helps to create a range of possibilities regarding established structures and disciplines. Empowerment exists across disciplines and epistemic traditions and among people through the field's position as a meeting place and contact zone. Individuals and groups can be empowered to explore digitally inflected research questions, activities, and infrastructure in a way that would not easily be possible without the digital humanities. We can also be empowered to change ourselves and to encourage real diversity. Infrastructural resources can shift perspectives, expressions, and subjects of study. At the same time, such resources are conditioned and constrained, as we must remain aware both while doing our own work and while doing critical work on these conditions.

Making Spaces

We tend to associate institution building and curating with physical environments. Most university departments have hallways with offices, and traditional curating is most likely to happen in a physical museum or gallery. Some examples of empowerment are similarly linked to physical space as a platform. At the same time, universities, cultural heritage institutions, and many other organizations are struggling with how to engage with an increasingly digital world. While massively open online courses or digital museums will not remove the need for physical space, they put considerable pressure not only on space but also on these institutions more broadly. What does it mean if university education does not require physical space in the form of a campus and buildings? Can browsing a museum website replace the experience of visiting a physical museum? Such institutions are strongly grounded in their physical spaces, so this is not an either/or question: we engage both with digital and physical materiality. The digital humanities can arguably contribute to the ongoing debate in this area. Material engagement is, however, also relevant for how the digital humanities organizes and builds itself: it is relevant for making the field.

Interest in space has recently been renewed, driven both by technological development and by an intellectual reengagement with space as a category.[43] Geographical information and positioning systems have become infrastructural cornerstones, and maps provide a convenient way of organizing and accessing digital information. These systems also have built-in notions of what space actually is and how it can be described and understood. The so-called spatial turn is often traced back to the work of Henri Lefebvre and his discussion of the production of space and of space as a social product.[44] Similarly, research has demonstrated that creative ideas "emerge and develop in complex, dynamic interaction between the creator and his or her environments."[45] Infrastructure is inevitably situated and is never purely immaterial. David N. Livingstone argues for the interrelation between spatially situated practice and knowledge production:

In important ways, scientific knowledge is always the product of specific spaces. To claim otherwise is to displace science from the culture of which it is so profoundly a part.[46]

It is critical to connect the ideational underpinning of any operation to material manifestations, whether physical or digital, and to appropriate infrastructure. Generally speaking, big digital humanities as a meeting place and contact zone will benefit from both physical and digital manifestations. These manifestations are increasingly merged, and the digital world no longer seems so separate from the physical world. Walking around at an airport talking to a face on a tablet screen may not yet be fully naturalized behavior, but we are no longer concerned with separate and decontextualized video conference setups and stationary computers. A range of technologies supports this development, including 3-D printing and various mobile technologies, but the most critical factor is the quick social and cultural uptake of such technologies.

Since the late 1990s, many resources have been invested in building digital and online spaces, but the integrity of such spaces is difficult to uphold in a diversified and mobile media ecology. In particular, the idea of separate online places divorced from our physical world no longer seems tenable as the distinctions between physical and digital materiality become increasingly blurred. Recent developments seem to indicate a reassertion of physical space, a decentering of the idea of the primacy of digital space in certain discourses, and a realization that as embodied beings, we are profoundly situated spatially and materially. Digital materiality shapes and interacts with physical materiality, and this interaction plays out in embodied space, which is constructed culturally, socially, institutionally, and of course through our bodies.

Humans are always physically situated, even when taking online courses or engaging in distributed computing. And the details of that situatedness are important. It is now common to see as many screens as customers in coffee shops. I am writing this at my favorite table in a Umeå café with my laptop, IPad, and phone on the table in front of me. I am somewhat closing off the world around me by using headphones and listening to music. I carefully choose where to sit in places like this—probably more carefully than most customers—but I am certainly not the only one who cares about space. People pick seats in these types of spaces based on factors such as availability of outlets, interest in communicating with other patrons, location of and interest in TV screens, and the presence of other customers. I have observed that in most coffee shops, patrons follow patterns in selecting certain seats first. In the coffee shop on the third floor of the Barnes and Noble bookshop in Union Square in New York City, a couple of tables close to the bay windows overlooking Union Square are usually taken first, often by the same people. Outsiders who wish to take these spots must not only arrive very early but also infringe on an established social order. Other positions are less popular in the long term. On one level, this is a matter of simple arithmetic, but if we take seriously the spatial situatedness of knowledge production, we need to consider such aspects when considering how to make the digital humanities.

A great deal of physical space is not necessarily required to implement the big digital humanities. Network models, multiple-campus platforms, working groups, and online environments can be critical to operationalizing the field. For small colleges and large, dispersed universities, it makes more sense to implement a network model or tap into platforms such as HASTAC than to build a physical digital humanities center. Even with designated space, it is a question of how much is needed. Make-do physical spaces such as a prototype lab or pop-up space can be more appropriate for many initiatives and projects. There is sometimes a sense that institutional space of this kind has to be vast, but small, well-grounded, and active spaces can often be attractive and functional.

It is not, however, necessary to choose between the physical and the digital. In most cases, any digital humanities operation has some kind of physical instantiation, and it is very unlikely that a physically situated operation would lack digital instantiation. One key challenge involves making the line between the physical and digital porous or maybe eliminating it altogether and encouraging different types of integration.

Physical space is extremely valuable in many contexts. Space partially structures our experience, and vice versa, and we coconstruct space with others and with our surrounding environment. Consequently, knowledge production, intellectual exchange, and development work are spatially situated.[47] From the point of view of big digital humanities, space can also be quite useful in terms of channeling resources, getting people together, manifesting work and ideas, and enabling deep collaboration. While space is an important parameter, we also need to be careful not to be deterministic about the function of space in knowledge production. Many other parameters condition and shape knowledge production. For example, the culture built around a place and institution plays a critical role. Also, a beautifully designed lab without people does not make much sense, and people can shape spaces to suit goals and visions even if the conditions are not optimal.

Space is institutional, symbolic, and ideational, as Shannon Mattern stresses in her work on public libraries and space:

> The architectural design process provides an unparalleled opportunity for institutional closet-cleaning and psychoanalysis. What better time to prioritize the institution's values, to reassess its purpose, to reconsider what ideas and ideals it embodies, and to refashion its image than when considering how to physically embody these values, to structurally accommodate the functions, to materially symbolize these ideas, and to reflect these images? Through the design and construction of a new home, libraries reassess or reaffirm who they are, they reconsider what they reflect on how to assert their continued relevance in an era in which their obituary has already been written by a myopic few.[48]

Mattern's work demonstrates the hopes and visions that can be ascribed to spatial reconfiguration. Much of her description does not concern space but rather prioritizing, reassessing, reconsidering, and refashioning operational ideas and ideals. Again, we need to be careful not to take this argument too far while acknowledging the institutional and symbolic power of space. And we need to ask who does the ideational work and for what reason.

As Mattern shows, reconfiguration is rarely a neutral process, as it is driven by different kinds of internal and external pressure. One example of current pressure is the role of the digital in relation to both public and research libraries. One of the main challenges faced by libraries and digital humanities initiatives is how to be simultaneously physical and digital. This challenge arises not so much from the distinction between the physical and the digital or from moving from one domain to another but rather from about thinking carefully about who one is and where one wants to go and adapting or creating material manifestations based on this ideational foundation.

We also need to take seriously material that is primarily digital. The exact materiality of the platforms and underlying architecture we use and create will shape us, our work, and our physical materiality. Widely used systems, such as presentation software and learning platforms, have an enormous impact on how we manifest ourselves and carry out our work. The fact that the most commonly used piece of presentation software is built on a slide paradigm (serial presentation of slides) is significant. For one thing, it means that thousands of talks, lectures, and discussions carried out at any point in time are facilitated by a platform that structures the presentation situation in terms of presenter and audience and that does not easily accommodate multiple threads, multiple screens, distributed "live" collaboration, or a different presentation situation. This platform, in turn, is built into other technical systems and into expectations of what it means to give a talk, have a dialogue, or make a presentation.

What does this mean for the digital humanities? First, we should not underestimate the importance of the material qualities of spaces and platforms that are core to our operation, regardless of whether they are physical or digital. The details of these configurations matter and are linked to our vision and goals as well as to questions of identity and well-being. Second, we need to take the complexity of our operations into account when creating space and infrastructure. Doing so is particularly important when moving between physical and digital materiality, as we run the risk of forgetting important qualities when we move mostly physical operations in a digital direction, especially when those qualities are not clearly instrumental or necessarily computational. Third, ideas, space, and infrastructure are worth little if not used, negotiated, and changed by people. Individual people's engagement plays a crucial role, just like people-centered processes such as curatorship and empowerment.

Collaborations in Space

In HUMlab, we have experimented since the early 2000s with incorporating distributed resources in the physical space, including virtual worlds, remote participants, and Twitter and chat feeds. For an operation grounded both in physical and digital materiality, this approach makes sense, and it has been important to integrate these distributed materials and presences in the lab environment in such a way as to not make them separated or too instrumental. In the early 2010s, we started to bring in remote people via Skype on big screens—portable screens measuring between fifty and sixty inches. One of the first times we did this, at a 2011 conference, the speaker's screen was wheeled in on a mobile stand. His presentation material was shown on the main screen (just like with the speakers who were physically present). The material configuration and movement of the screen played a significant role, just like the prominent slot given to the remote speaker. If he had appeared on the main screen along with slides, the effect would have been quite different in terms of size, comparison to the local speakers, separation from the slides, and embodied presence. It turns out that screen stands can have an almost uncanny human sensibility.

We have also used wall- and pillar-mounted screens to accommodate remote participants (as well as for many other things), and here the localized sound plays an important role, enabling people to walk around and chat individually with the on-screen participants. HUMlab's new space on the Arts Campus has a wall of four asymmetrically positioned screens, two in portrait mode and two in landscape mode. For a spring 2013 workshop on the digital humanities, we used these four screens and a portable one to bring in five international participants.

Each event of this type is an experiment, and we have learned, for example, about the importance of giving feedback to the remote participants. They benefit if they can see the whole space as well as the other remote participants, and we use a ceiling-placed camera to give an overview and deliver this feed separately to the participants.

This example demonstrates how space can organize physical and digital materiality for the digital humanities. This is an intellectual-material argument, grounded in the assertion that space and infrastructure can be an important part of (and even prerequisite for) the arguments we make and the work we do. The digital humanities benefits from a strong spatial presence. This is particularly true for big digital humanities, which sits between disciplines, centers, and other actors; works with boundary objects; makes humanities infrastructure possible; and functions as a contact zone. Tension can arise between working with digital technology and being physically situated, but the case for space seems fairly strong. However, many other kinds of models exist for doing work in the field, and there is no one-size-fits-all model. Also, space is notoriously difficult to come by in most institutional contexts. But given that the value of such an environment goes far beyond the field itself, it might be possible to convince leaders of the importance of such prioritizations.

Having a space can be quite useful to university and regional leadership in terms of channeling humanities work and interaction and in providing a site to showcase to outside visitors. The humanities traditionally has few such sites, and being seen as an exciting place to visit can have clear value. In the fall of 2013, the king and queen of Sweden visited HUMlab. The royal family may no longer wield much power, but the king and queen were accompanied by university and regional leaders as well as many others, and all of these people heard the story of HUMlab. A week later, the minister of commerce came to HUMlab to discuss the digital humanities and entrepreneurship.

Space can also be shared institutionally. A fairly common strategy is to for digital humanities labs to work together with university libraries, who often have space and whose operations have changed fairly dramatically. Such joint ventures can be quite powerful and can help with the packaging of humanities infrastructure, but both parties must be willing to change and to devise a joint intellectual and material agenda. Dissonance can occur between the library model of infrastructure and what the digital humanities may need, but rightly done, both institutions can benefit from an alliance.

Other possible partners include humanities centers. A strong research-driven vision of humanities academic infrastructure can motivate the need for space. With external applications for infrastructure funding, the university may be convinced to put up space (among other things) as its contribution if the applications are successful. And even if such funding is mainly for re-search, it is unlikely that anyone would stop the inclusion of students and others in such an operation.

A good example of an argument for a digital humanities space in a library comes from a group of scholars at Columbia who wrote an open letter in favor of a digital humanities studio in which they noted that such spaces can facilitate THATcamps, open labs, and other "emerging models of getting together, sharing knowledge, and getting things done." Although some of these models are distributed, their function stresses the importance of a local constituency and associated space. The authors also emphasized the need for "a neutral, flexible space for experimentation in the humanities" based on such environments as art studios, startup spaces, maker spaces, and science laboratories, which are "characterized by open, grassroots architecture, a variety of working surfaces, the presence of projectors and whiteboards."[49] The resultant space, Studio@Butler, is described as "a collaboratory for educators, scholars and librarians" and a "bring-your-own-technology space."[50] The inclusion of librarians is significant, and long-term success is of course more likely if the collaboration between librarians and scholars is genuine.

It other cases it might be more useful to align with science labs to stress the need for more costly humanities infrastructure. Another supporting factor can be the interest in such spaces outside the humanities, and how these spaces matter for the university as a whole and for connecting to the world outside the university. One possibility is to write a five- to ten-page document that connects the underlying concept with the space as well as its importance for research and education.

Interlude 8: Operating on the Radar

In September 2013, the dean of the Faculty of Arts and Humanities at Umeå University called a meeting to discuss the allocation of doctoral positions for the next four years. This a very serious matter: in Sweden, doctoral students cannot be accepted unless there is funding. Almost all graduate positions are fully salaried for four years, but only a limited number of positions are available. Our standard practice had been to allocate positions based on indicators such as the throughput of students and the number of qualified advisers. At this time, between fifteen and eighteen positions were to be filled, a very significant investment for the faculty. In Sweden, a substantial part of research funding is spent on graduate students.

Other commitments had originally meant that I would not be attending the meeting, but some of those were rescheduled for other reasons, and by the time I realized that the others were less important than the meeting, I was twenty minutes late in arriving. When I got there, the room was overflowing: some faculty members were standing in the hallway and trying to peer into the room. I grabbed a chair from another classroom and found a spot inside. Many senior faculty were present as well as some junior scholars and others with an interest in the matter. The room was crackling with energy, and I realized that I had probably missed the most intense discussion, which was likely a good thing.

The dean had analyzed the present allocation system and found some basic problems. It was conservative in that the same disciplines tended to get the bulk of available positions, and it was not strategic in the sense that very few positions were geared toward specific areas. Furthermore, it was largely based on the conception of doctoral work as a series of individual projects and missed the idea of the students as part of a larger group. He offered a radical and surprising suggestion: allocate all the positions for one period to a strategically prioritized area. Each discipline would get at least one position, and about fifteen salaried four-year positions would be connected to one specific area. And the area he proposed was the digital humanities.

He was seeking not to take the positions away from the departments and disciplines but rather to make sure that all the positions had some type of digital inflection. He suggested that these positions would be tied to projects defined by the departments and dangled the possibility of external matching funding for such an initiative. Furthermore, the dean pointed to HUMlab as a platform and a competitive advantage but did not make it the center of the proposal. In an academic culture where prioritization is not necessarily easy and where large strategic assessments may not be plentiful, the dean's proposal was daring and quite provocative.

The proposal challenged the epistemic and institutional tradition of the humanities. Senior humanities faculty do not necessarily think of their graduate students' work as projects or as connected to a designated research theme. Other faculty members felt unease about the idea that the humanities should invest in something because external interest (from funding agencies and others) existed. Someone said that she was inclined to say no to money of this kind. Several other participants brought up the speed of the suggestion, which was not compatible with the way the humanities usually operates. Comparisons to the sciences were also made, and one person argued that if we were to adopt a science model, we should do so completely rather than trying to come up with our own halfhearted version of it. Others brought up the strong belief among Swedish humanists that ideas for thesis projects come from the doctoral students themselves. Allocating graduate positions based on a strategic focus is thus a fairly foreign concept. Yet other speakers brought up possible problems with competent supervision as well as the issue some potential applicants would be shut out because their planned work was not digitally inflected.

The proposal was also provocative because of the choice of the digital humanities as a prioritized strategic area and the sense that the digital is a discipline-neutral area and boundary object. One junior faculty member declared that the field was really no longer as current. A senior faculty member likened the proposal to the royal warship *Vasa*, which sunk on its maiden voyage in 1628: "Remember this image!" Another senior scholar strongly opposed the idea that the digital can be a perspective, and someone else contended that the digital is already part of the disciplines.

Even though the discussion seemed unnecessarily pointed at times, I quite enjoyed it because it was the sort of open, strategic conversation not very often seen in academe. For my part, I tried to connect this initiative to past investments in the field (and HUMlab). I also suggested that it would be possible to have an open call for digital humanities graduate students without having the departments specify projects. Several moderate voices noted the rashness of making such a large move all at once, which seemed to be a sensible perspective. Many faculty members were not particularly happy, but there was also a great deal of support, some of which was not vocalized at the time.

Any institutional platform is also a story. In many ways, HUMlab's story has distinct appeal. Making the digital humanities is also about finding and articulating these stories. At the same time, as such stories are retold and packaged over time, they naturally tend to focus on the successful and exciting moments rather than the hardships and mistakes. HUMlab has had good support, and much of its story is positive, but it is also a story of institutional struggles, resistance, and disappointments. This story is also important, particularly in relation to building new platforms for the digital humanities. At the same time, we also need to avoid becoming caught up in a story that merely repeats institutional critique. Someone once pointed out that my presentations of HUMlab drew on a mild form of opposition to the faculty, and I have subsequently tried to be clear that HUMlab is part of the faculty rather than an outsider—not because I was afraid or felt pressured, but because it made sense.

This meeting reminded me of Sandy Stone's 2006 comment that as director of the ACTlab at the University of Texas, she preferred to "operate under the radar."[51] I was now quite aware that we were no longer operating under the radar—if we ever had been. Though interest in and support for HUMlab had grown over the years, the majority of faculty did not actively engage with us. The dean's proposal changed that fairly drastically. We were no doubt operating on the radar, and although the proposal was not primarily about securing resources for HUMlab, the suggested allocation model forced faculty to take an active position. The fact that the discussion took place at all says something about the relative openness of the faculty and the viability of big digital humanities. If HUMlab had been organized as a discipline and department rather than an intersectional lab, it would almost certainly have been impossible to secure more than just one or two doctoral positions. For developing the digital humanities, many doctoral positions are unquestionably better than a few—in part to forge connections to the disciplines and achieve long-term traction.

The humanities sometimes has difficulty applying its critical awareness to itself even though doing so is important. For example, the argument that it is important to allow students to choose the topics of their doctoral work is important, but it is also embedded in a system where many students are vetted locally (they earn their undergraduate degrees from the same department) and where the senior professors (and their research interests) are likely to be quite influential. Doctoral candidates are not working with a blank slate, and a bias may well exist in favor of local students at the expense of external ones. I am not suggesting that faculty are not concerned with getting students of the highest quality; rather, we get locked into epistemic mind-sets and can lose the critical perspective. Moreover, criticality must be balanced by an interest in structural development and change or the humanities will never evolve. Meetings such as this one may lay bare existing positions and power structures and offer rare opportunities to discuss important matters such as the role of doctoral programs across a number of departments and disciplines.

Finally, the dean's approach would seem to be a productive strategy. By remaining calm and not argumentative, he probably made something possible that would not have happened otherwise. Provocation can sometimes be useful. A certain degree of daring is important in institution building, and long-term change and influence are secured by being moderate, constructive, sharp, and persistent. I became aware that I could now hold my ground fairly effortlessly in a weighty and concentrated context—and actually could enjoy the discussion and the heat. Shortly thereafter, we invited faculty members to participate in a workshop, Sorting the Digital Humanities Out. Instead of operating under the radar, we were confidently involved in an ongoing local and international dialogue.

Digital Humanities as a Site for Learning

So, what happens when one starts out from a conceptual foundation and builds competent institutions, curates the digital humanities, empowers the humanities, and makes appropriate spaces? Learning happens.

Because learning is essentially what higher education is about, claiming that the digital humanities is a site for learning is hardly a controversial or surprising move. It is a useful and relevant way to think about the field, however, allowing us to bring together a number of threads already considered as well as perspectives that may not receive enough emphasis in the literature or in online discussions.

The digital humanities can be seen as a curiosity-driven site for learning. Learning across epistemic traditions and intersectional junctions can be facilitated in the digital humanities as a contact zone. Such zones are not free from power structures, traditional assumptions about learning, or epistemic commitments, but they deliberately challenge and discuss some of those assumptions and empower alternative modes of thinking and making. Learning in epistemically and structurally different environments has the potential to change the way we think. For example, accommodating many modes of engagement with the digital creates opportunities for deep-going intellectual-material engagement across disciplines and professional areas. Furthermore, critically based exploration through making can empower us as scholars and intellectuals and help us approach complex, real-world problems and opportunities. Also, curatorship can play an important role in creating conditions for learning through facilitating encounters, suggesting intellectual themes or discussions to be had, connecting to fields and domains outside of the humanities, and pointing to differences as something useful and important to explore.

Education has surfaced as an important point of discussion in the digital humanities, and a sense seems to exist that this perspective is underdeveloped.[52] However, several recent initiatives emphasize digital pedagogy, among them *Digital Pedagogy in the Humanities: Concepts, Models, and Experiments*, a U.S.-based online open-access collection, and the edited volume *Digital Humanities Pedagogy*.[53]

Learning and pedagogy are not separate from other activities but rather form the core of the field. Such learning is not generic but is oriented around the intersection of the humanities and the digital. Furthermore, we are concerned not merely with one type of learning but with a range of types of knowledge building that span education and research. These learning processes are situated in an intersectional and technologically engaged context that differs from many traditional academic settings. Knowledge production and learning are spatially situated, and space and infrastructure can be used to signal and manifest alternative types of learning and knowledge production. Such infrastructure is both physical and digital, and the capacities of networking learning, Cathy N. Davidson and David Theo Goldberg discuss, are quite significant.[54] They refer both to knowledge about networking tools and networks and to the possibilities of shaping learning processes through networking technologies and cultures. Another important factor is the multiple-mode engagement between the humanities and the digital, which presents us with a range of different types of knowledge building and epistemic positions.

Big digital humanities is in many ways ideally placed to constitute an exploratory site for learning. There is power in drawing on disciplinary depth while encouraging intersectional engagement. There is power in an inviting and open organization that sits outside the established departments and is not part of the organized higher education pedagogy. There is power in a strong digital engagement and a long humanistic scholarly tradition. The processes of empowerment and curatorship are also key pedagogical strategies, as is opening up both the traditional classroom and the seminar room. What if a stronger flow existed between such institutional platforms? What if students and faculty engaged in knowledge making in the same environment? What if academic installations were to replace 10 percent of traditional publications? What if students built alternative database ontologies to challenge the platforms used by faculty? I am arguing not for the replacement of replacing current structures but rather for complementing and to some degree reshaping them. The digital humanities can play an important role in providing hope, innovation, and infrastructure.

Different environments support different types of learning and put different demands on learning. Contact zones would seem to require continuous learning in relation to different epistemic traditions, emergent themes, and technological development. For example, structuring and encoding data typically is closely linked to particular materials or research questions. According to Geoffrey Bowker and Susan Leigh Star, "Classifications should be recognized as the significant site of political and ethical work that they are."[55] Ursula Heise shows how biodiversity databases are cultural as well as scientific constructions. Database structures are important to Heise's work, and she is clear about the necessity and value of working with digital humanists to produce analyses using appropriate tools.[56] Such collaborations do not involve one party who knows only technology and another party who knows only his or her own research and material. Rather, they are intellectual-technological exchanges about learning and building knowledge.

Such exchanges do not have to be based on a clearly identified and instrumental need but can emerge in a shared environment that supports learning and facilitates meetings and infrastructure. Humanities scholars working on individual book projects in such an environment are also likely to be influenced by the infrastructure and learn from the people present, not necessarily in a shallow or trivial way. The technologist, conversely, is likely to learn from talking to such scholars about their individual projects. In terms of advising on structuring data and encoding materials, the technologist will have accumulated experience and knowledge from different projects in different epistemic traditions. Such knowledge is invaluable.

Digital humanists have realized that their field needs to engage more strongly with undergraduate education.[57] Digital humanities centers have largely focused on research and development projects and have typically had little involvement in undergraduate affairs. One obvious reason is that most of these centers have not had departmental status and a discipline of their own. Consequently, extensive discussion of the field tended not to concentrate on educational issues. The massive *Companion to Digital Humanities* (2004), includes the word *education* only thirty-three times, more than a third of them in one chapter (on art history). In contrast, the word *research* appears 509 times in thirty-six of the book's thirty-seven chapters. In the decade-plus since that volume was published, however, the situation has changed quite drastically, with a larger institutional footprint for the digital humanities that is increasingly linked to undergraduate education. By 2012, *education* appeared 100 times in *Debates in the Digital Humanities*, while *research* appeared 153 times. While in this book I have used *research* about three times more than *education*, *learning* also appears rather frequently.

It should not come as a surprise that the digital humanities shows more interest in educational matters at a time when the field has leverage and institutionalization work is in progress. Building undergraduate and graduate programs is part and parcel of establishing a stronger institutional platform and a steady income stream in much of higher education.

Another factor connecting the digital humanities to learning is the resurgence of online education as a topic of discussion. In 2012–13, Stanford University president John Hennessy said that he planned to "think hard about . . . distance learning":

> Stanford, like newspapers and music companies and much of traditional media a little more than a decade ago, is sailing in seemingly placid waters. But Hennessy's digital experience alerts him to danger. He says, "There's a tsunami coming."[58]

The topic of online learning and massively open online courses (MOOCs) was particularly current at this time, and had Hennessy taken his sabbatical two years later, he might have had different priorities. However, the topic remains important. Given an inclusive notion of the digital humanities, it may not be surprising that online learning sometimes seems to fall under the field's umbrella. Online learning is a clearly a matter of technology and culture, and some might assume that digital humanists would bring competence to this discussion as well as possibly the know-how to build conceptually grounded platforms for online learning. However, given that the digital humanities has not been particularly invested in education and learning tools, there may well be better candidates for taking on this task. Or it could be argued that there is need for a humanities-based sensibility in thinking deeply about online learning and in devising other ways of carrying out such education. Indeed, if present-day online learning systems are lacking conceptually, intellectually, pedagogically and technologically, the digital humanities might be able to help fill the gap.

Online Learning and the Digital Humanities

The spread of MOOCs and other online platforms has highlighted the intersection of the digital humanities and online learning. While, on one level, MOOCs do not necessarily differ substantially from earlier examples of distributed learning, they are also clearly not the same thing. Scale is a major difference: MOOCs were designed to accommodate vast numbers of students. Furthermore, many MOOCs are freely available (although generally embedded in commercial structures and uncertain business models), which means that they contrast with some other online learning platforms. The shift from fifty students to fifty thousand students is arguably more a conceptual and marketing shift than a technological or pedagogical one. Much of the pedagogics and technology would seem to be the same aside from the infrastructure needed to handle so many students. MOOCs offer mass education on a scale not previously possible (or imagined). Just as important is the idea of learning taking place outside established educational systems, physical campuses, and current business models.

However, MOOCs are not necessarily characterized by high-quality, innovative thinking or progressive pedagogies. Just like many other learning platforms, MOOCs are built primarily around information distribution rather than constructivist or student-centered pedagogies. Even if the scale, accessibility, and pricing of MOOCs are important benefits for many learners, the pedagogical vision is usually very limited. According to the Coursera website,

> Key ideas include mastery learning, to make sure that you have multiple attempts to demonstrate your new knowledge; using interactivity, to ensure student engagement and to assist long-term retention; and providing frequent feedback, so that you can monitor your own progress, and know when you've really mastered the material.[59]

The idea that materials must be mastered and that multiple tries and feedback systems will help students do so is reminiscent of 1980s arguments in favor of educational technologies.[60] Although we should not downplay the usefulness of such learning platforms in certain contexts, a mechanistic idea of learning lies at the heart of such pedagogy. The Coursera website argues that moving traditional lecturing to online platforms can free up time for active learning in the classroom. But do we still want or need the traditional lecture format (digitally mediated or not)? The digital humanities could be asking such questions.

Digital humanists could also voice concerns about the extent to which the hype around MOOCs is driven by market interests. Ian Bogost offers an excellent example of critical work in line with what the digital humanities could be:

> The growth of private MOOC companies is driven almost entirely from financial speculation, speculation with an interest in private, short-term gain via industrialized scale. It's worth imagining what other kinds of growth might be possible if we had the stomach for a different kind of speculation meant to benefit long-term social institutions like schools instead of just the market.[61]

We should learn from David N. Noble and other scholars who juxtapose earlier generations of distributed learning (for example, correspondence learning and video-based education) and online learning. For example, clear parallels exist between the discourse that surrounded correspondence education in the late nineteenth and early twentieth centuries and the current discussion of online learning. Correspondence education was said to be independent of time and space, adaptable to different learning styles, and highly individualized. But as Noble shows, correspondence education, like many other platforms for distributed learning, was also about rationalizing higher education and developing new business models.[62] This link between new technologies, predictions about radical impact, and rationalization efforts has always been strong. The discourse often does not highlight the will to rationalize and create business (in places where doing so is possible) but rather focuses on technologically driven visions and eliminating the constraints of time and place. While access and distributed learning are important, the pedagogical rationale for online learning platforms and most current MOOCs is rarely well worked out, and we would be hard-pressed to claim that they arise from a pedagogical vision.

Noble's harsh criticism of distributed learning has merit, but it is also clearly one-sided in blaming administrators and commercial interests. In addition, he idealizes traditional, classroom-based education, a common tendency in discussions of MOOCs.[63] As in the past, the polarities and many of the technologically driven dreams are strong. However, a broad push now comes from a range of factors, including financial pressure, space pressures, an increased sense of global education as opposed to exclusionary models, and a certain level of technological maturity. MOOCs have helped open up a conceptual space, a useful accomplishment whatever the shortcomings in implementation. This means that President Hennessy's priorities were probably right and that the question of whether the digital humanities can and should be part of this discussion of online learning is both current and important.

The Dark Side of the Digital Humanities

The connection between the digital humanities and MOOCs came into focus after a roundtable session, The Dark Side of Digital Humanities, held at the 2013 MLA conference. The first of the session's four speakers, Wendy Chun, pointed to the dismal situation of the humanities (and the academy more generally), declaring that we have "capitulated to a bureaucratic technocratic logic." Nontechnological problems are rewritten into problems that can be fixed by technology, and MOOCs become a quick fix to education, preferable to dealing with the real problems of increasing costs, temporary positions, and the quantification of research and education. According to Chun, the same holds true for the digital humanities, and we need to address the "dark side" of the field, which includes omissions related to critical theory, critical race studies, and the negative aspects of the Internet.[64]

Not surprisingly, observers found Chun's statement provocative. She critiqued the digital humanities both for its failure to engage critically and for its use as a discursive means of approaching but not really solving serious higher education problems. Though Matthew Kirschenbaum, who was in attendance, perceived Chun as conflating the digital humanities and MOOCs, it is more accurate to say that she was making the point that both the discourse of MOOCs and the discourse of the digital humanities draw on technology to suggest solutions to large-scale problems.[65] The problem, however, is that humanities computing as digital humanities is normally not associated with a far-reaching will to change higher education. Chun's critique of the visionary sentiment of digital humanities therefore seems based on conflation of several traditions of digital humanities. Nevertheless, it also seems fair to say that humanities computing has bought into a technological logic without substantively engaging with critical theories of technology, environmental perspectives, or gender studies, thereby opening up the field to charges that it is neoliberal and uncritical (although Kirschenbaum and other scholars have undertaken work that extends across technological and critical engagement).

The second speaker was Richard Grusin, also the organizer of the roundtable, and he, too, was accused of conflating MOOCs with digital humanities. Grusin largely read the digital humanities as part of a neoliberal movement, and he made a strong connection between the digital humanities and the (alleged) crises of the humanities. Furthermore, he depicted interest in making in the digital humanities as reflecting the neoliberal agenda and devaluing critical work:

> At the same time that the market logic of neoliberalism has been used to decimate the mainstream humanities from within and without, this same logic has encouraged foundations, corporations, and university administrations to devote new resources to the digital humanities and beginning over the past year to the development of MOOCs and other online forms of "content delivery."[66]

Grusin attacked the digital humanities more forcefully than (though not necessarily as effectively as) Chun. Grusin's talk had a much greater tendency to look back, and he argued that the digital humanities should not engage with collaborative work because doing so could be perceived as playing into the hands of the neoliberal powers. This attitude seems counterproductive and fails to acknowledge the benefits of working together. None of these issues is either/or, but it makes sense to include different work practices and epistemic traditions in the digital humanities. Grusin's position also focuses on the United States, where issues of tenure, increases in temporary employment, and rising tuition are particularly worrying. Furthermore, his denouncement of "making" as instrumental and buying into a neoliberal system is quite problematic, as it devalues making and erects rather than dismantles the boundaries between different practices. Making can indeed be instrumental and uncritical, but this sort of making is not most important to the development of the digital humanities.

In her contribution to the roundtable discussion, Rita Raley also pointed to the digital humanities as a discursive panacea, asking whether the field can be everything to everyone. She then voiced one of the discussion's most sensible positions: "I teach and write about digital media, so clearly I should want to participate in working groups and pilot programs for online education."[67] This statement encapsulates the ideal intersection of the digital humanities and learning; not without critical awareness, but with an interest in engaging.

This roundtable is interesting for several reasons. The panel did not include any old-time digital humanists—that is, people who have been heavily involved in the institutional work of the field. Nevertheless, many people from the traditional digital humanities community apparently attended. This tradition largely controls the organizations, journals, and many other digital humanities channels, and the session represents one of the few instances where the community came to the table but did not have any speaker slots. The roundtable seems to exemplify one-sided curatorship rather than to constitute a genuine attempt to bring together different perspectives in a productive manner. I see no problem with discussing the dark side of the digital humanities and using speakers outside the digital humanities proper, but this session seems to me to have been too one-sided and confrontational to constitute more than a provocation.

Indeed, this roundtable session, like some traditional digital humanities orchestrations, can be useful in helping us think about the future. Making the digital humanities is about curatorship, and better curatorship exists that is less aggressive than what was evident at MLA panel. The roundtable failed to find that respectful place in between. The digital humanities needs to involve the interweaving of critical work and making work as well as work practices that are more firmly placed in the book-writing or technology-building categories. It needs to accommodate both text encoding and the search for a future for the humanities and the academy. It needs to be unafraid, assertive, receptive, critical, humble, and forward-looking—all at the same time.

Conclusion

The digital humanities needs to be big to make possible the things that the field empowers us to imagine and to take on the challenges facing us. This bigness does not involve hiding in big digital humanities tents or building large institutional structures but rather involves being open to multiple modes of engagement between the digital and the humanities and to the bigness of the humanities itself. Curatorship and empowerment can be key strategies for facilitating this expansive vision.

I see making the digital humanities as a humanistic responsibility that includes embracing key intellectual questions, expanding our critical-material vocabulary and expressive practices, and exploring what it means to be human. This work must necessarily engage with the technological and always be driven by curiosity. Such an undertaking may not be small, but it is important and exciting.

Making December Events

December days are short in northern Sweden. In Umeå, the sun rises sometime after 9:00 A.M. and sets before 2:00 P.M. for most of the month. This is a good time for indoor work and connection building, and HUMlab has taken to organizing scholarly events during this month. These events have become one of our trademarks, channeling much energy and engagement over two or three days. They provide an opportunity to manifest, enact, and question the digital humanities and offer ideal case studies for examining how ideas and practice meet in big digital humanities. In addition, event making is a curatorial practice, so examining this process and the texture of these events can highlight the workings of the curatorial process.

Events bring people together, allow intellectual and technological exploration, and channel considerable amounts of energy into specific endeavors. A side effect of organizing large-scale events is that they motivate many other accomplishments—infrastructure is installed, projects are finalized, and the whole lab becomes refreshed and ready.

In a way, a platform such as HUMlab comes to life during such events. Curating the event can create a dynamism and experimental quality that is vital: What themes are chosen? Who is invited? How is the event carried out? How is technology utilized and integrated? Significant advantages can result from carrying out such events in a dedicated venue rather than in a generic university space or a conference hotel. Similarly, having staff and faculty who embody the basic ideas of the operation and demonstrate kindness, sharpness, and engagement is invaluable.

The networks that are created and developed through such events are anchored in HUMlab as an idea and operation. Such networks encompass physically present participants, distributed networks (sometimes represented on Twitter walls), streaming of content (when possible), and remote participants appearing on screens via Skype or similar platforms. As participants learn from each other and create new knowledge together in a conditioned environment, they form a kind of knowledge infrastructure.

At the same time, events are transitory, take a great deal of work to organize and implement, and may disappoint in that they rarely have dramatic long-term impact. Nevertheless, they are critical to an operation such as HUMlab. I agree with Jonathan Sterne's position regarding edited volumes: he declines many requests that reflect primarily interest from a press, but he believes that field-defining volumes arising from strong scholarly engagement can play a vital role.[1] Not every conference can be field-changing, but scholarly events make much more sense if they set out to make a difference, move beyond the state of the art, engage passionately with the questions raised, and be experimental (or at least not frozen) in terms of structure and the modalities employed.

On December 5–7, 2012, HUMlab hosted a conference, Infrastructure | Space | Media, that focused on themes such as knowledge production, making, architecture, infrastructure, and framing and was attended by a range of intellectuals and makers. Exactly a year later, on December 5–6, 2013, HUMlab sponsored a workshop, Sorting the Digital Humanities Out, that took a five- to seven-year perspective on the development of the field of digital humanities. Most participants were junior faculty members. And one week after that, on December 12, we held a discussion session on possible new master's degree programs at the intersection of the arts and science/technology/engineering/mathematics (STEM).

On one level, these events can be seen as exemplifying and demonstrating the digital humanities given particular intentions and conditions that roughly correspond to the idea of big digital humanities as presented in this book. Primarily, however, they were scholarly activities with specific themes and goals. The 2012 conference explored two principal questions: How is knowledge production shaped by infrastructure (and notions of infrastructure), and vice versa? And how does digital materiality change notions of space and architectural theory as well as of built space itself? Johanna Drucker, for example, talked about the renewed rise of positivism, pointed to how our understanding of spatial experience is anachronistic, and critiqued digital projects such as Rome Reborn as based on a number of lies.[2] While the research questions remained the focus of the conference, a related and sometimes fierce discussion of the digital humanities also occurred.

If the events themselves constitute attempts to model the digital humanities, their implementation can provide a sense of what big digital humanities can be and what might be difficult to realize in practice. For example, although we had wanted the 2012 conference to include a significant number of representatives invested in making and coding, most of the participants came from analytical traditions (English, information studies, and cinema studies). This bias was balanced to some degree by the presence of several architects, who are both critically invested and engaged in making and practice. A showcase demonstrated ongoing projects and technologies, and Chris Speed of the University of Edinburgh encouraged participants to use the app Comob to trace social negotiations of space.

Inviting and attracting diverse participants is one of HUMlab's major challenges in staging these events. The 2013 workshop deliberately focused on Sweden and the United States but also included attendees from Norway, Denmark, England, Australia, India, and France. Given that the task was to sort the digital humanities out, this would seem to be a fairly limited array of participants. However, some fifteen disciplines and areas were represented. In any case, it is important to go beyond established networks and try to get the best people regardless of where they are situated. Doing so is not easy, in large part because we rely on our existing networks, and moving one or two steps away from those networks may not create substantial diversity. Open and inclusion-aware calls for proposals can be a useful strategy, as can efforts to draw on the diversity of perspectives and backgrounds available within the university (including the student population) and the local community.

Events can be organized and orchestrated in a way that supports diversity, but avoiding micromanagement can also at times be helpful in this and other regards. For the discussion session on master's programs, HUMlab sent out a general invitation to the whole university to join us in exploring the possibility of creating high-quality, internationally competitive master's programs in between science/engineering and humanities/art. The inspiration was partly the U.S.-based STEAM movement, which has added the arts to the STEM framework. We were not entirely sure what to expect, but the discussion session drew participants from the Center for Arctic Research, linguistics, literature, medicine, computer science, engineering, the Institute of Design, art, archaeology, a local school's technology center, the business school, the Department of Tourism program at Otago University, and a physics simulation company. A dean attended, as did artists, professors, graduate students, undergraduate students, and practitioners.

I had planned the STEAM discussion but had not had the time to prepare as carefully as I would have liked. In terms of curatorial practice, however, underpreparing can sometimes offer advantages. Planners run the risk of having everything so much in place that some possible directions are stifled. The structure of an event can make some conversations very likely and others not. If certain people, competencies, and backgrounds are not present (or do not receive space), certain narratives and exchanges are unlikely to develop. The STEAM session was perceived as a success partly because of the participants' diversity and their willingness to engage. They spoke about societal challenges, offered experiences and perspectives on doing work across the arts and sciences, and made suggestions about what might attract students to such programs. Participants believed in the importance of having students maintain a sense of agency throughout the process as well as of strong disciplinary grounding and the need to go far beyond merely selecting existing courses from different departments. All in all, the atmosphere was very constructive and explorative.

The humanities and the digital humanities took the lead in planning this event. The initiative came from HUMlab and the Dean's Office, with support from university administrators. We demonstrated our interest, informed others about the process, and invited people to come together. The connection between the arts and the sciences will likely play an increasingly important role in the context of institutional structures and large-scale worldly challenges, and the digital humanities can be one suitable platform for carrying out such work. One participant, John Maeda (at the time with the Rhode Island School of Design), pointed to the importance of in-between platforms for doing this kind of intersectional work. As he noted, the MIT Media Lab was driven not only by Nicholas Negroponte but also by Jerome Wiesner, a former president of MIT and science adviser to President John F. Kennedy. According to Maeda, Wiesner was convinced that the arts would be important to MIT's future development. In addition, the MIT Media Lab had early success because it was institutionally placed under the radar. The Machine Architecture group and what is now the School of Architecture and Planning were not seen as major or influential institutions at the time, which made it easier to implement an intersectional and innovative enterprise such as the Media Lab.[3] Considerable advantages accrue from seeing the digital humanities as an intersectional operation, and doing so requires an appropriate institutional position.

Maeda was traveling halfway around the world from Sweden, so we brought him in on a large screen, an approach that worked well and one that we have come to use regularly. Situating off-location people in a physical environment can be quite powerful, especially if careful attention has been paid to the material conditions of such setups and if the physical environment is not a sterile white-wall videoconference room.

The 2012 conference had little remote video participation, and what did occur resulted from a raging winter storm and illness. The 2013 workshop, conversely, featured several remote participants. The organizer of a session on critical making, Matt Ratto, appeared on an enormous triptych wall screen with a second feed from his document camera, which essentially showed his hands demonstrating how the manual work should be carried out. This feed was shown on the floor screen next to the triptych screen. The communication between the remote session leader and his graduate student (ginger coons, who did much of the practical work) felt very natural and functional. It helped that they knew each other well and that we had a good audio system in place. The remote leader and the local participants communicated throughout the session.

The setup was atypical in that, for much of the time, the participants and the session leader were focused on building—looking at paper-folding projects or at each other—so the remote presence became peripheral or subdued despite the size of the screen on which Ratto appeared. It was fascinating to watch him focus on the paper building rather than on his Skype connection. He even left at one point to take care of his crying child.[4]

The document camera feed, however, was not very useful, since people were dispersed in the space and not really proximal to the floor screen. Also, focusing simultaneously on both the talking head and the floor screen seems to be cognitively difficult. Furthermore, the workshop leaders would probably have benefited from a private channel for certain conversations. But we could not have known these things until we tried—material and experimental engagement are necessary to find out what works and does not when curating events and engaging with infrastructure.

This critical making session, Fixsels, sought to explore digital materiality by building "physical pixels" (the fixsels) out of origami paper and some circuitry. Matthew Kirschenbaum's work on forensic and formal materiality was central to the session, as was the framework suggested by Drucker in *SpecLab: Digital Aesthetics and Projects in Speculative Computing*.[5] It was entertaining to see a roomful of humanists struggling with scissors, glue, and complex folding as well as with the connection to a set of abstract ideas about materiality. Ratto usefully kept coming back to the theoretical framing, although the making part probably took a bit too long in this first fixel iteration. The session amply demonstrated the need for a methodology to robust critical making work. If the digital humanities is about making and thinking at the same time, then we need to create and enact such methodologies.

Without appropriate infrastructure, such enactment becomes difficult. The digital humanities needs infrastructure that manifests basic ideas and values associated with the field and that allows us to engage with ideas, technology, and people. Many digital humanities platforms and spaces do not enact an inclusive, intellectual, and technologically engaged digital humanities. And even a platform that does so can be employed in many different ways, as evidenced by the various formats of the HUMlab events.

The 2012 conference was the most conservative of the three events in terms of setup and conditions. We received very generous support from the Wallenberg Foundation on the condition that we create a high-quality meeting with some of the best scholars in the world. There was also an assumption that the conference would be organized around a number of keynotes. However, we suggested a format where keynotes were kept relatively short and were followed by more junior scholars who spoke on related themes and questions. The themes included knowledge production, making, infrastructures, framing, and pre- and postdigital architectures. Each such session finished with a thirty-minute discussion. This format was successful, and the early-career scholars (some of whom were actually quite senior) made important contributions to the conversation. The professional moderator did not have to use his prepared questions and comments. Keynote speaker Tara McPherson took it is a very good sign that she found herself wishing that the "junior" scholars would do the keynotes.[6] She spoke about scholarly publishing in the session on knowledge production and was followed by Shannon Mattern on inhabiting knowledge, Cecilia Lindhé on medieval interfaces, and Zephyr Frank on bridging scales in the digital humanities. This is more than a matter of program design. Encouraging a multivocal dialogue requires creating appropriate conditions.

The 2013 workshop furthered this strategy. Most of the participants were junior scholars with a stake in the future of the digital humanities. We sought to create an event with a more active and cocreative format than a series of talks, and we orchestrated it in a much different way than the 2012 conference. A cocreative format means engaging not just with other participants but also with infrastructure and technology. In addition to Ratto's critical making session, there was a lightning talk session using the eleven-screen screenscape, and three batches of eight six-minute presentations, each followed by a discussion among the presenters and the rest of the participants. Each presenter was allowed only one slide, and the participants walked from screen to screen, meaning that all of the slides for each batch were visible at the same time. This configuration differs substantially from a sit-down presentation where the presentation surface gets erased between each contribution. The digital humanities needs to experiment with formats, expressions, and ideas in different kinds of arenas.

Scholarly conferences embed many values and modalities that the digital humanities could challenge—rigid hierarchies and other power structures, stratification, preestablished networks, disciplinarity, gatekeeping, and explicit and implicit socializing of junior scholars as well as formats such as the decontextualized conference venue, the lecture format, a single-screen presentation paradigm, and a limited focus on making. Traditional conferences also seem at times to feature a sense of disengagement and lack of curiosity, openness, and substantial progress.

Andrew Prescott notes that the conference format comes from the nineteenth century and that poster sessions are archaic, but he continues: "unconferences don't really cut the mustard. Need something more truly connective & interactive."[7] He suggests that the digital humanities can take the lead. Indeed, given the criticisms that have been directed at the ADHO Conference, it would make an excellent test case for manifesting and enacting a new kind of digital humanities. Big digital humanities (especially if grounded in strong curatorship and spatial thinking) can be a leader in challenging and realigning the format of scholarly meetings.

Technology and presentation and communication modalities impose constraints. For example, presentation software is typically based on a slide-by-slide paradigm, most display screens are single and have a cinematic aspect ratio, lightning talks impose time limit, and conference proceedings are almost always textual. Traditional conference talks are locked into very specific structural and physical conditions. Presenters are expected to stand at the front of the room, use some kind of slide software, and respond to moderated questions and comments. Institutional websites often are not just expected to look a certain way but must follow a template. Such templates lend consistency but do so at the cost of experimentation, interaction, and expressiveness, and they have become so entrenched that they do not get questioned. Such conventions are not just a matter of form but structure the way we make critical arguments and interact with others.

While working with available platforms and systems, the digital humanities needs to challenge some of these templates and restrictions, perhaps by imposing new conditions, constraints, and challenges. HUMlab's triptych screen exemplifies this approach. Most software has been designed for single rectangular screens, and the first time I tried to do a presentation using the triptych screen, some of the digital content ended up where there was no screen. And what does it mean to display and interpret research data using a center and periphery in this way? During the 2013 workshop, the faceted browser system that HUMlab has developed to interrogate rich datasets was deployed across the triptych screen and the floor screen, essentially distributing the application over several viewports. The faceted browser experiment and the triptych screen itself raise questions about our obsession with rectangular screens and single web browser windows.

We carried out another—unplanned—experiment during the 2013 workshop as a result of a late decision to show conference tweets on the triptych screen. I spent the evening before looking for an appropriate application, and I found one that worked perfectly for our purposes. It showed a collection of tweets (in this case with the hashtag #sortingDH) in the form of the images associated with the Twitter accounts. The size of the images varied according to the number of tweets that account had generated. Actual tweets (the text) were shown one at a time in large format, visually expanding out from the image associated with that Twitter account. We ran this for some time, but I was also following tweets from a conference in Hanover, Germany, (Digital) Humanities Revisited—Challenges and Opportunities in the Digital Age. I decided to shift the content of our display wall by changing the hashtag to the one used for the German conference. This simple move might not have had a major impact on the conference, but the conceptual leap is significant. There is a strong tendency to use digital mediation to strengthen existing networks and to look inward. Doing so can be useful, but there is certainly a place for rethinking some of these patterns.

This close engagement with technology and the idea that constraints can be useful helped shape one of the key activities of the 2013 workshop. The task was to devise an implementation plan for the digital humanities for a five- to seven-year time frame. The objectives and presentation format were clearly defined, and we asked everyone to reflect critically on the constraints. The preformed groups were asked to present their implementation plans using the large HUMlab space that houses the eleven-screen screenscape they had used for the lightning talks. They thus were familiar with the space, although the constraints had changed. Each group had access to the whole space and all the screens. However, only one image could be deployed per screen, and we had created a visual web interface to allow easy upload of content to the screens. The ten-minute presentations followed by discussion sessions were broadcast live. Each group had about three hours to work out ideas and come up with a presentation.

The eight groups tackled the challenge in very different ways, but none of them deployed a mostly textual implementation plan across the eleven screens or traditional PowerPoint-like presentations. Indeed, as far as I can remember, there was not a single bullet point. Again, the material conditions really matter: if there is no bullet-point template and no expectation of standard slideware presentations, chances are good that the effort will result in different kinds of expressions and narratives. In this case, the presentations were dynamic, varied, and embodied. People used their bodies, moved through the space, declared their convictions, and made narratives by meshing the group's work and the infrastructure.

The pink team, whose members came from media studies, ancient history, anthropology, art, and gender studies,[8] devised a game system, DH 2020, in which the digital humanities moved from day-to-day pragmatics to world domination fighting the old traditional scholars (OGs). A map recurred on several of the screens, and various minigames involved networking (to get influence points), spreading knowledge (to get knowledge points), fundraising, gaining disciples, and finding places to do research. The game was meant to be thought-provoking and experiential and to help players (among them junior scholars) to think through and experience the process of working institutionally, understand the roles involved in an attempted spread of the digital humanities, and teach certain mechanisms. A more generic version of such a game could be useful for graduate seminars in the humanities more generally.

The black group took a similar approach, although it based its story on an individual rather than the institutional structures.[9] The group enacted the career and challenges of Diana, a postdoc with a classics degree from the University of Budapest who was working on a project to establish the location of Troy. She had to grapple with institutional constraints, translating her work to a grant committee, methodology, expectations that the digital was limited to websites, pressures from standardized assessments, attracting funding, using crowdsourcing, and building networks. In addition, her postdoc time is ending and her desperation is increasing (demonstrated by one participant running back and forth between screens).

The guerrilla group presented an antimanifesto based on the presumption that the digital humanities is needed and does not necessarily have to act from a passive position.[10] The message was that we can make demands and set parameters before the discussion starts: "We have their loved ones!" The delivery was characterized by coordination, cooperation in the presentation, and an aesthetics taken from protest signs. The group loudly declared its manifesto, and its points (one per screen) included respect for the idea that digital objects are people too (we need to accommodate the agency of information objects and nonhuman organic forms), embracing the dark side of corporate information control (working with media companies), moving beyond the prototype (to make real change in society), letting research and education meet (drawing on Humboldt), and working with many languages (the world is multilingual). Again, the format expressed a particular perspective, and the coordination of the group's declarations carried meaning. Near the end, one group member noted that the team had sought to take a "bit of an aggressive stance," positioning itself as a guerrilla group with convictions as well as a willingness to negotiate.

One of the other groups explored the long-term validity of the term digital humanities.[11] Their initial screen featured an animation that alternately crossed out *digital* and *humanities* while ruminating on the interrelation of these terms. The animation represented a successful modification of the presentation format within the technical constraints of the system. In addition, the group used two screens to show the image search results for *digital humanities* on Google and Bing. The fact that these results differed significantly made the point that an important role of the digital humanities is to look critically at the tools we and others use. Toward the end of the presentation, a technologist talked about the separation of the digital and humanities. Two cartoon slides brilliantly illustrated the difference between having a process where scholars order solutions from technologists and a process that is integrated from the outset. He talked about the humanities in a way that I suspect humanists often talk about the technology side of things. Though made humorously, the point was crystal clear, important to the workshop, and highly relevant for the digital humanities.

I had been reluctant to include all the technology staff as participants in the workshop since they were needed to organize and implement the event. I may also have been stuck in my conception of different roles in the lab. The event coordinator convinced me to open up the event, and I am happy we did. Finding ways of working together across competencies, roles, and projects is critical for the digital humanities.

We could never have foreseen what would result from this exercise, but the fact that the results were not predictable is one of the most important points. We had structures, conditions, constraints, infrastructure, and carefully put-together groups, but we had no blueprint. And moving away from standard presentation formats had a major influence on the outcome. This is not to say that the session was perfect or that it could not be improved; rather, we realized that doing it this way was the right choice.

The field of digital humanities is facing many choices, some of which will be difficult. Becoming larger, opening up to other epistemic traditions, and engaging more broadly with the digital, the academy, and the world outside does not come easily. We need to make a case for big digital humanities based on the intellectual and technological challenges of the next decade. Many of them will require the humanities to engage with the digital in many different ways, to recruit the best early-career scholars and experts, and to create humanistic infrastructure.

We need technological and intellectual engagement to come together. We need to approach challenges across the technological and humanistic. We need to take on the responsibility of creating hope for early-career faculty and of making a real difference within the humanities and the academy. We need to work with the world outside academia.

Big digital humanities is a response to these and other challenges. It is not a panacea or a single solution but a set of ideas, practices, and values centered on the digital humanities as an intellectual-material meeting place across epistemic traditions and multiple modes of engagement with the digital.

At the end of the 2013 workshop, Johanna Drucker participated in a mini-panel with five remote guests, each of whom had three minutes to speak. Drucker stated that until digital humanities work is cited and used in other fields because of the arguments made, it will be marginalized. We can only reach this goal by working with the humanities writ large as equal partners, and I think we are starting to do so. Strong scholarship with digital inflection is being produced both inside and outside the core community of the digital humanities. We need to meld the intellectual and the technological in all kinds of ways, and we need to draw on the meaningful coming together of different traditions and energies. Much more remains to be done.

Notes

Preface

1. Jeffrey Schnapp, Twitter post, January 16, 2013, 8:08 p.m., https://twitter.com/jaytiesse
2. Mark Sample, Twitter post, January 18, 2013, 6.15 a.m., https://twitter.com/samplereality
3. Ted Underwood, Twitter post, January 18, 2013, 7:41 p.m., http://twitter.com/Ted_Underwood/
4. Cecire, "Introduction."
5. Liminal here describes a disciplinary and spatial position rather than a temporal stage.
6. Whitney Trettien to Humanist Mailing List, January 6, 2013, 8:24 a.m., http://www.dhhumanist.org/cgi-bin/archive/archive_msg.cgi?file=/Humanist.vol26.txt&msgnum=648&start=90882/
7. Bethany Nowviskie, "Digital Humanities in the Anthropocene," *Bethany Nowviskie*, July 10, 2014, http://nowviskie.org/2014/anthropocene/
8. Goldberg, *Afterlife*, sec. IV.
9. Ong, "Expanding Humanities," 1.
10. Ekström and Sörlin, *Alltings Mått*, 23.
11. Goldberg, *Afterlife*, sec. VI.

Chapter 1

1. Eisenstein, *Printing Press*; Febvre and Martin, *Coming of the Book*, 143–47.
2. Dahlström, "Critical Editing."
3. For a very illuminating discussion of library catalogs, see Andrew Prescott, "The Function, Structure, and Future of Catalogues," *Digital Riffs*, January 11, 2013, http://digitalriffs.blogspot.se/2013/01/the-function-structure-and-future-of.html
4. Drucker, "Humanities Approaches."
5. White, *What Is Spatial History?*
6. Kirschenbaum, *Mechanisms*, 12–13.
7. Sterne, "Example."

8. Fitzpatrick, *Planned Obsolescence*, 2–5.

9. Swedish Research Council (Vetenskapsrådet), Ämnesöversikter 2010.

10. Turner, "Family of Man."

11. See, e.g., Chittum, "NYT's $150 Million-a-Year Paywall"; Royal, "We Need a Digital-First Curriculum."

12. Hayles, *How We Think*, 2–3.

13. Lindhé, "Medieval Materiality."

14. Svensson, "Virtual Worlds."

15. Hockey, "History of Humanities Computing," 16.

16. University of California Humanities Research Institute, "HASS Cyberinfrastructure."

17. Mukerji, "Me? A Digital Humanist?"

18. Natalia Cecire, "When DH Was in Vogue; or, THATcamp Theory," *Natalia Cecire's Blog*, October 19, 2011, http://nataliacecire.blogspot.se/2011/10/when-dh-was-in-vogue-or-thatcamp-theory.html

19. Ibid.

20. See also Porsdam, *Too Much "Digital," Too Little "Humanities"?*

21. Digital Humanities Conference, "<audio>Digital Humanities</audio>."

22. Jonathan Sterne, "Audio in Digital Humanities Authorship: A Roadmap (version 0.5)," *Superbon!*, July 24, 2011, http://superbon.net/?p=1915

23. Cárdenas, "Is the Digital Humanities a Hot, Sellable Commodity?"

24. See, e.g., Risam, "On Disruption, Race, and the Digital Humanities."

25. Ted Underwood, "How Everyone Gets to Claim They Do DH," *The Stone and the Shell*, September 22, 2012, http://tedunderwood.com/2012/09/22/how-everyone-gets-to-claim-they-do-dh/

26. Stommel, "Public Digital Humanities."

27. Jen Guiliano, "Why You Shouldn't Be a Digital Humanist," *Just Another Day of DH 2013 Site*, April 8, 2013, http://dayofdh2013.matrix.msu.edu/jenguiliano/2013/04/08/why-you-shouldnt-be-a-digital-humanist/

28. Goldberg, "World as Platform"; Mattern, "Library as Infrastructure."

29. Balsamo, "Engineering Cultural Studies."

30. Liu, "Where Is Cultural Criticism?," 491.

31. For more examples, see, e.g., Prescott, "Consumers, Creators, or Commentators?"

32. Kirsch, "Limits of the Digital Humanities."

33. For a useful account of digital-humanities-based critiques of Kirsch's article, see Mark Sample, "Difficult Thinking about the Digital Humanities," *Sample Reality*, May 12, 2014. http://www.samplereality.com/2014/05/12/difficult-thinking-about-the-digital-humanities/

34. Paraphrased from an e-mail conversation with David Theo Goldberg.

35. Gitelman, *Paper Knowledge*.

36. *Infrastructure, Space, and Media*, 71.

37. White, *What Is Spatial History?*

38. Sterne, *MP3*.

39. Asaro, "On Banning Autonomous Lethal Systems."

40. "Love Machine," *Peter Asaro's WWW*, accessed November, 27, 2013, http://www.peterasaro.org/lovemachine/lovemachine.htm

41. Palm and Larsson, "Rock Carvings at Nämforsen."

42. Roy Rosenzweig Center, "What Is Digital History?"

43. Kaci Nash, "Digital Historical Scholarship and the Civil War," *Digital History Project*, January 8, 2012, http://digitalhistory.wordpress.com/2012/01/08/digital-historical-scholarship-and-the-civil-war/

44. Cameron Blevins, "The Perpetual Sunrise of Methodology," *Cameron Blevins*, January 5, 2015, http://www.cameronblevins.org/posts/perpetual-sunrise-methodology/

45. Donahue, *Great Meadow*.

46. See, e.g., Anderson, "Quantitative History."

47. Hayles, *How We Think*, 183.

48. Terras, "Digital Classicist," 172.

49. Hayles, *How We Think*, 183–92.

50. Frank, "Spatial History," 420–21.

51. Seed, "Map Is Not a Picture."

52. *Rome Reborn*.

53. Dylla et al., "Rome Reborn 2.0."

54. Drucker, "Humanities Approaches," par. 1.

55. Betts, "Towards a Multisensory Experience."

56. Ibid, 132.

57. Saldana and Johanson, "Procedural Modeling for Rapid-Prototyping of Multiple Building Phases."

58. Guldi, "Time Wars."

59. Armitage, "What's the Big Idea?," 507.

60. Ibid.

61. Hayles, *How We Think*, 27–28.

62. See, e.g., Lindgren, "Introducing Connected Concept Analysis," 1–4.

63. Maker Lab, "About."

64. McCarty et al., "Questioning, Asking, and Enduring Curiosity."

65. Alliance for Networking Visual Culture.

66. Ratto, "Critical Making."

67. Svensson, "From Optical Fiber to Conceptual Cyberinfrastructure."

68. University of Minnesota Press, "Debates in the Digital Humanities."

69. Kirschenbaum, "Digital Humanities."

70. Palgrave Macmillan, "Understanding Digital Humanities."

71. University of Chicago Press, "How We Think."

72. Matthew Kirschenbaum, Twitter post, March 20, 2012, 3:48 p.m., http://www.twitter.com/mkirschenbaum/

Chapter 2

1. Willard McCarty to Humanist Mailing List, May 14, 1987, 8:17 p.m., http://dh-humanist.org/Archives/Virginia/v01/8705.1324.txt/

2. Alvarado, "Digital Humanities Situation."

3. 4Humanities.

4. Julie Thompson Klein, e-mail message to author, January 31, 2013.

5. Weingart, "Short History," 6.

6. Whitney Trettien, "So, What's Up with MLA?," *Diapsalmata*, January 25, 2013, http://blog.whitneyannetrettien.com/2013/01/so-whats-up-with-mla.html

7. Andrew Prescott, "Making the Digital Human: Anxieties, Possibilities, Challenges," *Digital Riffs*, July 5, 2012, http://digitalriffs.blogspot.se/2012/07/making-digital-human-anxieties.html

8. Pannapacker, "No DH, No Interview."

9. Ibid.

10. ACH Panel, "Humanities Computing."

11. Klein, *Crossing Boundaries*, 57.

12. Busa, foreword, xvi. Attempts at tracing the history within the tradition of humanities computing include McCarty, "Humanities Computing," 1224–35; Vanhoutte, "Gates of Hell."

13. Eisenstein, *Printing Press*.

14. Julianne Nyhan, "Gender, Knowledge, and Hierarchy: On Busa's Female Punch Card Operators," *Arche Logos*, May 3, 2014, http://archelogos.hypotheses.org/135

15. Jones, "Network Inside Out."

16. Svensson, "Humanities Computing."

17. Functional words, generic adjectives, and "humanities" were removed from the frequency list.

18. Svensson, "Humanities Computing."

19. Deegan, "Report," 1.

20. Vanhoutte, *Editor's Report*, 3.

21. *Literary and Linguistic Computing*, http://llc.oxfordjournals.org/

22. Svensson, "Landscape of Digital Humanities."

23. Stephen Ramsay, "DH Types One and Two," *Stephen Ramsay's Blog*, May 3, 2013, http://stephenramsay.us/2013/05/03/dh-one-and-two/

24. ADHO, "About."

25. "About page," http://hastac.org/about, accessed January 15, 2013.

26. J. Rice, "A HASTAC Revolution?," *Yellow Dog*, October 18, 2010, http://ydog.net/?p=792/

27. See Andrew Prescott, "Small Worlds and Big Tents," *Digital Riffs*, May 5, 2013, http://digitalriffs.blogspot.se/2013/05/small-worlds-and-big-tents.html

28. David Golumbia, "'Digital Humanities': Two Definitions," *Uncomputing*, January 20, 2013, http://www.uncomputing.org/?p=203

29. Stephen Ramsay, comment on Golumbia, "'Digital Humanities': Two Definitions."

30. Ibid.

31. Alex Reid, comment on Golumbia, "'Digital Humanities': Two Definitions."

32. Hayles, *How We Think*, 26–27.

33. Ibid., 27.

34. Burdick et al., *Digital_Humanities*, 122.

35. Ibid.

36. Ibid.

37. McPherson, "Introduction."

38. Davidson, "Humanities 2.0," 711–12.

39. Ibid., 715.

40. Ramsay, "DH Types One and Two."

41. McCarty, *Humanities Computing*, 3.

42. Vanhoutte, "Gates of Hell," 131.

43. McCarty, "Becoming Interdisciplinary," 94.

44. Kirschenbaum, "What Is Digital Humanities?," 6; Schreibman, Siemens, and Unsworth, *Companion*.

45. Ramsay, comment on Golumbia, "'Digital Humanities': Two Definitions."

46. Ramsay, "DH Types One and Two."

47. John Unsworth to adhoc mailing list, August 16, 2002, http://lists.village.virginia.edu/lists_archive/adhoc/0000.html

48. Svensson, "Humanities Computing," par. 35.

49. Lisa Lena Opas-Hanninen to adhoc mailing list, April 13, 2005, http://lists.village.virginia.edu/lists_archive/adhoc/0167.html

50. Matthew Kirschenbaum, June 18, 2011, 6:15 p.m., comment on Alex Reid, "Digital Humanities Tactics," *Digital Digs*, June 17, 2011, http://www.alex-reid.net/2011/06/digital-humanities-tactics.html

51. EADH, Twitter post, September 19, 2012, 10:37 a.m., https://twitter.com/eadh_org/status/248475849551142916/

52. EADH, *ALLC Annual General Meeting*.

53. EADH, "About."

54. Vanhoutte, "Gates of Hell," 129.

55. EADH, "EADH Membership Report."

56. EADH, *ALLC Committee Meeting*.

57. Fiormonte, "Towards a Cultural Critique."

58. "Governance Protocol."

59. EADH, "Mission."

60. "Digital Humanities," *Wikipedia*, http://en.wikipedia.org/wiki/Digital_humanities/

61. Hockey, "History of Humanities Computing," 3.

62. de Smedt, "Some Reflections," 95.

63. Smith, "Human Touch Software," 4.

64. Victorian Women Writers Project, "Encoding Overview"; Willett, "Victorian Women Writers Project."

65. "Women Writers in Context," The Women Writers Project, http://www.wwp.northeastern.edu/context/#. See also "Exhibit," The Women Writers Project, http://www.wwp.northeastern.edu/research/publications/exhibits/. Cf. also Risam, "On Disruption, Race, and the Digital Humanities."

66. See, e.g., McCarty, *Humanities Computing*.

67. Vanhoutte, "Gates of Hell," 139.

68. Juola, "Killer Applications," 83.

69. Terras, "Disciplined," 236.

70. Hockey, "History of Humanities Computing," 15.

71. Sterne, "Audio in Digital Humanities Authorship."

72. McCarty, *Humanities Computing*, 136.

73. Hockey, "History of Humanities Computing," 3.

74. Unsworth to adhoc mailing list, August 16, 2002.

75. See EADH, "ALLC: Proposed Name Change," December 20, 2011, http://eadh. org/news-events/allc-proposed-name-change; EADH, *ALLC Annual General Meeting*.

76. "Admissions Protocol ADHO: Alliance of Digital Humanities Organisations: Admission of new organisations," http://adho.org/administration/admissions-committee/admissions-protocol (2008).

77. Association for Computers and the Humanities, "ACH Annual General Meeting."

78. CenterNet, "Join."

79. Ibid.

80. Fraistat, "Function," 288, 281.

81. Mark Sample, "On the Death of the Digital Humanities Center," *Sample Reality*, March 26, 2012, http://www.samplereality.com/2010/03/26/on-the-death-of-the-digital-humanities-center/

82. Zorich, "Digital Humanities Centers," 70–71.

83. CenterNet, "CenterNet to Join ADHO."

84. CenterNet, "Join."

85. CenterNet, "International Directory."

86. Prescott, "Small Worlds and Big Tents."

87. Fiormonte, "Towards a Cultural Critique."

88. CHCI Network, "Digital Humanities Initiative."

89. O'Donnell, "Report."

90. Ben W. Brumfield, Twitter post, February 4, 2013, 8:12 a.m., http://twitter.com/benwbrum/

91. Ortega, "Crisscrossing Borders."

92. Monclova, "Transformative Mediations?"

93. Alexis Lothian, "#transformDH and Transformativity," *Queer Geek Theory*, January 9, 2012, http://www.queergeektheory.org/2012/01/transformdh-and-transformativity/

94. #transformDH Collective Blog, "About #transformDH."

95. Based on a Google search ("adho movement digital humanities") and going through the first one hundred hits, March 26, 2015.

96. THATcamp, "About."

97. Roger Whitson, "Does DH Really Need to Be Transformed? My Reflections on #mla12," *Roger T. Whitson Ph.D.*, January 8, 2012, http://www.rogerwhitson. net/?p=1358

98. Andrew Prescott, "#transformDH," *Digital Riffs*, February 2012. http://digitalriffs.blogspot.se/2012/02/transformdh.html

99. CUNY DHI, Twitter post, February 12, 2013, 12:16 p.m., https://twitter.com/cunydhi/status/301424574074060800

100. Prescott, "#transformDH."

101. #transformDH.
102. Vanhoutte, "Gates of Hell," 144.
103. Digital Humanities 2011, "General CFP."
104. See Svensson, "Humanities Computing."
105. Alex Reid, "The Digital Humanities Divide," *Digital Digs*, February 17, 2011, http://www.alex-reid.net/2011/02/the-digital-humanities-divide.html
106. Hugh Cayless, "DH Tea Leaves," *Scriptio Continua*, December 28, 2010, http://philomousos.blogspot.com/2010/12/dh-tea-leaves.html
107. Whitney Trettien, "Digital Humanities vs. the Digital Humanist," *Hyperstudio*, April 26, 2010, http://hyperstudio.mit.edu/blog/thoughts/digital-humanities-vs-the-digital-humanist/
108. ADHO, "Minutes: ADHO Steering Committee Meeting, 2015 (Sydney)," June 28–29, 2015. http://adho.org/administration/steering/minutes-adho-steering-committee-meeting-2015-sydney
109. Risam, "Beyond the Margins."

Chapter 3

1. Alan Liu, "'Why I'm in It' x 2—Antiphonal Response to Stephan Ramsay on Digital Humanities and Cultural Criticism," *Alan Liu*, September 13, 2013, http://liu.english.ucsb.edu/why-im-in-it-x-2-antiphonal-response-to-stephan-ramsay-on-digital-humanities-and-cultural-criticism/
2. Svensson, "Building a Virtual World."
3. Shanks, "Media as Modes of Engagement."
4. Vanhoutte, "Gates of Hell."
5. Michel et al., "Quantitative Analysis."
6. Haber, "Data and Desire in Academic Life."
7. Bolter and Gromala, *Windows and Mirrors*, 15. See also Wiberg, *Interaction Society*, which discusses the development of information technology use from crunching numbers to social interaction.
8. See Golumbia, *Cultural Logic*.
9. Hopkins, "Future U."
10. Laue, "How the Computer Works," 159.
11. DigiPal, "Home."
12. DigiPal, "About."
13. Gitelman and Jackson, introduction, 1.
14. Manovich, "Cultural Analytics." The extent of qualitative analysis in cultural analytics is debatable. Lev Manovich tends to present a strong quantitative model; for a discussion of quantitative cultural analysis, see, e.g., Manovich, "How to Follow." For a discussion of qualitative elements, see Eduardo Navas, "Notes on Cultural Analytics Seminar, December 16–17, 2009, CALIT2, San Diego," *Remix Theory*, December 29, 2009, http://remixtheory.net/?p=408
15. Manovich, "How to Follow."
16. See, e.g., Douglass, "Cultural Analytics."

17. Kitchin, "Big Data."

18. Thomas LaMarre to empyre@lists.cofa.unsw.edu.au, February 8, 2010, "Visualization as the New Language of Theory," http://lists.cofa.unsw.edu.au/pipermail/empyre/2010-February/002557.html

19. See Kirschenbaum, "'So the Colors Cover the Wires.'"

20. Drucker, *SpecLab*, 6.

21. Kagan, *Three Cultures*, 4.

22. Janlert and Jonsson, "Kulturlaboratoriet [The Culture Laboratory]."

23. Catherine D'Ignazio, "What Would Feminist Data Visualization Look Like," Blog entry, MIT Center for Civic Media, December 20, 2015. https://civic.mit.edu/feminist-data-visualization

24. Ratto, "Epistemic Commitments," 60.

25. Klein, *Humanities, Culture, and Interdisciplinarity*, 24–28.

26. Davidson and Goldberg, "Engaging the Humanities," 49.

27. Drucker, *SpecLab*, 28.

28. KTH, Division of History, Science, Technology and Environment, "Views from a Distance."

29. Bogost and Montfort, "Platform Studies."

30. Piet Zwart Media Design Master, "Software Studies," http://pzwart3.wdka.hro.nl/wiki/Software_Studies/

31. HaCCS Lab, "About."

32. Parikka, "On Designerization."

33. Leorke, "Rebranding the Platform," 266–67.

34. David M. Berry, "Digital Humanities: First, Second, and Third Wave," *Stunlaw*, January 14, 2011, http://stunlaw.blogspot.com/2011/01/digital-humanities-first-second-and.html

35. Stanford Humanities Center, "How Is Humanities Research Conducted?"

36. Modern Language Association, "Guidelines."

37. "About DHQ". *Digital Humanities Quarterly*. http://www.digitalhumanities.org/dhq/about/about.html

38. Schnapp and Shanks, "Artereality," 134.

39. Robles-Anderson and Svensson, "'One Damn Slide After Another': PowerPoint at every Occasion for Speech."

40. Manovich, *Software Takes Command*, 134.

41. Ibid., 142.

42. *Issuu*, accessed December 1, 2013, http://issuu.com/

43. Lindgren, "Social Science"; Sterne, "Footnotes."

44. Holmberg, "Forgotten Encyclopedia." The video trailer has not been published.

45. Linn Holmberg, personal communication with the author, November 2014.

46. Sousanis, *Unflattening*.

47. Dobson, "Blendie."

48. McPherson, "Introduction," 120.

49. Swedish Higher Education Authority, "Quality."

50. REF2014, "Research Excellence Framework."

51. Prescott, "Small Worlds and Big Tents."

52. Ippolito et al., "New Criteria."

53. McPherson, "We Need Some Transitional Models."

54. Sousanis, *Unflattening.*

55. Daniel, "Public Secrets."

56. Raley, *Tactical Media,* 14.

57. Drucker, *SpecLab,* 31, 29.

58. Postcolonial Digital Humanities, "Rewriting Wikipedia Project."

59. These particular topics were discussed during the event "Ideas in Circulation: Libraries, Presses, Platforms," organized by the Futures Initiative, CUNY Graduate Center, February 5, 2016. https://www.eventbrite.com/e/ideas-in-circulation-open-scholarship-for-social-justice-tickets-20792182979

60. Ratto and Ree, "Materialization of Information."

61. IATH, "'Is Humanities Computing an Academic Discipline?'"

62. Flanders and Unsworth, "Evolution of Humanities Computing Centers."

63. Galison, *Image and Logic*; Galison, "Trading with the Enemy," 27.

64. Galison, "Trading with the Enemy," 36.

65. Pratt, "Arts of the Contact Zone," 34.

66. Bey, T.A.Z.

67. Thomassen, "Uses and Meaning."

68. Iedema et al., "Corridor Work," 239.

69. Collins, Evans, and Gorman, "Trading Zones."

70. Ibid.

71. Star and Griesemer, "Institutional Ecology."

72. Ibid., 408.

73. Ibid., 387.

74. Ratto, "Critical Making: Conceptual and Material Studies."

75. Ramsay and Rockwell, "Developing Things."

76. Ratto, "Critical Making: Conceptual and Material Studies," 258.

77. Livingstone, *Putting Science in Its Place.*

78. See, e.g., "HASS Committee on the Humanities Library, Final Report," Humanities Library Report, MIT, 2001.

79. See Ratto, "Critical Making: Conceptual and Material Studies."

80. Roser and Merson, "Have Academics Forgotten?"

81. See Shannon Christine Mattern, "DH: The Name That Does No Favors," *Words in Space,* February 17, 2011, http://www.wordsinspace.net/wordpress/2011/02/17/dh-the-name-that-does-no-favors/

82. Fraistat, "Function."

83. Walsh and Ungson, "Organizational Memory," 69.

84. Klein, *Crossing Boundaries,* 101.

85. See Svensson, "From Optical Fiber to Conceptual Cyberinfrastructure."

86. See, e.g., Turner, *From Counterculture to Cyberculture*; Streeter, *Net Effect.*

87. Svensson, "Envisioning the Digital Humanities."
88. Hacking the Academy, "What This Is."
89. David Parry, "The MLA, @briancroxall, and the Non-Rise of the Digital Humanities," *AcademHack*, January 6, 2010, http://academhack.outsidethetext.com/home/2010/the-mla-briancroxall-and-the-non-rise-of-the-digital-humanities/
90. E.g., Nussbaum, *Not for Profit*; Donoghue, *Last Professors*.
91. Taylor, *Crisis on Campus*; Nussbaum, *Not for Profit*; Stanley Fish, "Will the Humanities Save Us?," *Opinionator* (*New York Times*), January 6, 2008, http://opinionator.blogs.nytimes.com/2008/01/06/will-the-humanities-save-us/; Parker, "Humanities' 'Peculiar' . . . or All Important . . . 'Practices.'"
92. Wayne Bivens-Tatum, "The 'Crisis' in the Humanities," *Academic Librarian*, November 5, 2010, https://blogs.princeton.edu/librarian/2010/11/the_crisis_in_the_humanities/
93. Johanna Drucker and Patrik Svensson, "The Why and How of Middleware" (accepted for publication by *Digital Humanities Quarterly*).
94. Ralón, "Interview."
95. Omeka, "Omeka."
96. Shannon Christine Mattern, "Intellectual Furnishing: The Physical and Conceptual Architectures of Our Knowledge Institutions," *Words in Space*, February 26, 2014, http://www.wordsinspace.net/wordpress/2014/02/26/7542/
97. Latour, *Politics of Nature*; Stengers, *Power and Invention*.

Chapter 4

1. Rockwell, "As Transparent as Infrastructure."
2. Maria Börjesson, Jonas Eliasson, and Per Kågeson, "Tågens höghastighetsbanor en dålig affär för samhället," *Dagens Nyheter*, January 1, 2016. http://www.dn.se/debatt/tagens-hoghastighetsbanor-en-dalig-affar-for-samhallet/
3. See, e.g., Atkins et al., *Revolutionizing Science and Engineering*.
4. Swedish Research Council (Vetenskapsrådet), "Function."
5. Swedish Research Council (Vetenskapsrådet), "Projektdatabas [Project Database]."
6. Swedish Research Council (Vetenskapsrådet), "Människa, Kultur och Samhälle [Humanity, Culture and Society]."
7. Starosielski, "Warning: Do Not Dig."
8. Chemical Biological Centre, "Welcome to KBC."
9. ESFRI, *Strategy Report*, 7.
10. *Merriam-Webster Online*, s.v. "infrastructure," http://mw4.merriam-webster.com/dictionary/infrastructure
11. Edwards et al., "Introduction," 365.
12. See Borgman, *Scholarship*.
13. CISE, "About ACI."
14. Borgman, *Scholarship*, 22–23.
15. Kitchin, "Big Data," 8–9.

16. See Rockwell, "As Transparent as Infrastructure."

17. Moulin, "Research Infrastructures," 4.

18. Rockwell, "As Transparent as Infrastructure"; Green, "Cyberinfrastructure."

19. Atkins et al., *Revolutionizing Science and Engineering*, 31.

20. Borgman, *Scholarship*, 30.

21. American Council of Learned Societies, *Our Cultural Commonwealth*.

22. As demonstrated by the NSF's funding of various workshops and initiatives. See, e.g., HASTAC, "Expanding Cyber-Communities," http://www.hastac.org/node/496/

23. Hey and Trefethen, "E-Science," 15.

24. Andrew Prescott, "Thinking about Infrastructure," *Digital Riffs*, February 2012, http://digitalriffs.blogspot.se/2012/02/thinking-about-infrastructure.html

25. E.g., Swedish Research Council (Vetenskapsrådet), "Samhällen och Kulturer i Förändring [Societies and Cultures in Change]"; Turner, "Burning Man at Google."

26. Moulin, "Research Infrastructures," 3.

27. See, e.g., ibid., 15–16.

28. American Council of Learned Societies, *Our Cultural Commonwealth*, 6.

29. Drucker, "Blind Spots."

30. Blackwell and Crane, "Conclusion."

31. Bentkowska-Kafel, "Needs."

32. See, e.g., Roper, "New Humanities Workstation," 131; Gibbons et al., *New Production of Knowledge*, 94.

33. Parker, "Speaking Out," 51–52.

34. Fraistat, "Function," 281.

35. I-CHASS, "About Us."

36. Burnette, Gillis, and Cochran, "Humanist and the Library," 182.

37. Grafton, *Worlds Made by Words*, 2–5.

38. AHRC, "Digital Transformations in the Arts and Humanities—Big Data Projects Call."

39. AHRC, "Digital Transformations in the Arts and Humanities: Big Data Research."

40. Ibid., 3.

41. Ibid., 4.

42. Gitelman and Jackson, introduction, 4.

43. See, e.g., Bonnett, Rockwell, and Kuchmey, "High Performance Computing."

44. Rockwell and Meredith-Lobay, "Mind the Gap."

45. American Council of Learned Societies, *Our Cultural Commonwealth*, 8.

46. Sterne, "Digital Media and Disciplinarity," 251.

47. Bowker, *Memory Practices*, 123.

48. Prescott, "Thinking about Infrastructure."

49. Bowker and Star, *Sorting Things Out*, 33.

50. Melissa Terras to Humanist Mailing List, July 27, 2009, no. 7, http://lists.digital-humanities.org/pipermail/humanist/2009-July/000622.html

51. Ratto, "Epistemic Commitments."

52. Ratto, "Already False, Potentially True."

53. See Erickson and Kellogg, "Social Translucence."
54. Dourish and Bly, "Portholes," 541.
55. Merkel, "Folkloristics"; Jamieson et al., "Place and Space"; Gonsalvez and Atchison, "Implementing Studios."
56. See Mitchell, "Places for Learning."
57. Ibid.
58. Fällman, "Supporting Studio Culture," 5.
59. Buren, "Function of the Studio," 160.
60. See Manovich, "Archeology of a Computer Screen."
61. Franklin and Rodriguez'G, "Next Big Thing."
62. Defanti et al., "OptIPortal."
63. Friedberg, *Virtual Window*, 3; Manovich, "Archeology."
64. Brooks, "What's Real?"
65. Manovich, "Archeology."
66. Sandin interviewed in Russett, *Hyperanimation*, 183.
67. Bolter and Gromala, *Windows and Mirrors*, 54.
68. Oculus VR, "Oculus Rift."
69. Lindhé, "Medieval Materiality."
70. Friedberg, *Virtual Window*, 205, 232.
71. Colomina, "Enclosed by Images."
72. Jacobs, *Opening Doors*, 1.
73. See Arnheim, *Power of the Center*, 73.
74. John Hope Franklin Humanities Institute, Duke University, "Humanities Laboratories"; HASTAC.

Chapter 5

1. STEM to STEAM.
2. "Interview: Natalie Jeremijenko," Center for the Study of the Drone, Bard College, November 13, 2013. http://dronecenter.bard.edu/interview-natalie-jeremijenko/
3. Vyas et al., "Collaborative Practices," 156.
4. Lindhé, "Rethinking Medieval Spaces."
5. Ratto, "Critical Making: Conceptual and Material Studies."
6. Menand, *Marketplace of Ideas*, 62.
7. Gouglas et al., "Before the Beginning."
8. Giroux, "Public Intellectuals."
9. Ingeno, "Crowdfunding Academic Research."
10. Walker, "Curator as a Custodian," 292.
11. Association of Art Museum Curators, "Professional Practices."
12. Galison and Schnapp, "Science Museum Futures."
13. Ralón, "Interview."
14. See, e.g., Higgs, "Between the Audience and the Stage"; Donegan, "Between Zones."

15. Star and Griesemer, "Institutional Ecology."
16. Flanders and Muñoz, "Introduction."
17. Constantopoulos and Dallas, "Aspects of a Digital Curation Agenda," 2.
18. Drabinski, "Queering the Catalog," 108.
19. Burdick et al., *Digital_Humanities*, 34.
20. Cook, "Immateriality and Its Discontents," 28.
21. "Digital Pedagogy in the Humanities: Concepts, Models, and Experiments," MLA Commons, accessed January 23, 2016. https://digitalpedagogy.commons.mla.org/
22. Glass, "Social Paper."
23. Gil, "Ed: A Minimal Edition Theme for Jekyll."
24. Chelsea Emelie Kelly, "What Does It Mean to 'Curate'?," *Under the Wings*, June 15, 2012, http://blog.mam.org/2012/06/15/what-does-it-mean-to-curate/
25. TED, "Curating Speakers."
26. John Hope Franklin Humanities Institute, Duke University, "Audiovisualities Lab."
27. Graham and Cook, *Rethinking Curating*, 10.
28. Shaw, *"Who's Driving?."*
29. Shared Horizons, "About."
30. Barker and Smithen, "New Art, New Challenges," 95; American Association of Museums, Curators Committee, "Code of Ethics."
31. Graham and Cook, *Rethinking Curating*, 10.
32. Crow, "Research University," 214.
33. Duke University Press Log, "Nicholas Mirzoeff Extends His Book."
34. Deegan and McCarty, *Collaborative Research*, back cover.
35. Sue Stone, "Humanities Scholars."
36. Bey, T.A.Z.
37. Galison, "Trading Zone," 137.
38. James Cronin to Humanist mailing list, September 1, 2010, no. 2, http://lists.digitalhumanities.org/pipermail/humanist/2010-September/008350.html
39. See, e.g., Repko, *Interdisciplinary Research*, 44.
40. Shanks, "Digital Humanities."
41. Risam, "Beyond the Margins."
42. Orgega, "Crisscrossing Borders."
43. Warf and Arias, introduction to *Spatial Turn*.
44. Lefebvre, *Production of Space*.
45. Meusburger, "Milieus of Creativity," 97.
46. Livingstone, *Putting Science in Its Place*, 86.
47. See ibid., 179; Burke, *Social History of Knowledge*, 56; Martin, *Organizational Complex*, 183.
48. Mattern, *New Downtown Library*, viii.
49. Connelly, Dames, and Tenen, "Open Letter."
50. Studio@Butler, "Frequently Asked Questions."

51. Sandy Stone, "On Being Trans."
52. Hirsch, "</Parentheses>," 3.
53. Rebecca Frost Davis et al., "Announcing *Digital Pedagogy in the Digital Humanities: Concepts, models, and experiments*," accessed March 21, 2015, https://github.com/curate-teaching/digitalpedagogy/blob/master/announcement.md/; Hirsch, *Digital Humanities Pedagogy*.
54. Davidson and Goldberg, *Future of Thinking*, 199.
55. Bowker and Star, "Invisible Mediators," 147.
56. Ursula Heise, personal communication with the author, November 2013.
57. Brian Croxall, "DH2013: The Future of Undergraduate Digital Humanities," *Research, Teaching, Technology*, July 17, 2013, http://www.briancroxall.net/events/9/the-future-of-undergraduate-digital-humanities/; Kolowich, "Behind the Digital Curtain."
58. Auletta, "Get Rich U."
59. Coursera, "About Coursera."
60. Svensson, *Språkutbildning i en Digital Värld*.
61. Ian Bogost, "What Grows When MOOCs Grow?," *Videogame Theory, Criticism, Design*, August 18, 2013, http://www.bogost.com/blog/what_grows_when_moocs_grow.shtml
62. Noble, *Digital Diploma Mills*.
63. P-O. Rehnquist, "Storskaliga Öppna Nätkurser—MOOC—Det Går Inte Över!," October 3, 2013, http://peosblogg.wordpress.com/2013/10/03/storskaliga-oppna-natkurser-mooc-det-gar-inte-over/
64. Wendy Hui Kyong Chun, "The Dark Side of the Digital Humanities—Part 1," *Thinking C21*, January 9, 2013, http://www.c21uwm.com/2013/01/09/the-dark-side-of-the-digital-humanities-part-1/
65. Matthew Kirschenbaum, Twitter post, January 4, 2013, 10:50 a.m., http://www.twitter.com/mkirschenbaum. Kirschenbaum tweeted, "Four minutes into #s307, and the conflation of MOOCs and DH has begun. #mla13."
66. Richard Grusin, "The Dark Side of the Digital Humanities—Part 2," *Thinking C21*, January 9, 2013, http://www.c21uwm.com/2013/01/09/dark-side-of-the-digital-humanities-part-2/
67. Rita Raley, "The Dark Side of the Digital Humanities—Part 4," *Thinking C21*, January 9, 2013, http://www.c21uwm.com/2013/01/09/the-dark-side-of-the-digital-humanities-part-4/

Epilogue

1. Jonathan Sterne to Air-L (Association of Internet Researchers) mailing list, "Book Prices," March 9, 2011, http://skryb.info/m/air-l@listserv.aoir.org/569CC7B9-7D2F-43DC-A4DE-3D731CD3E19B@mcgill.ca
2. Drucker, "Making Space into Place."
3. Maeda, "Master's programs at Umeå University across science-technology-engineering and humanities-arts?", Workshop, Decembe 12, 2013. http://www.umu.

se/english/about-umu/news-events/calendar/display-page/new-research-in-interactive-architecture-to-be-presented-at-international-conference.cid86258?eventId=6666

4. Ratto, "Critical making workshop: fixsels," "Sorting the Digital Humanities Out," December 6, 2013. http://www.humlab.umu.se/en/research-development/events/archive/sorting-the-digital-humanities-out/program/

5. Kirschenbaum, *Mechanisms*; Drucker, *SpecLab*.

6. Tara McPherson, Twitter post, December, 6, 2012, 1:28 p.m., https://storify.com/JimBarrett/media-places-2012-day-two

7. Andrew Prescott, Twitter post, December 15, 2013, 11:00 a.m., https://twitter.com/Ajprescott/status/412296170787323905

8. This group included Eric Carlsson, Mathias Crawford, Carl-Erik Engqvist, Anna Foka, and Helga Sadowski.

9. This group included Cameron Blevins, Finn Brunton, Tomas Karlsson, Fredrik Palm, and Lindsay Thomas.

10. This group included James Barrett, Paul Conway, Marin Dacos, Matts Lindström, Thomas Nygren, and Hanna Zipernovszky.

11. This group included Jonas Ingvarsson, Virginia Langum, Mattis Lindmark, Mats Malm, Jennie Olofsson, and Andrew Reinhard.

Bibliography

4Humanities: Advocating for the Humanities. http://4humanities.org/

ACH Panel. "Humanities Computing and the Rise of New Media Centers: Synergy or Disjunction?" 1999. http://www2.iath.virginia.edu/ach-allc.99/proceedings/renear-ach.html

ADHO. "About." http://adho.org/about

ADHO. "Minutes: ADHO Steering Committee Meeting, 2015 (Sydney)," June 28–29, 2015. http://adho.org/administration/steering/minutes-adho-steering-committee-meeting-2015-sydney

Alliance for Networking Visual Culture. http://scalar.usc.edu/

Alvarado, Rafael C. "The Digital Humanities Situation." In Debates in the Digital Humanities, edited by Gold, 50–55.

American Association of Museums, Curators Committee. "A Code of Ethics for Curators." 2009. http://www.aam-us.org/docs/continuum/curcomethics.pdf?sfvrsn=0

American Council of Learned Societies. Our Cultural Commonwealth: The Report of the American Council of Learned Societies Commission on Cyberinfrastructure for the Humanities and Social Sciences. 2006. http://www.acls.org/uploadedFiles/Publications/Programs/Our_Cultural_Commonwealth.pdf

Anderson, Margo. "Quantitative History." In The SAGE Handbook of Social Science Methodology, edited by William Outhwaite and Stephen P. Turner, 246–63. London: Sage, 2007.

Armitage, David. "What's the Big Idea? Intellectual History and the Longue Durée." History of European Ideas 38, no. 4 (December 2012): 493–507.

Arnheim, Rudolf. The Power of the Center: A Study of Composition in the Visual Arts. Rev. ed. Berkeley: University of California Press, 1983.

Arts and Humanities Research Council (AHRC). "Digital Transformations in the Arts and Humanities—Big Data Projects Call." http://www.ahrc.ac.uk/Funding-Opportunities/Pages/Big-Data-Projects-Call.aspx

Arts and Humanities Research Council (AHRC). "Digital Transformations in the Arts and Humanities: Big Data Research." 2013. http://www.ahrc.ac.uk/Funding-Opportunities/Documents/Big-Data-projects-call-document.pdf

Asaro, Peter. "On Banning Autonomous Lethal Systems: Human Rights, Automation, and the Dehumanizing of Lethal Decision-Making." *International Review of the Red Cross* 94, no. 886 (Summer 2012): 687–709.

Association for Computers and the Humanities. "ACH Annual General Meeting, Stanford 2011." http://ach.org/2011/06/21/ach-annual-general-meeting-stanford-2011/

Association of Art Museum Curators. "Professional Practices for Art Museum Curators." New York, 2007. http://www.collegeart.org/pdf/AAMC_Professional_Practices.pdf

Atkins, Daniel E., Kelvin K. Droegemeier, Stuart I. Feldman, Hector Garcia-Molina, Michael L. Klein, David G. Messerschmitt, Paul Messina, Jeremiah P. Ostriker, and Margaret H. Wright. *Revolutionizing Science and Engineering through Cyberinfrastructure: Report of the National Science Foundation Blue-Ribbon Advisory Panel on Cyberinfrastructure.* January 2003. http://www.nsf.gov/cise/sci/reports/atkins.pdf

Auletta, Ken. "Get Rich U." *New Yorker*, April 30, 2012. http://www.newyorker.com/reporting/2012/04/30/120430fa_fact_auletta

Balsamo, Anne. "Engineering Cultural Studies: The Postdisciplinary Adventures of Mindplayers, Fools, and Others." In *Doing Science + Culture*, edited by Roddey Reid and Sharon Traweek, 259–74. New York: Routledge, 2000.

Barker, Rachel, and Patricia Smithen. "New Art, New Challenges: The Changing Face of Conservation in the Twenty-First Century." In *New Museum Theory and Practice: An Introduction*, edited by Janet Marstine, 86–102. Oxford: Blackwell, 2006.

Bentkowska-Kafel, Anna. "Needs of the 3D Visualisation Community." JISC 3D Visualisation of the Arts Network Report. 2007. http://3dvisa.cch.kcl.ac.uk/needs/3DVisA%20Report_Needs.pdf

Berry, David M. *Stunlaw* (blog). http://stunlaw.blogspot.com/

Betts, Eleanor. "Towards a Multisensory Experience of Movement in the City of Rome." In *Rome, Ostia, and Pompeii: Movement and Space*, edited by Ray Laurence and David J. Newsome, 118–32. Oxford: Oxford University Press, 2011.

Bey, Hakim. *T.A.Z.: The Temporary Autonomous Zone, Ontological Anarchy, Poetic Terrorism: Anarchy and Terrorism.* Brooklyn, NY: Autonomedia, 1991.

Bivens-Tatum, Wayne. *Academic Librarian* (blog). https://blogs.princeton.edu/librarian/

Blackwell, Christopher, and Gregory Crane. "Conclusion: Cyberinfrastructure, the Scaife Digital Library and Classics in a Digital Age." *Digital Humanities Quarterly* 3, no. 1 (2009). http://digitalhumanities.org/dhq/vol/3/1/000035/000035.html

Blevins, Cameron. *Cameron Blevins* (blog). http://www.cameronblevins.org/posts/

Bogost, Ian. *Videogame Theory, Criticism, Design* (blog). http://www.bogost.com/

Bogost, Ian, and Nick Monfort. "Platform Studies: Frequently Questioned Answers." *Digital Arts and Culture 2009.* UC Irvine: Digital Arts and Culture, 2009. https://escholarship.org/uc/item/01r0k9br/

Bolter, Jay David, and Diane Gromala. *Windows and Mirrors: Interaction Design, Digital Art, and the Myth of Transparency.* Cambridge: MIT Press, 2003.

Bonnett, John, Geoffrey Rockwell, and Kyle Kuchmey. "High Performance Computing in the Arts and Humanities." 2007. https://www.sharcnet.ca/my/research/hhpc

Borgman, Christine L. *Scholarship in the Digital Age: Information, Infrastructure, and the Internet.* Cambridge: MIT Press, 2007.

Börjesson, Maria, Jonas Eliasson, and Per Kågeson. "Tågens höghastighetsbanor en dålig affär för samhället." *Dagens Nyheter*, January 1, 2016. http://www.dn.se/debatt/tagens-hoghastighetsbanor-en-dalig-affar-for-samhallet/

Bowker, Geoffrey C. *Memory Practices in the Sciences*. Cambridge: MIT Press, 2005.

Bowker, Geoffrey C., and Susan Leigh Star. "Invisible Mediators of Action: Classification and the Ubiquity of Standards." *Mind, Culture, and Activity* 7, nos. 1–2 (2000): 147–63.

Bowker, Geoffrey C., and Susan Leigh Star. *Sorting Things Out: Classification and Its Consequences*. Cambridge: MIT Press, 1999.

Brooks, Fredrick B., Jr. "What's Real about Virtual Reality?" *IEEE Computer, Graphics and Applications, Special Report* (November–December 1999): 16–27. http://www.cs.unc.edu/~brooks/WhatsReal.pdf

Burdick, Anne, Johanna Drucker, Peter Lunenfeld, Todd Presner, and Jeffrey Schnapp. *Digital_Humanities*. Cambridge: MIT Press, 2012.

Buren, Daniel. "The Function of the Studio." In *The Studio Reader: On the Space of Artists*, edited by Mary Jane Jacob and Michelle Grabner, 156–62. Chicago: University of Chicago Press, 2010.

Burke, Peter. *A Social History of Knowledge: From Gutenberg to Diderot*. Cambridge: Polity, 2000.

Burnette, Michaelyn, Christina M. Gillis, and Myrtis Cochran. "The Humanist and the Library: Promoting New Scholarship through Collaborative Interaction between Humanists and Librarians." In *Reference Services in the Humanities*, edited by Judy Reynolds, 181–91. New York: Hayworth Press, 1994.

Busa, Roberto A. Foreword to *Companion to Digital Humanities*, edited by Schreibman, Siemens, and Unsworth, xvi–xxi.

Cárdenas, Micha. "Is the Digital Humanities a Hot, Sellable Commodity? Or a Place for Counter Hegemonic Critique?" *Micha Cárdenas's Blog*. http://hastac.org/blogs/michacardenas/

Cayless, Hugh. *Scriptio Continua* (blog). http://philomousos.blogspot.com/2010/12/dh-tea-leaves.html

Cecire, Natalia. "Introduction: Theory and the Virtues of Digital Humanities." *Journal of Digital Humanities* 1, no. 1 (Winter 2011). http://journalofdigitalhumanities.org/1-1/introduction-theory-and-the-virtues-of-digital-humanities-by-natalia-cecire/

Cecire, Natalia. *Natalia Cecire's Blog*. http://nataliacecire.blogspot.se/

Center for the Study of the Drone, Bard College. "Interview: Natalie Jeremijenko." November 13, 2013. http://dronecenter.bard.edu/interview-natalie-jeremijenko/

CenterNet. "CenterNet to Join ADHO." http://dhcenternet.org/2011/08/centernet-to-join-adho/

CenterNet. "The International Directory of Digital Humanities Centers." http://www.dhcenternet.org/centers

CenterNet. "Join." http://dhcenternet.org/join/

CHCI Network. "Digital Humanities Initiative." http://chcinetwork.org/our-members/regional-and-affinity-groups/digital-humanities/

Chemical Biological Centre. "Welcome to KBC." http://www.kbc.umu.se/

Chittum, Ryan. "The NYT's $150 Million-a-Year Paywall." *Columbia Journalism Review.* August 1, 2013. http://www.cjr.org/the_audit/the_nyts_150_million-a-year_pa.php

CISE. "About ACI." http://www.nsf.gov/cise/aci/about.jsp

Collins, Harry, Robert Evans, and Mike Gorman. "Trading Zones and Interactional Expertise." *Studies in History and Philosophy of Science Part A* 38, no. 4 (December 2007): 657–66.

Colomina, Beatriz. "Enclosed by Images: The Eamseses' Multimedia Architecture." *Grey Room* 2 (Winter 2001): 6–29. http://csis.pace.edu/~marchese/TextImage/colomina_eames.pdf

Connelly, Matthew J., Nicholas J. Dames, and Dennis Tenen. "Open Letter in Support of the Digital Humanities Studio Space at Butler Library." http://academiccommons.columbia.edu/catalog/ac:157744

Constantopoulos, Panos, and Costis Dallas. "Aspects of a Digital Curation Agenda for Cultural Heritage." In *Proceedings of the IEEE International Conference on Distributed Human-Machine Systems,* 317–22. Prague: IEEE Systems, Man, and Cybernetics Society and Czech Technical University in Prague, 2008. http://www.academia.edu/931035/Aspects_of_a_Digital_Curation_Agenda_for_Cultural_Heritage

Cook, Sarah. "Immateriality and Its Discontents: An Overview of Main Models and Issues for Curating New Media." In *New Media in the White Cube and Beyond: Curatorial Models for Digital Art,* edited by Christiane Paul, 26–50. Berkeley: University of California Press, 2008.

Coursera. "About Coursera." https://www.coursera.org/about

Crow, Michael M. "The Research University as Comprehensive Knowledge Enterprise: A Prototype for a New American University." In *University Research for Innovation,* edited by Luc E. Weber and James J. Duderstadt, 211–25. London: Economica, 2010. http://www.glion.org/pdf_livres/g10_University_reserach_for_innovation.pdf

Croxall, Brian. *Research, Teaching, Technology* (blog). http://www.briancroxall.net/

Dahlström, Mats. "Critical Editing and Critical Digitization." In *Text Comparison and Digital Creativity: The Production of Presence and Meaning in Digital Text Scholarship,* edited by Wido van Peursen, Ernst D. Thoutenhoofd, and Adriaan van der Weel, 79–97. Leiden: Brill, 2010.

Daniel, Sharon. "Public Secrets." *Vectors.* http://vectors.usc.edu/projects/index.php?project=57

Davidson, Cathy N. "Humanities 2.0: Promise, Perils, Predictions." *Publications of the Modern Language Association of America* 123, no. 3 (May 2008): 707–17.

Davidson, Cathy N., and David Theo Goldberg. "Engaging the Humanities." *Profession* (2004): 42–62.

Davidson, Cathy N., and David Theo Goldberg. *The Future of Thinking: Learning Institutions in a Digital Age.* Cambridge: MIT Press, 2010.

Davis, Rebecca Frost, Matthew K. Gold, Katherine D. Harris, and Jentery Sayers. "Announcing *Digital Pedagogy in the Digital Humanities: Concepts, Models, and Experiments.*" https://github.com/curateteaching/digitalpedagogy/blob/master/announcement.md/

Deegan, Marilyn. "Report for ALLC, ADHO, and ACH Committee Meetings." June 16, 2008. http://www.docstoc.com/docs/102704044/Literary-and-Linguistic-Computing-Literary-and-Linguistic-Computing

Deegan, Marilyn, and Willard McCarty, eds. *Collaborative Research in the Digital Humanities*. Farnham: Ashgate, 2012.

DeFanti, Thomas A., Jason Leigh, Luc Renambot, Byungil Jeong, Alan Verlo, Lance Long, Maxine Brown, et al. "The OptIPortal, a Scalable Visualization, Storage, and Computing Interface Device for the OptiPuter." *Future Generation Computer Systems* 25 (2009): 114–23.

de Smedt, Koenraad. "Some Reflections on Studies in Humanities Computing." *Literary and Linguistic Computing* 17, no 1 (April 2002): 89–101.

DigiPal. "About." http://www.digipal.eu/about/

DigiPal. "Home." http://www.digipal.eu/

Digital Humanities 2011. "General CFP." https://dh2011.stanford.edu/?page_id=97

Digital Humanities at MIT. *Hyperstudio* (blog). http://hyperstudio.mit.edu/category/blog/

Digital Humanities Conference. "<audio>Digital Humanities</audio>: The Intersections of Sound and Method." Panel discussion, Lausanne, Switzerland, 2014. http://dharchive.org/paper/DH2014/Panel-817.xml

Digital Humanities Quarterly. "About DHQ". http://www.digitalhumanities.org/dhq/about/about.html

"Digital Pedagogy in the Humanities: Concepts, Models, and Experiments," MLA Commons, accessed January 23, 2016. https://digitalpedagogy.commons.mla.org/

D'Ignazio, Catherine. "What Would Feminist Data Visualization Look Like," Blog entry, MIT Center for Civic Media, December 20, 2015. https://civic.mit.edu/feminist-data-visualization

Dobson, Kelly. "Blendie." http://web.media.mit.edu/~monster/blendie/

Donahue, Brian. *The Great Meadow: Farmers and the Land in Colonial Concord*. New Haven: Yale University Press, 2004.

Donegan, Rosemary. "Between Zones, Spaces, and Sites: A Methodology of Curating." In *Naming a Practice: Curational Strategies for the Future*, edited by Peter White, 105–13. Banff: Banff Center Press, 1996.

Donoghue, Frank. *The Last Professors: The Corporate University and the Fate of the Humanities*. New York: Fordham University Press, 2008.

Douglass, Jeremy. "Cultural Analytics: Webcomics and Video Games (Guest Material during Lev Manovich Keynote Address)." June 22, 2009. http://jeremydouglass.com/cv/Douglass,%20Jeremy.%20Digital%20Humanities%202009%20keynote%20guest%20spot.pdf

Dourish, Paul, and Sara Bly. "Portholes: Supporting Awareness in a Distributed Work Group." In *Proceedings of the SIGCHI Conference on Human Factors in Computing Systems*, 541–47. New York: ACM, 1992. http://www.dourish.com/publications/1992/chi92-portholes.pdf

Drabinski, Emily. "Queering the Catalog: Queer Theory and the Politics of Correction." *Library Quarterly* 83, no. 2 (April 2013): 94–111.

Drucker, Johanna. "Blind Spots: Humanists Must Plan Their Digital Future." *Chronicle of Higher Education*. April 3, 2009. http://chronicle.com/article/Blind-Spots/9348/

Drucker, Johanna. "Humanities Approaches to Graphical Display." *Digital Humanities Quarterly* 5, no. 1 (2011). http://digitalhumanities.org/dhq/vol/5/1/000091/000091.html

Drucker, Johanna. "Making Space into Place: Probabilistic Materiality and Experiential Metadata." Keynote presentation, Media Places 2012: Infrastructure | Space | Media, Umeå University, December 6, 2012.

Drucker, Johanna. *SpecLab: Digital Aesthetics and Projects in Speculative Computing*. Chicago: University of Chicago Press, 2009.

Duke University Press Log. "Nicholas Mirzoeff Extends His Book with New Digital Project on Scalar." June 25, 2012. http://dukeupress.typepad.com/dukeupress-log/2012/06/nicholas-mirzoeff-extends-his-book-with-new-digital-project-on-scalar.html

Dylla, Kimberly, Bernard Frischer, Pascal Mueller, Andreas Ulmer, and Simon Haegler. "Rome Reborn 2.0: A Case Study of Virtual City Reconstruction Using Procedural Modeling Techniques." http://romereborn.frischerconsulting.com/rome_reborn_2_documents/papers/Dylla2_Frischer_Rome_Reborn.pdf

Edwards, Paul N., Geoffrey C. Bowker, Steven J. Jackson, and Robin Williams. "Introduction: An Agenda for Infrastructure Studies." *Journal of the Association for Information Systems* 10, no. 5 (2009): 364–74.

Eisenstein, Elizabeth L. *The Printing Press as an Agent of Change: Communications and Cultural Transformations in Early-Modern Europe*. Cambridge: Cambridge University Press, 1997.

Ekström, Anders, and Sverker Sörlin. *Alltings Mått: Humanistisk Kunskap i Framtidens Samhälle*. Stockholm: Norstedts, 2012.

Erickson, Thomas, and Wendy A. Kellogg. "Social Translucence: An Approach to Designing Systems That Support Social Processes." *ACM Transactions on Computer-Human Interaction* 7, no. 1 (2000): 50–83.

European Association for Digital Humanities (EADH). "About." http://eadh.org/about/

European Association for Digital Humanities (EADH). *ALLC Annual General Meeting at Hamburg*. July 2012. http://eadh.org/sites/eadh.org/files/pdf/ALLC_AGM_at_Hamburg_minutes.pdf

European Association for Digital Humanities (EADH). *ALLC Committee Meeting, Stanford* June 18, 2011. http://eadh.org/sites/eadh.org/files/pdf/stanfordminutes.pdf

European Association for Digital Humanities (EADH). "EADH Membership Report, July 2014." http://eadh-static.adho.org/sites/default/files/pdf/eadh_membership_report_july_2014.pdf

European Association for the Digital Humanities (EADH). "Mission." http://www.allc.org/about/mission

European Strategy Forum on Research Infrastructure (ESFRI). *Strategy Report on Research Infrastructures: Roadmap 2010*. Luxembourg: European Union Publications Office, 2011. http://ec.europa.eu/research/infrastructures/pdf/esfri-strategy-report_and_roadmap.pdf

Fällman, Daniel. "Supporting Studio Culture in Design Research." In *Proceedings of IASDR 2007, International Association of Societies of Design Research*. https://dl.dropboxusercontent.com/u/599778/resources/papers/studioresearch-IASDR-final.pdf

Febvre, Lucien, and Henri-Jean Martin. *The Coming of the Book: The Impact of Printing, 1450–1800*. Translated by David Gerard. London: Verso, 2010.

Fiormonte, Domenico. "Towards a Cultural Critique of the Digital Humanities." *Historical Social Research* 37, no. 3 (2012): 59–76. http://www.academia.edu/1932310/Towards_a_Cultural_Critique_of_Digital_Humanities/

Fitzpatrick, Kathleen. *Planned Obsolescence: Publishing, Technology, and the Future of the Academy*. New York: New York University Press, 2011.

Flanders, Julia, and John Unsworth. "The Evolution of Humanities Computing Centers." *Computers and the Humanities* 36, no. 4 (2002): 379–80.

Flanders, Julia, and Trevor Muñoz. "An Introduction to Humanities Data Curation." *DH Curation Guide*. http://guide.dhcuration.org/intro/

Fraistat, Neil. "The Function of Digital Humanities Centers at the Present Time." In *Debates in the Digital Humanities*, edited by Gold, 281–91.

Frank, Zephyr. "Spatial History as Scholarly Practice." In *Between Humanities and the Digital*, edited by Svensson and Goldberg, 411–28.

Franklin, Kevin, and Karen Rodriguez'G. "The Next Big Thing in Humanities, Arts and Social Science Computing: Cultural Analytics." *HPCwire*. July 29, 2008. http://archive.hpcwire.com/hpcwire/2008-07-29/the_next_big_thing_in_humanities_arts_and_social_science_computing_cultural_analytics.html

Friedberg, Anne. *The Virtual Window: From Alberti to Microsoft*. Cambridge: MIT Press, 2006.

Galison, Peter. *Image and Logic: A Material Culture of Microphysics*. Chicago: University of Chicago Press, 1997.

Galison, Peter. "Trading with the Enemy." In *Trading Zones and Interactional Expertise: Creating New Kinds of Collaboration*, edited by Michael E. Gorman, 25–52. Cambridge: MIT Press, 2010.

Galison, Peter. "Trading Zone: Coordinating Action and Belief." In *The Science Studies Reader*, edited by Mario Biagioli, 137–60. New York: Routledge, 1999.

Galison, Peter, and Jeffrey Schnapp. "Science Museum Futures." http://www.ahva.ubc.ca/EventPDFs/PeterGalison_JCI_Mar12_12.pdf

Gibbons, Michael, Camille Limoges, Helga Nowotny, Simon Schwartzman, Peter Scott, and Martin Trow. *The New Production of Knowledge: The Dynamics of Science and Research in Contemporary Societies*. London: SAGE, 1994.

Gil, Alex. "Ed: A Minimal Edition Theme for Jekyll." Website, accessed January 23, 2016. https://github.com/elotroalex/ed

Giroux, Henry A. "Public Intellectuals against the Neoliberal University." *Truthdig*. November 1, 2013. http://www.truthdig.com/report/item/public_intellectuals_against_the_neoliberal_university_20131101

Gitelman, Lisa. *Paper Knowledge: Toward a Media History of Documents*. Durham: Duke University Press, 2014.

Gitelman, Lisa, and Virginia Jackson. Introduction to *"Raw Data" Is an Oxymoron*, edited by Lisa Gitelman, 1–14. Cambridge: MIT Press, 2013.

Glass, Erin. "Social Paper: Retooling Student Consciousness." *Scholarly and Research Communication* 6, no. 4 (2015).

Global Outlook::Digital Humanities. "Minimal Computing." http://www.globaloutlookdh.org/minimal-computing/

Gold, Matthew K., ed. *Debates in the Digital Humanities*. Minneapolis: University of Minnesota Press, 2012.

Goldberg, David Theo. *The Afterlife of the Humanities*. Irvine: University of California Humanities Research Institute, 2014. http://humafterlife.uchri.org/

Goldberg, David Theo. "World as Platform." *Medium*, January 13, 2015. https://medium.com/genres-of-scholarly-knowledge-production/world-as-platform-da7f8a1f042e/

Golumbia, David. *The Cultural Logic of Computation*. Cambridge: Harvard University Press, 2009.

Golumbia, David. *Uncomputing* (blog). http://www.uncomputing.org/

Gonsalvez, Christabel, and Martin Atchison. "Implementing Studios for Experimental Learning." *Proceedings of the Australasian Conference on Computing Science Education* 8 (2000): 116–23.

Gouglas, Sean, Geoffrey Rockwell, Victoria Smith, Sophia Hoosein, and Harvey Quamen. "Before the Beginning: The Formation of Humanities Computing as a Discipline in Canada." *Digital Studies* 3, no. 1 (2012). http://www.digitalstudies.org/ojs/index.php/digital_studies/article/view/214/290

"Governance Protocol of the Alliance of Digital Humanities Organizations (ADHO)." http://people.brandeis.edu/~unsworth/ifdish_2.html

Grafton, Anthony. *Worlds Made by Words: Scholarship and Community in the Modern West*. Cambridge: Harvard University Press, 2009.

Graham, Beryl, and Sarah Cook. *Rethinking Curating: Art after New Media*. Cambridge: MIT Press, 2010.

Green, David. "Cyberinfrastructure for Us All: An Introduction to Cyberinfrastructure and the Liberal Arts." *Academic Commons*, December 16, 2007. http://www.academiccommons.org/2007/12/cyberinfrastructure-for-us-all-an-introduction-to-cyberinfrastructure-and-the-liberal-arts/

Guiliano, Jen. *Just another Day of DH 2013 Site* (blog). http://dayofdh2013.matrix.msu.edu/jenguiliano/

Guldi, Jo. "Time Wars of the Twentieth Century and the Twenty-First Century Toolkit." In *Between Humanities and the Digital*, edited by Svensson and Goldberg, 253–65.

Haber, Benjamin. "Data and Desire in Academic Life: A Review of Erez Aiden and Jean-Baptiste Michel, *Uncharted: Big Data as a Lens on Human Culture* (Riverhead Books, reprint edition, 2014)". *Boundary2*, December 23, 2015. http://boundary2.org/2015/12/23/data-and-desire-in-academic-life/

HaCCS Lab. "About." http://haccslab.com/?page_id=2/

Hacking the Academy. "What This Is and How to Contribute." http://hackingtheacademy.org/what-this-is-and-how-to-contribute/

HASTAC. http://www.hastac.org/

Hayles, Katherine. *How We Think: Digital Media and Contemporary Technogenesis.* Chicago: University of Chicago Press, 2012.

Hey, Tony, and Anne Trefethen. "E-Science, Cyberinfrastructure, and Scholarly Communication." In *Scientific Collaboration on the Internet,* edited by Gary M. Olsen, Ann Zimmerman, and Nathan Bos, 15–31. Cambridge: MIT Press, 2008.

Higgs, Matthew. "Between the Audience and the Stage." In *The Edge of Everything: Reflections on Curational Practice,* edited by Catherine Thomas, 15–24. Banff: Banff Center Press, 2002.

Hirsch, Brett D., ed. *Digital Humanities Pedagogy: Practices, Principles, and Politics.* Cambridge: Open Book, 2012.

Hirsch, Brett D. "</Parentheses>: Digital Humanities and the Place of Pedagogy." In *Digital Humanities Pedagogy: Practices, Principles, and Politics,* edited by Brett D. Hirsch, 3–30. Cambridge: Open Book, 2012. http://www.openbookpublishers.com/reader/161

Hockey, Susan. "The History of Humanities Computing." In *Companion to Digital Humanities,* edited by Schreibman, Siemens, and Unsworth, 3–19.

Holmberg, Linn. "The Forgotten Encyclopedia: The Maurists' Dictionary of Arts, Crafts, and Sciences, the Unrealized Rival of the *Encyclopédie* of Diderot and d'Alembert." Ph.D. diss. Umeå University, 2014. http://umu.diva-portal.org/smash/get/diva2:715277/FULLTEXT02.pdf

Hopkins, Curt. "Future U: Rise of the Digital Humanities." *Ars Technica,* June 17, 2012. http://arstechnica.com/business/2012/06/future-u-rise-of-the-digital-humanities/

I-CHASS. "About Us." http://chass.illinois.edu/?page_id=9

Iedema, Rick, Debbi Long, Katherine Carroll, Maree Stenglin, and Jeffrey Braithwaite. "Corridor Work: How Liminal Space Becomes a Resource for Handling Complexities of Multi-Disciplinary Health Care." *APROS 11: Asia-Pacific Researchers in Organization Studies: 11th International Colloquium, Melbourne, Australia, 4–7 December 2005* (2005): 238–47.

Infrastructure, Space, and Media: A Book from the Media Places Symposium in Umeå December 5–7, 2012. Stockholm: Peter Wallenberg Foundation, 2013. https://www.wallenberg.com/pws/sites/default/files/files/pdf/media_original_inlaga_rgb.pdf

Ingeno, Lauren. "Crowdfunding Academic Research." *Inside Higher Ed,* June 10, 2013. http://www.insidehighered.com/news/2013/06/10/academic-researchers-using-crowdfunding-platforms/

Institute of Advanced Technology in the Humanities, University of Virginia (IATH). "'Is Humanities Computing an Academic Discipline?' An Interdisciplinary Seminar." http://www.iath.virginia.edu/hcs/

Ippolito, Jon, Joline Blais, Owen F. Smith, Steve Evans, and Nathan Stormer. "New Criteria for New Media." *Leonardo* 42, no. 1 (February 2009): 71–75.

Issuu. http://issuu.com/

Jacobs, Lynn F. *Opening Doors: The Early Netherlandish Triptych Reinterpreted.* University Park: Pennsylvania State University Press, 2012.

Jamieson, Peter, Kenn Fisher, Tony Gilding, Peter G. Taylor, and A. C. F. (Chris) Trevitt. "Place and Space in the Design of New Learning Environments." *Higher Education Research and Development* 19, no. 2 (2000): 221–36.

Janlert, Lars-Erik, and Kjell Jonsson. "Kulturlaboratoriet [The Culture Laboratory]." *Tvärsnitt* 1 (2000): 54–61.

John Hope Franklin Humanities Institute, Duke University. "Audiovisualities Lab." http://www.fhi.duke.edu/labs/audiovisualities

John Hope Franklin Humanities Institute, Duke University. "Humanities Laboratories." http://www.fhi.duke.edu/labs

Jones, Steven. "The Network Inside Out and the New Digital Humanities." Keynote Talk at Digital Humanities Forum, September 12, 2014. https://www.youtube.com/watch?v=yTWsdmOqwEo

Juola, Patrick. "Killer Applications in Digital Humanities." *Literary and Linguistic Computing* 23, no. 1 (April 2008): 73–83.

Kagan, Jerome. *The Three Cultures: Natural Sciences, Social Sciences, and the Humanities in the Twenty-First Century.* Cambridge: Cambridge University Press, 2009.

Kelly, Chelsea Emelie. *Under the Wings* (blog), Milwaukee Arts Museum. http://blog.mam.org/

Kirsch, Adam. "The Limits of the Digital Humanities." *New Republic*, May 2, 2014. http://www.newrepublic.com/article/117428/limits-digital-humanities-adam-kirsch/

Kirschenbaum, Matthew. "Digital Humanities As/Is a Tactical Term." In *Debates in the Digital Humanities*, edited by Gold, 414–28.

Kirschenbaum, Matthew. *Mechanisms: New Media and the Forensic Imagination.* Cambridge: MIT Press, 2008.

Kirschenbaum, Matthew. "'So the Colors Cover the Wires': Interface, Aesthetics, and Usability." In *Companion to Digital Humanities*, edited by Schreibman, Siemens, and Unsworth, 523–42.

Kirschenbaum, Matthew. "What Is Digital Humanities and What's It Doing in English Departments?" In *Debates in the Digital Humanities*, edited by Gold, 3–11.

Kitchin, Rob. "Big Data, New Epistemologies, and Paradigm Shifts." *Big Data and Society* 1, no. 1 (June 2014): 1–12. http://bds.sagepub.com/content/1/1/2053951714528481/

Klein, Julie Thompson. *Crossing Boundaries: Knowledge, Disciplinarities, and Interdisciplinarities.* Charlottesville: University of Virginia Press, 1996.

Klein, Julie Thompson. *Humanities, Culture, and Interdisciplinarity: The Changing American Academy.* Albany: State University of New York Press, 2005.

Kolowich, Steve. "Behind the Digital Curtain." *Inside Higher Ed*, January 27, 2012. http://www.insidehighered.com/news/2012/01/27/could-digital-humanities-undergraduates-could-boost-information-literacy

KTH, Division of History, Science, Technology, and Environment. "Views from a Distance: Remote Sensing Technologies and the Perception of the Earth." http://www.kth.se/en/abe/inst/philhist/historia/Forskning/bilder-pa-avstand-fjarranalys-och-forestallningar-om-jorden-1.503469/

Latour, Bruno. *Politics of Nature: How to Bring the Sciences to Democracy.* Cambridge: Harvard University Press, 2004.

Laue, Andrea. "How the Computer Works." In *Companion to Digital Humanities*, edited by Schreibman, Siemens, and Unsworth, 143–60.

Lefebvre, Henri. *The Production of Space*. Translated by Donald Nicholson-Smith. Oxford: Blackwell, 1991.

Leorke, Dale. "Rebranding the Platform: The Limitations of 'Platform Studies.'" *Digital Culture and Education* 4, no. 3 (2012): 257–68. http://www.digitalcultureandeducation.com/cms/wp-content/uploads/2012/12/dce1073_leorke_2012.pdf

Lindgren, Simon. "Introducing Connected Concept Analysis—Confronting the Challenge of Large Online Texts through a Qualitative Approach to Quantity." Paper presented at IPP2012: Big Data, Big Challenges, University of Oxford, September 20–21, 2012.

Lindgren, Simon. "Social Science in Sixty Seconds." https://www.youtube.com/playlist?list=PLWMJI2ZhNY_CQSMhweRuwQOynEziKRGE1/

Lindhé, Cecilia. "Medieval Materiality through the Digital Lens." In *Between Humanities and the Digital*, edited by Svensson and Goldberg, 193–204.

Lindhé, Cecilia. "Rethinking Medieval Spaces in Digital Environments." May 2, 2013. http://vimeo.com/68517975

Liu, Alan. *Alan Liu* (blog). http://liu.english.ucsb.edu/

Liu, Alan. "Where Is Cultural Criticism in the Digital Humanities?" In *Debates in the Digital Humanities*, edited by Gold, 490–509.

Livingstone, David N. *Putting Science in Its Place: Geographies of Scientific Knowledge*. Chicago: University of Chicago Press, 2003.

Lothian, Alexis. *Queer Geek Theory* (blog). http://www.queergeektheory.org/

Maker Lab in the Humanities. "About." http://maker.uvic.ca/about/

Manovich, Lev. "An Archeology of a Computer Screen." *NewMediaTopia*. Soros Center for Contemporary Art, Moscow, 1995. http://manovich.net/index.php/projects/archeology-of-a-computer-screen

Manovich, Lev. "Cultural Analytics." Software Studies Initiative, University of California, San Diego. June 20, 2009. http://lab.softwarestudies.com/2008/09/cultural-analytics.html

Manovich, Lev. "How to Follow Global Digital Cultures; or, Cultural Analytics for Beginners." In *Deep Search: The Politics of Search beyond Google*, edited by Felix Stalder and Konrad Becker. Innsbruck: Studien, 2009. http://softwarestudies.com/cultural_analytics/cultural_analytics_overview_final.doc

Manovich, Lev. *Software Takes Command*. London: Bloomsbury, 2013. http://issuu.com/bloomsburypublishing/docs/9781623566722_web

Martin, Reinhold. *The Organizational Complex: Architecture, Media, and Corporate Space*. Cambridge: MIT Press, 2003.

Mattern, Shannon Christine. "Library as Infrastructure." *Places Journal*, June 2014. https://placesjournal.org/article/library-as-infrastructure/

Mattern, Shannon Christine. *The New Downtown Library: Designing with Communities*. Minneapolis: University of Minnesota Press, 2007.

Mattern, Shannon Christine. *Words in Space* (blog). http://www.wordsinspace.net/wordpress/

McCarty, Willard. *Humanities Computing.* New York: Palgrave, 2005.

McCarty, Willard. "Humanities Computing." In *Encyclopedia of Library and Information Science,* edited by Miriam Drake, 1224–35. 2nd ed. New York: Marcel Dekker, 2003. http://www.mccarty.org.uk/essays/McCarty,%20Humanities%20computing.pdf

McCarty, Willard. "Becoming Interdisciplinary." In *A New Companion to Digital Humanities,* edited by Susan Schreibman, Ray Siemens, and John Unsworth, 88-99. England: Wiley-Blackwell, 2016.

McCarty, Willard, Julianne Nyhan, Anne Welsh, and Jessica Salmon. "Questioning, Asking, and Enduring Curiosity: An Oral History Conversation between Julianne Nyhan and Willard McCarty." *Digital Humanities Quarterly* 6, no. 3 (2012). http://www.digitalhumanities.org/dhq/vol/6/3/000134/000134.html

McPherson, Tara. "Introduction: Media Studies and the Digital Humanities." *Cinema Journal* 48, no. 2 (Winter 2009): 119–23.

McPherson, Tara. "We Need Some Transitional Models in B/W Tradition and Innovation." February 5, 2009. http://www.hastac.org/forums/hastac-scholars-discussions/future-digital-humanities

Menand, Louis. *The Marketplace of Ideas.* New York: W.W. Norton, 2010.

Merkel, Cecilia. "Folkloristics of Educational Spaces: Material Lore in Classrooms with and without Walls." *Library Trends* 47, no. 3 (1999): 417–38.

Meusburger, Peter. "Milieus of Creativity: The Role of Places, Environments, and Spatial Contexts." In *Milieus of Creativity: An Interdisciplinary Approach to Spatiality of Creativity,* edited by Peter Meusburger, Joachim Funke, and Edgar Wunder, 97–153. Dordrecht: Springer, 2009.

Michel, Jean-Baptiste, Yuan Kui Shen, Aviva Presser Aiden, Adrian Veres, Matthew K. Gray, the Google Books Team, Joseph P. Pickett, Dale Hoiberg, Dan Clancy, Peter Norvig, Jon Orwant, Steven Pinker, Martin A. Nowak, and Erez Lieberman Aiden. "Quantitative Analysis of Culture Using Millions of Digitized Books." *Science* 331, no. 6014 (January 14, 2011): 176–82. http://www.sciencemag.org/content/331/6014/176.abstract/

Minassian, Levon. "UC, Campus Looks to Expand Online Education Program." *Daily Californian,* July 22, 2012. http://www.dailycal.org/2012/07/22/ucs-online-involvement/

Mitchell, William. "Places for Learning: New Functions and New Forms." Lecture at MIT, video, 56:06. March 7, 2003. http://video.mit.edu/watch/places-for-learning-new-functions-and-new-forms-9884/

Modern Language Association. "Guidelines for Evaluating Work in Digital Humanities and Digital Media." http://www.mla.org/guidelines_evaluation_digital/

Monclova, Marta S. Rivera. "Transformative Mediations? Ethnic and Queer Studies and the Politics of the Digital (ASA, 2011)." *PhDeviate,* January 13, 2012. http://www.phdeviate.org/presentations/asatransformdh/

Moulin, Claudine, ed. "Research Infrastructures in the Digital Humanities." *Science Policy Briefing* 42 (September 2011). http://www.esf.org/fileadmin/Public_documents/Publications/spb42_RI_DigitalHumanities.pdf

Mukerji, Chandra. "Me? A Digital Humanist?" In *Between Humanities and the Digital,* edited by Svensson and Goldberg, 41–53.

Nash, Kaci. *Digital History Project* (blog). http://digitalhistory.wordpress.com/

Navas, Eduardo. *Remix Theory* (blog). http://remixtheory.net/

Noble, David F. *Digital Diploma Mills: The Automation of Higher Education.* New York: Monthly Review Press, 2001.

Nowviskie, Bethany. *Bethany Nowviskie* (blog). http://http://nowviskie.org/

Nussbaum, Martha C. *Not for Profit: Why Democracy Needs the Humanities.* Princeton: Princeton University Press, 2010.

Nyhan, Julianne. *Arche Logos* (blog). http://archelogos.hypotheses.org/135

Oculus VR. "Oculus Rift: Next-Gen Virtual Reality." http://www.oculus.com/rift/

O'Donnell, Daniel. "Report to the ADHO Steering Committee for GO::DH." *Global Outlook::Digital Humanities.* January 29, 2013. http://www.globaloutlookdh.org/report-to-the-adho-steering-committee-for-godh/

Omeka. "Omeka: Serious Web Publishing." http://omeka.org/about/

Ong, Walter J. "The Expanding Humanities and the Individual Scholar." *PMLA* 82, no. 4 (September 1967): 1–7.

Opinionator (blog). *New York Times.* http://opinionator.blogs.nytimes.com/

Ortega, Élika. "Crisscrossing Borders: GO::DH Regional Networks in Dialogue." Blog entry, 2016. MLA 2016 presentation. http://elikaortega.net/2016/01/13/mla-dh-at-the-borders/

Palgrave Macmillan. "Understanding Digital Humanities." http://www.palgrave.com/products/title.aspx?pid=493310/

Palm, Fredrik, and Thomas Larsson. "Rock Carvings at Nämforsen." Umeå: Umeå University, 2011. http://rockart.humlab.umu.se/

Pannapacker, William. "No DH, No Interview." *Chronicle of Higher Education,* July 22, 2012. http://chronicle.com/article/No-DH-No-Interview/132959/

Parikka, Jussi. "On Designerization of Media Culture in the Age of Software." *Cultural Politics* 10, no. 3 (2014): 415–19.

Parker, Jan. "Humanities' 'Peculiar' . . . or All Important . . . 'Practices.'" Paper presented at the Warwick-Duke Conference, August 2009.

Parker, Jan. "Speaking Out in a Digital World: Humanities Values, Humanities Processes." In *Humanities in the Twenty-First Century: Beyond Utility and Markets,* ed. Eleonora Belfiore and Anna Upchurch, 44–62. Basingstoke: Palgrave Macmillan, 2013.

Parry, David. *AcademHack* (blog). http://academhack.outsidethetext.com/home/

Porsdam, Helle. *Too Much "Digital," Too Little "Humanities"? An Attempt to Explain Why Many Humanities Scholars Are Reluctant Converts to Digital Humanities.* Working Paper, Arcadia Project Reports, Arcadia Programme, University of Cambridge, 2011. http://www.dspace.cam.ac.uk/handle/1810/244642/

Postcolonial Digital Humanities. "The Rewriting Wikipedia Project." http://dhpoco.org/rewriting-wikipedia/

Pratt, Mary Louise. "Arts of the Contact Zone." *Profession* (1991): 33–40.

Prescott, Andrew. "Consumers, Creators, or Commentators? Problems of Audience and Mission in the Digital Humanities." *Arts and Humanities in Higher Education* 11, nos. 1–2 (February–April 2012): 61–75. http://ahh.sagepub.com/content/11/1-2/61/.

Prescott, Andrew. *Digital Riffs* (blog). http://digitalriffs.blogspot.se/

Raley, Rita. *Tactical Media*. Minneapolis: University of Minnesota Press, 2009.

Ralón, Laureano. "Interview with Johanna Drucker." *Figure/Ground Communication*. May 27, 2013. http://figureground.org/interview-with-johanna-drucker/

Ramsay, Stephen. *Stephen Ramsay's Blog*. http://stephenramsay.us/

Ramsay, Stephen, and Geoffrey Rockwell. "Developing Things: Notes toward an Epistemology of Building in the Digital Humanities." In *Debates in the Digital Humanities*, edited by Gold, 75–84.

Ratto, Matt. "Already False, Potentially True: Epistemic Commitments, Virtual Reality, and Archaeological Representation." HUMlab seminar, Umeå University. December 12, 2006. http://blog.humlab.umu.se/?p=426

Ratto, Matt. "Critical Making." In *Open Design Now*, edited by Bas van Abel, Roel Klaassen, Lucas Evers. and Peter Troxler. Amsterdam: BIS, 2011. http://opendesignnow.org/index.php/article/critical-making-matt-ratto/

Ratto, Matt. "Critical Making: Conceptual and Material Studies in Technology and Social Life." *Information Society* 27, no. 4 (2011): 252–60. http://com327ncsu.files.wordpress.com/2013/01/ratto_criticalmaking.pdf

Ratto, Matt. "Epistemic Commitments and Archaeological Representation." In *Book of Abstracts of the XV World Congress, International Union for Prehistoric and Protohistoric Sciences, Lisbon, September 4–9, 2006*. http://www.uispp.ipt.pt/UISPPprogfin/Livro2.pdf

Ratto, Matt, and Robert Ree. "The Materialization of Information and the Digital Economy: Knowledge Synthesis Report." Report submitted to Social Sciences and Humanities Research Council. University of Toronto, 2010. http://thingtanklab.com/wp-content/uploads/2011/02/SSHRC_DigEcon_DDF.pdf

REF2014. "Research Excellence Framework." http://www.ref.ac.uk/

Reid, Alex. *Digital Digs* (blog). http://www.alex-reid.net/

Repko, Allen F. *Interdisciplinary Research: Process and Theory*. Los Angeles: SAGE, 2008.

Rice, J. *Yellow Dog* (blog). http://ydog.net/

Risam, Roopika. "On Disruption, Race, and the Digital Humanities." *Disrupting the Digital Humanities*. January 5, 2015. http://www.disruptingdh.com/on-disruption- race-and-the-digital-humanities/

Risam, Roopika. 2015. "Beyond the Margins: Intersectionality and the Digital Humanities." *Digital Humanities Quarterly* 9:2 (2015). http://www.digitalhumanities.org/dhq/vol/9/2/000208/000208.html

Robles-Anderson, Erica, and Patrik Svensson. "'One Damn Slide After Another': PowerPoint at Every Occasion for Speech." *Computational Culture*, Issue 5 (2016).

Rockwell, Geoffrey. "As Transparent as Infrastructure: On the Research of Cyberinfrastructure in the Humanities." In *Online Humanities Scholarship: The Shape of Things to Come*, edited by Jerome McGann, 461–87. Houston: Rice University Press, 2010. http://cnx.org/content/m34315/1.2/

Rockwell, Geoffrey, and Megan Meredith-Lobay. "Mind the Gap." Draft Report. May 2010. https://docs.google.com/document/preview?id=1wSEesXjAKj8x56AoqfF_fwSkCQuBXp82C0IWJrVgDTQ&pli=1

Rome Reborn: A Digital Model of Ancient Rome. http://romereborn.frischerconsulting.com/

Roper, John P. G. "The New Humanities Workstation." *Literary and Linguistic Computing* 6, no. 2 (1991): 131–33.

Roser, David, and John Merson. "Have Academics Forgotten How to Talk to Each Other?" *The Ecologist,* July 21, 2009. http://www.theecologist.org/blogs_and_comments/commentators/other_comments/290244/have_academics_forgotten_how_to_talk_to_each_other.html

Royal, Cindy. "We Need a Digital-First Curriculum to Teach Modern Journalism." *PBS,* August 26, 2013. http://www.pbs.org/mediashift/2013/08/we-need-a-digital-first-curriculum-to-teach-modern-journalism

Roy Rosenzweig Center for History and New Media, George Mason University. "What Is Digital History?" http://chnm.gmu.edu/

Russett, Robert. *Hyperanimation: Digital Images and Virtual Worlds.* New Barnet: John Libbey, 2009.

Saldana, M., and C. Johanson. "Procedural Modeling for Rapid-Prototyping of Multiple Building Phases." *ISPRS—International Archives of the Photogrammetry, Remote Sensing and Spatial Information Sciences,* vol. XV-5/W1 (February 13, 2013): 205–10.

Sample, Mark. *Sample Reality* (blog). http://www.samplereality.com/

Schnapp, Jeffrey T., and Michael Shanks. "Artereality (Rethinking Craft in a Knowledge Economy)." In *Art School (Propositions for the 21st Century),* edited by Steven Henry, 141–57. Cambridge: MIT Press, 2009.

Schreibman, Susan, Ray Siemens, and John Unsworth, eds. *A Companion to Digital Humanities.* Oxford: Blackwell, 2004.

Seed, Patricia. "A Map Is Not a Picture: How the Digital World Threatens the Validity of Printed Maps." HUMlab video, 44:09. October 18, 2012. http://stream.humlab.umu.se/

Shanks, Michael. "Digital Humanities—A Vision." 2008. http://documents.stanford.edu/michaelshanks/386/

Shanks, Michael. "Media as Modes of Engagement." Paper presented at Society for the Social Study of Science Meetings, Vancouver, November 2006. http://documents.stanford.edu/michaelshanks/140/

Shared Horizons. "About." http://mith.umd.edu/sharedhorizons/about/

Shaw, Becky. "*Who's Driving?* The Artist as Curator." *Taxi Gallery.* http://www.radiotaxi.org.uk/abbeytaxi/taxigallerywebsite/whosedriving.pdf

Smith, Martha Nell. "The Human Touch Software of the Highest Order: Revisiting Editing as Interpretation." *Textual Cultures* 2, no. 1 (Spring 2007): 1–15.

Sousanis, Nick. *Unflattening.* Cambridge, MA: Harvard University Press, 2015.

Stanford Humanities Center. "How Is Humanities Research Conducted?" http://shc.stanford.edu/how-humanities-research-conducted/

Star, Susan Leigh, and James R. Griesemer. "Institutional Ecology, 'Translations,' and Boundary Objects: Amateurs and Professionals in Berkeley's Museum of Vertebrate Zoology, 1907–39." *Social Studies of Science* 19, no. 3 (August 1989): 387–420.

Starosielski, Nicole. "'Warning: Do Not Dig': Negotiating the Visibility of Critical Infrastructures." *Journal of Visual Culture* 11, no. 1 (April 2012). http://vcu.sagepub.com/content/11/1/38/

STEM to STEAM. http://stemtosteam.org/

Stengers, Isabelle. *Power and Invention.* Minneapolis: University of Minnesota Press, 1997.

Sterne, Jonathan. "Digital Media and Disciplinarity." *Information Society* 21, no 4 (2005): 249–56.

Sterne, Jonathan. "The Example: Some Historical Considerations." In *Between Humanities and the Digital,* edited by Svensson and Goldberg, 17–33.

Sterne, Jonathan. "Footnotes to a Manifesto for Diminished Voices." VIMEO video, 5:22. Presented at the 2014 Encuentro conference, Montreal, October 13, 2014. https://vimeo.com/108830830/

Sterne, Jonathan. *MP3: The Meaning of a Format (Sign, Storage, Transmission).* Durham: Duke University Press, 2012.

Stommel, Jesse. "The Public Digital Humanities." *Disrupting the Digital Humanities.* January 9, 2015. http://www.disruptingdh.com/the-public-digital-humanities/

Stone, Sandy. "On Being Trans, and under the Radar: Tales from the Actlab." http://sandystone.com/radar.shtml

Stone, Sue. "Humanities Scholars: Information Needs and Uses." *Journal of Documentation* 38, no. 4 (1982): 292–313.

Streeter, Thomas. *The Net Effect: Romanticism, Capitalism, and the Internet.* New York: New York University Press, 2011.

Studio@Butler. "Frequently Asked Questions." https://studio.cul.columbia.edu/faq/

Svensson, Patrik. "Building a Virtual World for Learning, Collaboration, and Experience." Project Report. Umeå University, 2002. https://gupea.ub.gu.se//bitstream/2077/18108/1/gupea_2077_18108_1.pdf

Svensson, Patrik. "Envisioning the Digital Humanities." *Digital Humanities Quarterly* 6, no. 1 (2012). http://digitalhumanities.org/dhq/vol/6/1/000112/000112.html

Svensson, Patrik. "From Optical Fiber to Conceptual Cyberinfrastructure." *Digital Humanities Quarterly* 5, no. 1 (2011). http://www.digitalhumanities.org/dhq/vol/5/1/000090/000090.html

Svensson, Patrik. "Humanities Computing as Digital Humanities." *Digital Humanities Quarterly* 3, no. 3 (2009). http://digitalhumanities.org/dhq/vol/3/3/000065/000065.html

Svensson, Patrik. "The Landscape of Digital Humanities." *Digital Humanities Quarterly* 4, no. 1 (2010). http://digitalhumanities.org/dhq/vol/4/1/000080/000080.html

Svensson, Patrik. *Språkutbildning i en Digital Värld: Informationsteknik, Kommunikation och Lärande* [Language Education in a Digital World: Information Technology, Communication, and Learning]. Stockholm: Norstedts Akademiska, 2008.

Svensson, Patrik. "Virtual Worlds as Arenas for Language Learning." In *Computer Assisted Language Learning: Critical Concepts in Linguistics,* edited by Philip Hubbard, 4:359–82. London: Routledge, 2009.

Svensson, Patrik, and David Theo Goldberg, eds. *Between Humanities and the Digital.* Cambridge: MIT Press, 2015.

Swedish Higher Education Authority. "The Quality of Higher Education Programmes." http://www.uk-ambetet.se/qualityassurance/thequalityofhighereducationprogrammes.4.4149f55713bbd91756380004975.html

Swedish Research Council (Vetenskapsrådet). *Ämnesöversikter* 2010. Kommittén för Konstnärlig Forskning och Konstnärligt Utvecklingsarbete. http://www.vr.se/download/18.65001ace131e9a45eea8000304/1314106133565/KFoU+-amnesoversikt.pdf/

Swedish Research Council (Vetenskapsrådet). "Function." http://www.vr.se/inenglish/researchinfrastructure/function.4.2b56827a13380c5abfd80001458.html

Swedish Research Council (Vetenskapsrådet). "Människa, Kultur och Samhälle [Humanity, Culture, and Society]." http://www.vr.se/omvetenskapsradet/verksamhet/forskningensframtid/webbforumforskningsinfrastruktur/tillstandetforinfra/manniskakulturochsamhalle.4.355ecfa414811ac638aa9a59.html

Swedish Research Council (Vetenskapsrådet). "Projektdatabas [Project Database]." http://vrproj.vr.se/

Swedish Research Council (Vetenskapsrådet). "Samhällen och Kulturer i Förändring: Ämnesrådet för Humaniora och Samhällsvetenskaps Underlag till Vetenskapsrådets Forskningsstrategi 2009–2012 [Societies and Cultures in Change: The Strategic Plan for the Swedish Research Council: Humanities and Social Sciences, 2009–2012]." 2007. http://www.vr.se/download/18.61c03dad1180e26cb878000459/Strategi+HS+2007.pdf

Taylor, Mark C. *Crisis on Campus: A Bold Plan for Reforming Our Colleges and Universities.* New York: Alfred A. Knopf, 2010.

TED. "Curating Speakers." http://www.ted.com/pages/tedx_curating_speakers/

Terras, Melissa. "The Digital Classicist: Disciplinary Focus and Interdisciplinary Vision." In *Digital Research in the Study of Classical Antiquity*, edited by Gabriel Bodard and Simon Mahony, 171–89. Farnham: Ashgate, 2010.

Terras, Melissa. "Disciplined: Using Educational Studies to Analyse 'Humanities Computing.'" *Literary and Linguistic Computing* 21, no. 2 (June 2006): 229–46.

THATcamp. "About." http://thatcamp.org/about/

Thinking C21 (blog). http://www.c21uwm.com/

Thomas, Catherine, ed. *The Edge of Everything: Reflections on Curatorial Practice.* Banff: Banff Center Press, 2002.

Thomassen, Bjørn. "The Uses and Meaning of Liminality." *International Political Anthropology* 2, no. 1 (2009): 5–28.

#transformDH. http://transformdh.tumblr.com/

#transformDH Collective Blog. "About #transformDH." http://originaltransformdh.tumblr.com/about

Trettien, Whitney. *Diapsalmata* (blog). http://blog.whitneyannetrettien.com/

Turner, Fred. "Burning Man at Google: A Cultural Infrastructure for New Media Production." *New Media and Society* 11, nos. 1–2 (February–March 2009): 73–94.

Turner, Fred. "The Family of Man and the Politics of Attention in Cold War America." September 13, 2012. http://stream.humlab.umu.se/

Turner, Fred. *From Counterculture to Cyberculture: Stewart Brand, the Whole Earth Network, and the Rise of Digital Utopianism.* Chicago: University of Chicago Press, 2006.

Turner, Fred. "Where the Counterculture Met the New Economy: The WELL and the Origins of Virtual Community." *Technology and Culture* 46, no. 3 (July 2005): 485–512.

Underwood, Ted. *The Stone and the Shell* (blog). http://tedunderwood.com/

University of California Humanities Research Institute. "HASS Cyberinfrastructure." http://uchri.org/initiatives/hass-cyberinfrastructure/

University of Chicago Press. "How We Think." http://press.uchicago.edu/ucp/books/book/chicago/H/bo5437533.html

University of Minnesota Press. "Debates in the Digital Humanities." http://www.upress.umn.edu/book-division/books/debates-in-the-digital-humanities/

Vanhoutte, Edward. *Editor's Report January–June 2012: Journal of the Alliance of Digital Humanities Organizations*. Oxford: Oxford University Press, 2012.http://eadh.org/sites/eadh.org/files/pdf/LLCEditorsReportJuly2012.pdf

Vanhoutte, Edward. "The Gates of Hell: History and Definition of Digital | Humanities | Computing." In *Defining Digital Humanities*, edited by Melissa Terras, Julianne Nyhan, and Edward Vanhoutte, 119–56. Farnham: Ashgate, 2013.

Victorian Women Writers Project. "Encoding Overview." http://webapp1.dlib.indiana.edu/vwwp/projectinfo/encoding.do/

Vyas, Dhaval, Dirk Heylen, Anton Nijholt, and Gerrit van der Veer. "Collaborative Practices That Support Creativity in Design." In *ECSCW 2009: Proceedings of the 11th European Conference on Computer Supported Cooperative Work, 7–11 September 2009, Vienna, Austria*, edited by Ina Wagner, Hilda Tellioğlu, Ellen Balka, Carla Simone, and Luigina Ciolfi, 151–70. London: Springer, 2009.

Walker, Boyd W. "The Curator as a Custodian of Collections." *Curator: The Museum Journal* 6, no. 4 (October 1963): 292–95.

Walsh, James P., and Gerardo Rivera Ungson. "Organizational Memory." *Academy of Management Review* 16, no. 1 (January 1991): 57–91.

Warf, Barney, and Santa Arias, eds. *The Spatial Turn: Interdisciplinary Perspectives* London: Routledge, 2009.

Weingart, Peter. "A Short History of Knowledge Formations." In *The Oxford Handbook of Interdisciplinarity*, edited by Robert Frodeman, Julie Thompson Klein, and Carl Mitcham, 3–14. Oxford: Oxford University Press, 2010.

White, Richard. *What Is Spatial History?* Working Paper, Spatial History Project, Stanford University, 2010. http://www.stanford.edu/group/spatialhistory/cgi-bin/site/pub.php?id=29

Whitson, Roger. *Roger T. Whitson, Ph.D.* (blog). http://www.rogerwhitson.net/

Wiberg, Mikael, ed. *The Interaction Society: Practice, Theories, and Supportive Technologies*. Hershey: Information Science, 2005.

Willett, Perry. "The Victorian Women Writers Project: The Library as a Creator and Publisher of Electronic Texts." *Public-Access Computer Systems Review* 7, no. 6 (1996): 5–16.

Zorich, Diane M. "Digital Humanities Centers: Loci for Digital Scholarship." In *Working Together or Apart: Promoting the Next Generation of Digital Scholarship*, edited by Kathlin Smith and Brian Leney, 70–78. Washington, DC: Council on Library and Information Resources, 2009. http://www.clir.org/pubs/resources/promoting-digital-scholarship-ii-clir-neh/index.html/zorich.pdf

Index